THE PROFESSIONS
IN AMERICA

THE DAEDALUS LIBRARY

The Professions in America is the second in a series of
books published by Houghton Mifflin Company and the
American Academy of Arts and Sciences. The first title in
the series is:

> *A New Europe?*
> edited by Stephen R. Graubard

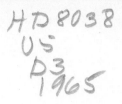

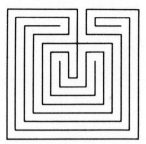

THE PROFESSIONS
IN AMERICA

EDITED BY KENNETH S. LYNN
AND THE EDITORS OF *Dædalus*

HOUGHTON MIFFLIN COMPANY BOSTON
THE RIVERSIDE PRESS CAMBRIDGE
1965

First Printing   R

PREFACE

THE PROFESSIONS are as characteristic of the modern world as the crafts were of the ancient. Alfred North Whitehead, in developing the distinction between the two, recognized the importance of specialization and institutionalization in creating the professions, but he saw these as secondary developments. For him there had been a prior necessity which was the leap from being satisfied with customary procedures to that of seeing the necessity of organizing and using intelligence in new ways. A craft, he explained, was "an avocation based upon customary activities and modified by the trial and error of individual practice." A profession, in contrast, was "an avocation whose activities are subject to theoretical analysis, and are modified by theoretical conclusions derived from that analysis." * An intellectual revolution separated these two activities, and Whitehead's concern was to document it, suggesting its importance for contemporary civilization.

Professions, while striving to be international, never entirely escape the effects of national and even parochial influence. A volume devoted to the professions must reflect this fact; it describes what is general, but also, inevitably, what is peculiar to a specific society. For various reasons, it seemed appropriate in the present instance to dwell on the American experience, with the result that many of the articles describe and interpret the professions as they exist in the United States today. An attempt has been made to deal both with the older professions, whose claim to that title no one thinks to contest, and certain of the newer ones which are only now beginning to assert their claims to this status.

Thanks are due to Mr. Kenneth Lynn, who served as Guest Editor for this issue.

Particular note ought to be given the fact that the Tamiment In-

* A. N. Whitehead, *Adventures of Ideas* (Great Britain: Pelican Books, 1948), pp. 73–74.

v

stitute has helped us with support for this volume. This is the sixth time that such aid has been forthcoming. We are proud of a collaboration which has contributed to the publication of the following issues of *Dædalus: Education in the Age of Science* (Winter 1959); *Mass Culture and Mass Media* (Spring 1960); *The Future Metropolis* (Winter 1961); *Youth: Change and Challenge* (Winter 1962); *American Foreign Policy—Freedoms and Restraints* (Fall 1962).

STEPHEN R. GRAUBARD

CONTENTS

Contents

awareness of the tremendous manpower requirements that a developing technology and an exploding population have enforced upon the professions, and of the rocketing costs of professional services which have alarmed even the world's most affluent society, we seem all but oblivious of the existence of a professional problem. Such disregard is surely dangerous, for in the mid-1960's the "problem of the professions" is nothing less than the "problem of America."

Manpower studies, for example, have endlessly played the "numbers game": America must increase the number of its professionals from x to y by the year z. But until recently the question of whether our reservoir of potential professionals was going to prove adequate to a constantly growing demand rarely came up. The problem of training more doctors, more lawyers and more engineers was treated as if it were analogous to training more automobile mechanics or welders. Ignoring the difference in intellectual rigor between professional and vocational training, we facilely assumed that if only funds and facilities were made available the nation could call into being as many professionals as it needed. In the summer of 1963, however, the research division of the National Education Association reported that despite all the efforts, particularly in the natural sciences, which have been made to persuade qualified young men and women to enter college teaching, demand has far outrun supply in the fields of mathematics, physics, chemistry, biology, economics, foreign languages (especially Russian), English and engineering. The result is that many colleges and universities have been forced to lower their teaching standards. The report further warned that this situation is getting worse, rather than better.[9] Experts on other callings have also begun to suggest that we are approaching the saturation point in our ability to multiply professional personnel.[10]

Because there are simply not enough professionals to go around, the practitioner of today is perforce burdened with too much work, thereby jeopardizing existing professional standards even further. It is notable how many of the contributors to this volume emphasize the multiplicity of demands that are made on the contemporary clergyman, teacher, doctor and scientist. Administrative demands increasingly divert them from their real work, while demands for their professional services are made not only by an ever expanding clientele, but by business and government, both of which have come to depend upon the advice of professional consultants. The closer the professional moves toward the center of American life, in sum, the more functions he is called on to perform. The clergyman becomes a marriage counselor and a political figure in the fight for Negro rights. The nuclear scientist becomes a military strategist, the college psychiatrist a dean and the school teacher a social worker. The personal gratification and the intellectual stimulation derived from these added duties are undoubtedly great, but so are the psychological and physical strains. Alma S. Wittlin, in her essay on "The Teacher," observes that our society expects a superhuman performance from its grade-school teachers, but has shown little interest in measuring the influence of overwork on the teacher's professional effectiveness and mental health. The same observation could be made, without exception, about all the other professions.

Because the professionals have been no more willing than the general public to face up to the predicament in which their triumph has placed them, they have clung to formal standards of professional training (*e.g.*, the educationists who steadfastly insist that without education courses a person could not possibly qualify as a school teacher) and have guarded their exclusive rights of performance (*e.g.*, the doctors who are loath to delegate significant authority to medical and psychiatric social workers) as if they had world enough and time for all their responsibilities. The prejudice against women in the professions also remains shockingly high. In the Soviet Union, 379,000 women are engineers and 332,400 women are doctors and surgeons, whereas there are only 14,000 women doctors in the United States and but a handful of women engineers.[11] For all their intellectual vitality and daring receptivity to new ideas, the American professions are enormously conservative when it comes to changing the club rules.

Such conservatism is clearly irresponsible in the America of the 1960's. It also runs counter to our oldest professional traditions. For as Professor Boorstin has pointed out, the professions in colonial America were distinguished by a marvelous fluidity. Unhampered by the institutional inheritance which narrowed and rigidified the development of the professions in England and on the Continent, the American professional blithely ignored such hallowed distinctions as that between barrister and attorney, or between apothecary and physician. Professionals were judged by the competency of their performance and not by the impressiveness of their credentials. Women played a far more important and diversified role in professional life than did their counterparts in Europe. Professionals moved with ease from one calling to another.[12]

Now, however, America also has an institutional inheritance. Built up over three centuries, it is the foundation on which the present achievement of the American professions rests, and no one in his right mind would suggest dismantling it. Our professional institutions are also an important stabilizing factor in our volatile society, and through their international associations they provide an important channel of communication with the intellectual leaders of other countries, thereby helping to maintain world order. Yet at the same time that they help to bridge the gulf between nations, the professions erect "No Trespassing" signs between themselves and other professional groups, especially the newer ones. And if they help to keep our society steady, they do not blaze new social pathways—at least, not as often as they should. To call for the recapture of the pioneering spirit is to issue the most sentimental of American battlecries; in this case, however, it ought to be heeded. For more than anything else, our professionals need to liberate themselves—just as their colonial predecessors did —from monopolistic notions of who should do what job and narrow-minded conceptions of their obligations to the community at large.

The authors of the following essays exemplify the proper spirit of inter-professional cooperation. Trained specialists, they devote themselves for the most part to analyses of their own particular callings. Yet in consenting to contribute to *The Professions* they have made possible a collective portrait of the professionalized society in which we now live. If they have eschewed the unmanageable ideal of comprehensiveness, they have surely achieved the Emersonian goal of showing us the "representative men" of our time.

KENNETH S. LYNN

REFERENCES

1. Godkin Lectures, Harvard University, Spring, 1963.

2. *The Class of 1962: Its Performance and Immediate Plans*, Cambridge, Mass., 1962, pp. 1, 25.

3. G. Franklin Edwards, *The Negro Professional Class*, Glencoe, Ill., 1959, p. 22.

4. Charles A. Quattlebaum, "Development of Scientific, Engineering, and Other Professional Manpower," *The Legislative Reference Service of the Library of Congress*, Washington, D.C., 1957, p. 11.

Introduction

5. A. M. Carr-Saunders and P. A. Wilson, *The Professions,* Oxford, 1933, p. iii.

6. The emerging studies by Donald Fleming are, however, beginning to fill this gap.

7. Daniel J. Boorstin, *The Americans. The Colonial Experience,* New York, 1958, p. 399.

8. A. N. Whitehead, *Science and the Modern World,* Cambridge, 1925, pp. 275–276.

9. As reported in the *New York Times,* June 24, 1963, p. 3.

10. See, for example, the recent studies of Derek J. de Solla Price.

11. Clare Boothe Luce, "But Some People Simply Never Get the Message," *Life,* June 28, 1963, p. 31.

12. Boorstin, *The Americans,* pp. 185–239.

EVERETT C. HUGHES

Professions

PROFESSIONS are more numerous than ever before. Professional people are a larger proportion of the labor force. The professional attitude, or mood, is likewise more widespread; professional status, more sought after. These are components of the professional trend, a phenomenon of all the highly industrial and urban societies; a trend that apparently accompanies industrialization and urbanization irrespective of political ideologies and systems. The professional trend is closely associated with the bureaucratic, although the queen of the professions, medicine, is the avowed enemy of bureaucracy, at least of bureaucracy in medicine when others than physicians have a hand in it.

A profession delivers esoteric services—advice or action or both —to individuals, organizations or government; to whole classes or groups of people or to the public at large. The action may be manual; the surgeon and the bishop lay on their hands, although in the one case manual skill is of the essence, while in the other it need not be great because the action is symbolic. (Yet some priests and religious healers become very effective in their manner of laying hands on the heads of people who seek confirmation or comfort.) Even when manual, the action—it is assumed or claimed—is determined by esoteric knowledge systematically formulated and applied to problems of a client. The services include advice. The person for or upon whom the esoteric service is performed, or the one who is thought to have the right or duty to act for him, is advised that the professional's action is necessary. Indeed, the professional in some cases refuses to act unless the client—individual or corporate—agrees to follow the advice given.

The nature of the knowledge, substantive or theoretical, on which advice and action are based is not always clear; it is often a mixture of several kinds of practical and theoretical knowledge. But

1

it is part of the professional complex, and of the professional claim, that the practice should rest upon some branch of knowledge to which the professionals are privy by virtue of long study and by initiation and apprenticeship under masters already members of the profession.

The Oxford Shorter Dictionary tells us that the earliest meaning of the adjective "professed" was this: "That has taken the vows of a religious order." By 1675, the word had been secularized thus: "That professes to be duly qualified; professional." "Profession" originally meant the act or fact of professing. It has come to mean: "The occupation which one professes to be skilled in and to follow. . . . A vocation in which professed knowledge of some branch of learning is used in its application to the affairs of others, or in the practice of an art based upon it. Applied specifically to the three learned professions of divinity, law and medicine; also the military profession." From this follows later the adjective "professional," with the meanings now familiar.

Professionals *profess*. They profess to know better than others the nature of certain matters, and to know better than their clients what ails them or their affairs. This is the essence of the professional idea and the professional claim. From it flow many consequences. The professionals claim the exclusive right to practice, as a vocation, the arts which they profess to know, and to give the kind of advice derived from their special lines of knowledge. This is the basis of the license, both in the narrow sense of legal permission and in the broader sense that the public allows those in a profession a certain leeway in their practice and perhaps in their very way of living and thinking. The professional is expected to think objectively and inquiringly about matters which may be, for laymen, subject to orthodoxy and sentiment which limit intellectual exploration. Further, a person, in his professional capacity, may be expected and required to think objectively about matters which he himself would find it painful to approach in that way when they affected him personally. This is why it is unfair to ask the physician to heal himself, the priest to shrive himself, or the teacher to be a perfect parent. A professional has a license to deviate from lay conduct in action and in very mode of thought with respect to the matter which he professes; it is an institutionalized deviation, in which there is a certain strain toward clear definition of situations and roles.

Since the professional does profess, he asks that he be trusted. The client is not a true judge of the value of the service he receives;

furthermore, the problems and affairs of men are such that the best of professional advice and action will not always solve them. A central feature, then, of all professions, is the motto—not used in this form, so far as I know—*credat emptor*. Thus is the professional relation distinguished from that of those markets in which the rule is *caveat emptor*, although the latter is far from a universal rule even in exchange of goods. The client is to trust the professional; he must tell him all secrets which bear upon the affairs in hand. He must trust his judgment and skill. In return, the professional asks protection from any unfortunate consequences of his professional actions; he and his fellows make it very difficult for any one outside —even civil courts—to pass judgment upon one of their number. Only the professional can say when his colleague makes a mistake.

The mandate also flows from the claim to esoteric knowledge and high skill. Lawyers not only give advice to clients and plead their cases for them; they also develop a philosophy of law—of its nature and its functions, and of the proper way in which to administer justice. Physicians consider it their prerogative to define the nature of disease and of health, and to determine how medical services ought to be distributed and paid for. Social workers are not content to develop a technique of case work; they concern themselves with social legislation. Every profession considers itself the proper body to set the terms in which some aspect of society, life or nature is to be thought of, and to define the general lines, or even the details, of public policy concerning it. The mandate to do so is granted more fully to some professions than to others; in time of crisis it may be questioned even with regard to the most respected and powerful professions.

These characteristics and collective claims of a profession are dependent upon a close solidarity, upon its members constituting in some measure a group apart with an ethos of its own. This in turn implies deep and lifelong commitment. A man who leaves a profession, once he is fully trained, licensed and initiated, is something of a renegade in the eyes of his fellows; in the case of the priest, even in the eyes of laymen. It takes a rite of passage to get him in; another to read him out. If he takes French leave, he seems to belittle the profession and his former colleagues. To be sure, not all occupations called professions show these characteristics in full measure. But they constitute the highly valued professional syndrome as we know it. Professions come near the top of the prestige-ratings of occupations.

Many occupations, some new, some old, are endeavoring so to change their manner of work, their relations to clients and public, and the image which they have of themselves and others have of them, that they will merit and be granted professional standing. The new ones may arise from the development of some scientific or technological discovery which may be applied to the affairs of others. The people who "process" data for analysis by computers are a recent example. Some of the specialties within medicine are due largely to the invention of some diagnostic instrument, or to an extension of biological or chemical knowledge. After the virus came the virologist, who works alongside the bacteriologist and the person who knows about fungi—together they are the microbiologists, who work with microscopes, and lately with the electronic one. Other new professions or specialties (and specialties follow much the same course of development as professions themselves) may arise from some change in society itself. As impersonal insurance replaced the older, more personal ways of spreading the risk of death, injury, illness, unemployment and loss of property, actuarial knowledge was of necessity developed, and a new profession arose. The professional social worker is a product of social changes. In an epoch of great technological and organizational change, new techniques and new social demands work in some sort of interaction to produce new esoteric occupations.

Perhaps the way to understand what professions mean in our society is to note the ways in which occupations try to change themselves or their image, or both, in the course of a movement to become "professionalized" (a term here used to mean what happens to an occupation, but lately used to refer also to what happens to an individual in the course of training for his occupation). Courses and seminars entitled Professions, Occupations, or Sociology of Work—which I have been holding for more than twenty-five years—invariably attract many people from outside sociology. As often as not, they want to write a paper to prove that some occupation—their own—has become or is on the verge of becoming a true profession. The course gives them a set of criteria for their demonstration. Librarians, insurance salesmen, nurses, public relations people, YMCA secretaries, probation officers, personnel men, vocational guidance directors, city managers, hospital administrators, and even public health physicians have been among them.

These people are serious, often quite idealistic. The changes they want to bring about or to document are directed to the same

4

terminus ad quem, but the starting points lie in different directions. The insurance salesmen try to free themselves of the business label; they are not selling, they are giving people expert and objective diagnosis of their risks and advising them as to the best manner of protecting themselves. They are distressed that the heads of families do not confide in them more fully. The librarians seek to make themselves experts on the effects of reading, on bibliography and reference, rather than merely custodians and distributors of books; in schools and colleges, librarians want status as members of the teaching staff. They insist that they are, or must become, jointly with social psychologists, investigators of communications. That is their science, or one of their sciences. People in business management work at developing a science of management which could presumably be applied to any organization, no matter what its purpose. The social workers earlier were at pains to prove that their work could not be done by amateurs, people who brought to their efforts naught but good will; it required, they said, training in casework, a technique based on accumulated knowledge and experience of human nature and its operation in various circumstances and crises. Their first goal was to establish the position of the professional and to separate it from the amateur friendly visitor or reformer. The nurse, whose occupation is old, seeks to upgrade her place in the medical system. Her work, she says, requires much more general education than formerly, and more special knowledge; as medicine advances, the physicians delegate more and more technical functions to the nurse, who delegates some of her simpler functions to practical nurses, aides and maids. The nurse wants a measure of independence, prestige and money in keeping with her enlarged functions, as she sees them. The YMCA secretary wants his occupation recognized not merely as that of offering young men from the country a pleasant road to Protestant righteousness in the city, but as a more universal one of dealing with groups of young people. All that is learned of adolescence, of behavior in small groups, of the nature and organization of community life is considered the intellectual base of his work. The vocational guidance people have trouble in bringing the teaching profession to recognize that theirs is a separate complex of skills, presumed to rest on psychology. The public health men have a double problem. They must convince other physicians that their work—which is generally not the diagnosing and treating of patients—is really medicine. They must also combat the belief of physicians that they should do for fees some of what the public health people do for a fixed salary.

In these examples appear the main themes of professionalization. Detachment is one of them; and that in the sense of having in a particular case no personal interest such as would influence one's action or advice, while being deeply interested in all cases of the kind. The deep interest in all cases is of the sort that leads one to pursue and systematize the pertinent knowledge. It leads to finding an intellectual base for the problems one handles, which, in turn, takes those problems out of their particular setting and makes them part of some more universal order. One aspect of a profession is a certain equilibrium between the universal and the particular. The priest who would fix his attention entirely on the universal aspects of religious behavior might find himself indifferent as to which religion he would attach himself to; and thus, a renegade and a heretic. Churches do not encourage such circulation of the elite. Great corporations, too, although they may seek men who know the science of management, want an executive's curiosity about and love of the universal aspects of human organization tempered with a certain loyalty and commitment to his employer. I suppose there may be a professional man so free-sweeping in his interests that he does not mind what client he serves and what aspects of the client's affairs he deals with. He would be a rarity—a rich outcast or a poor idealist.

The balance of the universal and the particular in a profession varies, but there is always some measure of both, with an appropriate equilibrium between detachment and interest. The balance between universal and particular is related to that between the theoretical and the practical. Branches of learning are not always very directly related to the ordinary business of life. If some occupations become professions by developing an intellectual interest, others do it by becoming more practical. A large number of chemists are now employed by industries. Psychologists are seeking and obtaining legislation giving them monopoly over the name and making it an offense for anyone to "practice" psychology without it. Some sociologists, especially those who do research by the "project" for "clients," would do likewise. Perhaps one should distinguish between professions in essence, such as medicine or engineering, which pursue knowledge to improve practice; and professions by accident, such as, say, archaeology, where the practices are merely the means to increasing knowledge. In both cases, the people engaged may make their living by their activities. There appears to be a trend in certain fields of knowledge for this distinction to disappear and for the learned societies to become professional guilds concerned with problems of practice, employment, licensing and distribution of their services. Many learned societies show strain between the intellectuals and the professionalizers.

This strain, incidentally, is found in some degree in all professions. A physician may be too devoted to research; a lawyer too concerned with comparative law; a social worker overcurious about the roots of human behavior. In fact, inside most professions there develops a tacit division of labor between the more theoretical and the more practical; once in a while conflict breaks out over issues related to it. The professional schools may be accused of being too "academic"; the academics accuse other practitioners of failure to be sufficiently intellectual.

Another set of themes in professionalizing movements has to do with a change of status of the occupation in relation to its own past, and to the other people—clients, public, other occupations— involved in its work drama. Changes sought are more independence, more recognition, a higher place, a cleaner distinction between those in the profession and those outside, and a larger measure of autonomy in choosing colleagues and successors. One necessary validation of such changes of status in our society is introduction of study for the profession in question into the universities. It may be as an undergraduate program, leading to a Bachelor's degree with a major in the theory and practice of the occupation. A large proportion of the university undergraduates in this country are in such professional courses. Other professions seek to have a Master's degree made the standard professional qualification; so it is in social work, hospital administration, business administration, laboratory technology, librarianship and many others. The Master's degree is also used as qualification for a professional or administrative elite in occupations for which the basic preparation is a Bachelor's degree. The Ph.D. or some substitute, such as the Doctor of Education, is also used as qualification for higher administrative and teaching positions in professional agencies and schools.

The older professions, law and medicine, have long been established in the universities; at present in this country, they can keep their aspirants in college for four years and in professional school for three or four years after that. Indeed, so sure are they of their place that they tend to encourage undergraduates to pursue what lines of study they will, so long as their achievements are high. One

7

way in which an occupation—or a college—can document its high status is by being able to take its pick of the young people about to enter the labor market, and then to keep them in school a long time before admitting them to the charmed circle.

Some combination of scholastic aptitude, ambition and financial means is required to accomplish this educational aim. The ambition must have been fostered in some social setting, generally in the middle class family, although occasionally in a working class family with the aid of a sponsoring schoolteacher who sets sights high. The financial means may come from the aspirant's family, a discounting in advance of the income to be made in the profession, or from an investment in talent by government, industry or the foundations. The latter is of increasing importance in allowing people to continue in higher professional training, especially for work thought to be of use to defense or related industrial development. It is probably effective only when reinforced by the expectation of good income and high prestige.

Not all occupations which aspire to professional standing can promise enough of either of these ingredients to get the most talented and then to keep them in school as long as do medicine, law and the sciences. Characteristically they seek to improve their position in both recruitment and the education system; in the earlier phases of their move toward professionalism, the people in an occupation may have to earn their way slowly and painfully to higher education, and the professional school may have difficulty in getting itself accepted in universities. It may take an operation bootstrap to get a corps of people in the occupation academically qualified to teach succeeding generations and grant them professional degrees.

This competition for status is accompanied by a trend toward prolonging the professional training at both ends: at the beginning by multiplying prerequisites for entry to professional school, at the finish by prolonging the course and the various apprentice or internship programs. This is held in check by the fact that many of the would-be professions cannot offer enough future income and prestige to get people early and keep them long in school. Parents of less income and education also press their children to seek security in known middle-level occupations. This pressure may also work against the movement to lift professional requirements.

Old and new alike, the professions cherish their recruits once they get them. Having picked their candidates with great care,

8

medical schools, for instance, gnash their teeth and tear their hair over a sheep lost from the fold. They wonder what they have done wrong to make the lamb stray. They make it clear to the professional recruit that he owes it to himself, the profession and the school to stick with his choice. Has it not been discovered by all the tests that this is the one right outlet for his talents? Is it not his duty to use his talents for his country in the best possible way? Have not the profession and the professional school made a great investment in him? Has he the right not to give full return on it? The day has passed when the youngsters entering professional school are told to look well at their neighbors in the classroom, for few of them will be there next year. The theme is mutual commitment, reinforced by students' auxiliaries sponsored by the professional associations, and by the use of such terms as "student-physician," which stress that the student is already in the professional family. One owes allegiance for life to a family.

Thus we have a high degree of competition among the professions for talent, combined with a great feeling of possessiveness over the recruits as soon as they have crossed the threshold. The professional student is, to some extent, already an organization man.

But that is not the only respect in which the modern professional is an organization man. Professions are more and more practiced in organizations. The *Freie Berufe* in Germany were considered free not merely because they were worthy of free men, but because those who followed them had no employer. Even the *freier Gelehrte,* or independent scholar, once he had acquired the right to teach, received his income in fees from his clients, the students. The university merely gave him his validation and his forum, as the court gives lawyers a playing field and a referee for their contest. The true professional, according to the traditional ideology of professions, is never hired. He is retained, engaged, consulted, etc., by some one who has need of his services. He, the professional, has or should have almost complete control over what he does for the client.

Especially in medicine, the protest against working in organizations and for salary is very strong. Yet in this country, more than in England, where there is a national plan of medical practice, physicians work in organizations. A decade ago it was reported that for every physician in the United States, there were between four and five people in the related or paramedical professions. There are more now; many people in the medical systems are in nonmedical

work such as accounting, housekeeping, engineering and maintenance, and actuarial work for medical insurance schemes. An increasing proportion of physicians are in specialties; the specialist
characteristically must work with other physicians. Some specialties
never get the first call from an ailing patient; they are reached only
after one or more referrals. Some specialties are, like pathology and
anaesthesiology, practiced only in hospitals or clinics. All physicians
now work at least a year for salary as interns; many work for a salary
for several years as residents. In some specialties—those far from
the first call of ailing people—work for an organization, possibly for
salary, is the rule. An increasing number of lawyers work in large
firms where duties and cases are assigned, not completely chosen by
the individual practitioner himself. The firm operates as a referral
system and allows the individual lawyer enough cases of one kind to
permit him to specialize. Many lawyers have but one client, a company; and when there is but one client, it becomes in fact an employer.

Law and medicine—the models which other professions try to
approximate—in spite of nourishing free practice of the individual
for a number of clients with a minimum of institutional apparatus,
are in fact far along the road to practice in complicated organizations which intervene in many ways between them and their clients. Engineers, applied scientists and people in most of the newer
professions nearly all work in organizations with others of their own
profession, and with many people of related occupations. Indeed,
it becomes hard to say who is the client in many cases; in the case
of medicine, is it the insurance company or the patient? In the
school, is it the child, the parent, the community at large or some
class of people within it? In social work, is it the agency—which
pays—or the so-called client, who is worked upon not always of his
own free will? It is characteristic of modern professions that they
do work in such institutional settings, often with capital goods which
they do not own and with a great variety of people. Professional
ideology prefers a two-party arrangement: the professional and his
client. It prefers the client who can speak for himself and pay for
himself. This is not the prevailing arrangement, nor is it likely to be.

Thus arise a great number of problems for professions. The
problem of finding a clientele becomes that of finding a place in a
system of organizations. The problem of colleague relationships becomes that of determining who, in a complex organization of many
professions, are indeed one's colleagues, and in what degree. The

problem of freedom becomes one of distinguishing between one's obligations to the person, if it be such a case, on which one performs some action or to whom one gives some advice, and to one's employer or organization. For example, does the college physician report the secrets of his student-patient to the dean and, if so, in what situations? There is also a problem of authority; what orders does one accept from an employer, especially one who is not a member of one's own profession and whose interests may not always be those of the professional and his clients?

The other side of this coin is that the employer, even in business, finds himself dealing with an increasing number of professional (staff) people, who will not be ordered about as freely as line people. Indeed, Robert Maynard Hutchins once said:

> . . . business may eventually be organized like a university, with the staff claiming a kind of academic freedom, participating in the formation of policy, and enjoying permanent tenure. When that happens the university administrators of America will derive a certain grim satisfaction from the struggles of those captains of industry who have had the habit of complaining about the mismanagement of universities.*

As the professions become more organized, business organizations become more professionalized. The result is the development of new patterns of organization. If the professional man giving staff services to business or industry sets a certain pattern of freedom not common among the employees of business, he has also lost a certain kind of freedom which inhered in the private practice of professions for clients of whom enough were solvent to assure him a good income and a fitting style of life.

But it may be possible that under present conditions the private practitioner of a profession does not have so much freedom, or at least not the same kinds of freedom as his colleague working in some sort of larger organization. In theory, the private practitioner is free to move at will; in fact, it is very chancy for a man established in practice in a given community to move. Reputations among the common run of clients are local and may depend upon conformity with local customs and beliefs concerning nonprofessional matters. The man who works in an organization may develop a wider reputation, even a national one; he may improve his lot by moving from time to time. He may be freer of social pressures. The man who practices privately may, in fact, be the choreboy of his clients, doing

* "The Administrator," in R. B. Heywood (ed.), *The Works of the Mind* (Chicago: University of Chicago Press, 1947), pp. 135–156.

11

only those things which they want in a hurry and which do not warrant the seeking out of a better known or more specialized practitioner, firm or other organization. He may thus have little or no choice of what kinds of work he will do. The man in the larger organization may apply himself to some line of work and become so proficient in it that he need not accept any work not to his taste. Perhaps the man in the organization may not pick his client, but he can often pick his problems. It may perhaps be that a few men at the very top of a profession can practice privately and as they wish, because of a great reputation throughout the profession and among sophisticated and affluent clients; while the bulk of people in private and "solo" practice will be choreboys without much reputation among clients and without any among their more specialized colleagues.

In between these two extremes there may be—and I believe there are—a large and increasing number of competent people who work in organized settings. They will, in order to be successful, develop reputations among their colleagues and will be, in case the profession is such as to demand it, known as effective with clients. They will work out new systems of relationships, which may be much the same in business, government agencies, universities, hospitals and clinics, and other kinds of organizations; among the relationships to be worked out are those of the balance between obligations to one's professional colleagues, both in and out of one's present organization, and the organizations in which one works. New formulae of freedom and control will be worked out. The people in organizations will be—although in some sense bureaucrats—the innovators, the people who push back the frontiers of theoretical and practical knowledge related to their professions, who will invent new ways of bringing professional services to everyone, not merely to the solvent or sophisticated few. Indeed, I think it likely that the professional conscience, the superego, of many professions will be lodged in that segment of professionals who work in complicated settings, for they must, in order to survive, be sensitive to more problems and to a greater variety of points of view.

On the other hand, the professionals will become more sensitive to outside opinion; and, like other organized groups, they will hire public relations people to perform for them the esoteric service of creating a satisfactory public image in the press, on television and in the schools, where young people learn about the careers open to them. It is all a rather confusing prospect. The professions will, in any case, be a large and influential element in our future, and in that of all societies which go the road of industrialization and urbanization; the organizational structures in which they will work will very likely resemble one another, no matter what the prevailing political ideologies in various countries of the same degree of industrialization.

In the meantime, there are large parts of the world which are not far along this road. In some of them there is an oversupply of professional people and an undersupply, or some lack of balance in the supply, of related professions. A recent paper reports that whereas in this country there are several nurses for each physician, in India there are seven physicians for one nurse. Oversupply means, of course, only more than can be supported by an economy. Lack of demand may be due to lack of money or to lack of acceptance of the very definition of wants to which a profession caters. It is generally both money and sophistication which are lacking. What will be the course of the rise of demand for medicine, education, legal protection and social services in the now poor and nonindustrial countries? It will not be the same course as in the older industrial countries, for the latter had no models to go by; people of the now developing countries know, or soon will know, that such personal services exist and are widely available in the older industrial economies. They will hardly pass through the same stages of professional practice, organization and distribution of services as we did.

Many of the institutions of a modern society depend upon an adequate supply of professionals who perform services for corporate bodies: people to plan and build water systems, communications, roads, industrial plants; people to train others in various trades and techniques and to organize public services. Professionals who do these things have, in the past, come to a new country from abroad as employees or representatives of colonial powers, business concerns or missionary agencies. They have not always sought native recruits or successors; nor have they always given full recognition to local colleagues where there have been some. We are evidently in a new situation with respect to the deploying of professional people over the world. It is not clear who will sponsor such a deployment, what sort of reception professionals from abroad will get in new nations, or how professionals from the highly urban and industrial countries will fit work abroad into their careers.

Again we face the problem of the relation of the particular, the culture-bound, aspect of professions to the universal aspect. The professional may learn some things that are universal in the physical, biological or social world. But around this core of universal knowledge there is likely to be a large body of practical knowledge which relates only to his own culture. The physician may recognize the rhythm of the beat of an East Indian woman's heart, yet lack the slighest knowledge of how to get her to accept his diagnosis of what ails her and his advice about how to live with it. Furthermore, the physician—or other professional—may have become so accustomed to his own society's particular way of practicing, of payment, of dividing labor with others that he will not and cannot adapt himself to these particularities of another society, especially a preindustrial and not highly literate one. An interlude in another part of the world might interrupt the accumulation of reputation, seniority and money so essential to his career at home; whatever he might learn in practice of his profession abroad might or might not be applicable to his future work at home. While professions are, in some of their respects, universal, in others they are closely ethnocentric. In many professions, careers are contained within a single economy and society. One of the interesting developments of the future will be new patterns of international exchange of professional knowledge and professional institutions.

BERNARD BARBER

Some Problems in the Sociology of the Professions

ALTHOUGH it is still only a partly developed field of specialized knowledge, the sociology of the professions is already too large a body of theoretical analysis and empirical research to be more than sketched in this paper. We shall therefore deal only with some of the central problems of the structure and functioning of the professions; even then, for lack of space, we shall concentrate on the general aspects of six of these problems: (1) Social sources of concern with the professions; (2) Toward a definition of the professions; (3) The role of the university professional school; (4) The emerging or marginal profession; (5) Professional roles and organizational necessities; and (6) Professionals and politics. Although these six problems touch upon the essential characteristics of professions in all societies, our illustrations are mostly from the United States, where the largest amount of empirical research on the professions has been carried out. Despite essential similarities, there are major differences among professions in different societies and at different historical times, and a more complete treatment of the professions would have to specify these comparative social and historical differences.

Social Sources of Concern with the Professions

A set of intricately interwoven moral, intellectual and practical concerns is responsible for the large amount of discussion, analysis and research on the nature and functions of the professions in modern society. The moral concerns have centered on the problem of the tensions and conflict between individual interest and community interest in modern society. Individualism, which is, as A. D. Lindsay has said, "a modern word," came to seem to some people a corrosive of all social ties and all social values. While individualism

15

was supposed, in the theory of Smith, Bentham and Mill, to contribute indirectly, through the "unseen hand," to the larger community interest, it obviously very often did not do so. And some moralists (who also had more or less intellectual concern in the matter) came to feel that individualism was fundamentally irreconcilable with the community welfare.

Business was, and it remains, of course, the vital center of individualism both in creed and practice.[1] The professions, by setting a pattern of more direct concern with the community interest, seemed to represent quite a different principle. In consequence, those who had the moral welfare of modern society much at heart often recommended the enlargement of the professions and the professionalization of business.[2] In France, for example, Emile Durkheim, speaking as a moral philosopher as well as a sociologist, recommended the corporative organization of professions in business as a way of raising standards of morality and of submitting individual interest to community welfare. In a course of lectures on professional ethics and civic morals given first at Bordeaux between 1890 and 1900 and repeated at the Sorbonne during the next two decades, Durkheim said: "There are professional ethics for the priest, the lawyer, the magistrate. . . . Why should there not be one for trade and industry?"[3] In England, the social theorist, historian and moralist R. H. Tawney made what was probably the most influential statement in that country on the desirability of the professionalization of business. A "functional society," according to Tawney, is one in which individual and community interest are harmoniously reconciled; an "acquisitive society" exists where the pursuit of individual interest subverts the community interest.[4] Cautioning us that "to idealize the professional spirit would be very absurd," he nonetheless recommends the enlargement of professionalism because of its necessity in a functional society. Finally, in the United States, at much the same time as Durkheim and Tawney, Louis D. Brandeis, then a Massachusetts social reformer and later a Justice of the United States Supreme Court, expressed the hope that "as the profession of business develops, the great industrial and social problems expressed in the present social unrest will one by one find solution."[5] In this same 1912 address he said: "Business should be, and to some extent already is, one of the professions."[6]

The primarily intellectual concern with the professions can be found in fullest measure in the sociology of the professions, which has become in the last twenty-five years a full-fledged field of special-

ization. Work in general, as well as professional work in particular, has been recognized as having great intellectual and practical significance for modern society.[7] Perhaps as good an indication as any of the significance that sociologists attach to the study of the professions can be found in the central place it has had in the work of Talcott Parsons.[8] He has used his study of the professions not only as a way of defining central characteristics of modern society but as a vehicle for developing a general scheme of analytical variables that apply to all social action.

Finally, and quite clearly, important practical concerns have been conductive to the study of the professions. In the United States, the "professionals" per 100,000 of the population have increased from 859 in 1870 to 3310 in 1950.[9] As W. J. Goode has put it, "An industrializing society is a professionalizing society."[10] Industrializing societies include, of course, the underdeveloped, "modernizing" societies.[11] All around the world, then, we see the growth in numbers and practical importance of the professional occupations.

Toward a Definition of the Professions

Theoretical and methodological consensus is not yet so great among sociologists that there is any absolute agreement on the definition of "the professions."[12] And of course among the public at large the debate over the boundary between "professional" and "nonprofessional" continues, a debate which is kept going by the fact that these terms carry an important assignment of differential occupational prestige. Still, considerable progress toward a definition has been made, and this section of the paper seeks to summarize that progress.[13]

A sociological definition of the professions should limit itself, so far as possible, to the *differentia specifica* of professional behavior. For example, concepts like style of life, corporate solidarity and socialization structures and processes, which apply to all other groups as well as to professional ones, are not the *differentia specifica*.

There is no absolute difference between professional and other kinds of occupational behavior, but only relative differences with respect to certain attributes common to all occupational behavior. Some occupational behavior, seen in the light of these attributes, which we discuss below, is fully professional; other behavior is partly professional; and some can be thought of as barely or not at

17

all professional. On this view, for example, there may be some professional elements in some kinds of business behavior. Similarly, on the same view, the medical profession is more professional than the nursing profession, and the medical doctor who does university research is more professional than the medical doctor who provides minor medical services in a steel plant. Professionalism is a matter of degree.

Professional behavior may be defined in terms of four essential attributes: a high degree of generalized and systematic knowledge; primary orientation to the community interest rather than to individual self-interest; a high degree of self-control of behavior through codes of ethics internalized in the process of work socialization and through voluntary associations organized and operated by the work specialists themselves; and a system of rewards (monetary and honorary) that is primarily a set of symbols of work achievement and thus ends in themselves, not means to some end of individual self-interest.[14] Some amplification of these four attributes will be useful.

All occupational behavior has some degree of knowledge as one of its attributes. As the phrase "the learned professions" vividly signifies, a high degree of generalized and systematic knowledge early became one of the commonly used defining characteristics of professional behavior. Generalized and systematic knowledge of professional degree exists in such diverse cultural realms as the physical and biological sciences, in religion or theology, in the law, literature, art, mathematics and philosophy. During the last one hundred years, the social sciences, including history, economics, psychology, anthropology and sociology, have developed generalized and systematic knowledge of a professional level.

Its relation to individual and community interest is another attribute of all occupational performance. Since generalized and systematic knowledge provides powerful control over nature and society, it is important to society that such knowledge be used primarily in the community interest. Where such knowledge exists, orientation primarily to community rather than individual interest is an essential attribute of professional behavior. Individual self-interest is, of course, not utterly neglected in professional behavior, but is subserved *indirectly*.

Social control depends in part, obviously, upon substantive understanding of the behavior to be controlled. In the case of behavior characterized by a high degree of knowledge, the requisite under-

standing is available in full measure only to those who have themselves been trained in and apply that knowledge. It follows that some kind of self-control, by means of internalized codes of ethics and voluntary in-groups, is necessary. In the realms of professional behavior, such codes and such associations for the setting and maintaining of standards proliferate. Further controls on professional behavior exist, of course, in the informal agencies of public opinion and in governmental-legal agencies. But these other forms of social control are less important than in nonprofessional areas.

Money income, general prestige and specific honors or symbols of achievement are among the different forms of social reward for occupational performance.[15] Since money income is a more appropriate reward for individual self-interest, and since prestige and honors are more appropriate for community interest, these latter types of reward are relatively more important in professional than in nonprofessional behavior. The actual reward system in the professions tends to consist, therefore, in a combination of prestige and titles, medals, prizes, offices in professional societies, and so forth, together with sufficient monetary income for the style of life appropriate to the honor bestowed. Although the professions are not so well paid, on the whole, as equal-ranking business roles in American society, all studies show that the public ranks the professions at the top of the occupational prestige hierarchy and that professionals themselves are more satisfied with their work-rewards than are other occupational groups.

These four essential attributes define a scale of professionalism, a way of measuring the extent to which it is present in different forms of occupational performance. The most professional behavior would be that which realizes all four attributes in the fullest possible manner. Justice of the United States Supreme Court, or professor of physics and Nobel Prize winner in a distinguished university, would be defined as very highly professional roles. A $100,000-a-year vice president in charge of legal affairs for a middle-size business corporation would be clearly less professional in these terms. And a $6000-a-year school teacher would be ranked as less professional still.

The Role of the University Professional School

In the light of our definition, we can now more easily see several aspects of the essential role that the university professional school

performs for the practicing profession it serves. Nearly all the well-established professions are located in some measure in the university; the more professional ones, according to our definition, having the more university-connected schools. Within a given profession, the "better" or more professional schools are more likely to be in a university, and the very best ones are typically in the very best universities. Where a well-established profession is not, for some special reasons, located in the university, it has usually sought to construct an institution that approximates one, as in the case of the war colleges for the training of top military personnel. This type of institution tries to staff itself, in part, with university caliber instructors and also to bring from various civilian universities, on at least a part-time basis, specialists in the different kinds of generalized and systematic knowledge it needs but cannot provide from among its own professionals. As we shall also see, the emerging or marginal professions, when they are trying to raise standards for themselves, seek to locate themselves in universities. If they already have a marginal connection there, they seek to improve their position in the university. Among the members of a profession, and probably also among the public at large, the university professional school staff tends to have as high occupational prestige as any in the professions, though typically not the highest income.

The university professional school has as one of its basic functions the transmission to its students of the generalized and systematic knowledge that is the basis of professional performance. Not only the substantive knowledge itself, but knowledge of how to keep up with continuing advances in professional knowledge is what the university school seeks to give its students. Where the body of professional knowledge is changing very rapidly, the university professional school may take a direct role in promoting the "adult" education of the members of its profession through postprofessional training courses, seminars and institutes.

Equally important is the university professional school's responsibility for the creation of new and better knowledge on which professional practice can be based. Its university position makes it possible for all members of its staff to be part-time scholars and researchers and for some to carry on these activities full time. The university professional school can borrow resources of knowledge from other university departments, either by co-opting full-time teaching and research personnel or through more informal, part-time cooperation in the university community. The better the uni-

versity professional school, the more likely it is to use resources from the other professional schools in the university and from all the other departments of basic knowledge insofar as they are relevant. In sum, the university professional schools are the leading, though not the sole, innovators and systematizers of ideas for their professions.

So far as normative standards of community orientation (or "ethics") are concerned, again the university professional school has certain essential functions. The university professional school sees to the ethical training of its students as well as to their other learning. Some of this ethical training is explicit, in the form of teaching professional codes; some of it is intermixed with what is ostensibly only the learning of substantive knowledge; and some of it is implicit in the behavior of the staff. University professional-school staff members often come to serve as ethical role-models for their students and even as guides to conscience after the students have themselves become mature practicing professionals.

The staff of the university professional school are often the leaders in the continual codification and improvement of standards of ethics for practicing professionals. They criticize, sometimes within professional circles and sometimes in public, inadequacy and deviation among practicing professionals. This criticism is the more powerful when it is based on careful research of the kind that university professionals are able to carry out. But more than negative means, in the form of criticism, is available to them. University members are often responsible for the award to praticing professionals of a variety of medals, prizes and other honors for high standards of ethics as well as for intellectual achievement in the profession. In these several ways, the university professional school is a moral watchdog for its profession.

For both its knowledge and its ethical functions, the relative insulation of the university professional school has certain advantages. It is relatively freer of those commitments to other organizations and other interests that practicing professionals have, and therefore it is more nearly able to maintain the highest intellectual and moral standards. Also, it can use the general insulation of the university from certain pressures to fortify itself in the performance of its functions, sometimes even in the face of resistance or opposition from the practicing professionals themselves.

So much for the positive functions of the university professional schools. Unfortunately, the literature has not pointed out that these

21

also have the defects of their virtues. The functions of the university professional school lead to a certain amount of "structured strain" between it and the practicing professionals. The university professional is ever pressing, with increasing knowledge and higher moral standards, on the practicing professional who has to meet other pressures, sometimes, as we shall see below, from nonprofessional organizations in which he works, but also from other cultural and social interests. These other pressures may have a legitimacy and a force that the practicing professional feels is equal to the legitimate pressure from his university colleagues. Even when he manages successfully to accommodate the opposed pressures, he is likely to feel a certain resentment against the "ivory-tower" university professionals whose relatively insulated situation and perspective have dysfunctions as well as functions for the man outside.

The Emerging or Marginal Profession

Since new levels and types of generalized and systematic knowledge are constantly being developed in modern society, there is a constant push both on and from within certain nonprofessional and quasiprofessional occupational groups to become more professional and to claim public recognition as such. Hence arises the phenomenon of the emerging or marginal profession, a phenomenon comprising a number of recurrent patterns, and of especial interest because it highlights the essential characteristics of professional behavior.[16]

The emerging or marginal profession is an occupation which is not so clearly high or so clearly low on both of the first two attributes of professionalism—generalized knowledge and community orientation—that its status is clearly defined by itself and others. The emerging profession may be middle-ranking on both of these dimensions or it may be higher on one dimension and lower on the other. Library work, social work, pharmacy and accountancy are all examples of the emerging or marginal profession.

It is typical of the structure of the occupational group that is emerging as a profession that its members are not homogeneous with respect to the amount of knowledge and community orientation they possess. In occupations like social work or library work, probably two thirds or more of the members are pretty clearly only marginally professional. But the elite of these occupations, such as the director of a university library or the dean of a major university school of social work, are clearly professional. It is the elite of an emerging profession that takes the lead in pushing for the advancement of professionalism in its occupational group and in claiming public recognition of its new status.[17] Toward these ends, they typically engage in behavior showing the following patterns.

The leaders of an emerging profession may acknowledge the present and obvious inadequacies of their group, but they compare these inadequacies to ones that existed in the past among professions now fully established. Thus the professionally aspiring leader of the American Management Association says, "It's something like medicine years ago, when the doctors came to the realization that working in a drug store was not sufficient training for their profession. Now management is going through a similar transition." [18] The implication is that the emerging profession too can progress to full professional status.

In the attempt to express and strengthen the community orientation of their group, the leaders take pains to construct and publish a code of ethics. Unfortunately, because the knowledge on which their occupational performance is based is not highly developed, the codes they construct are full of vague generalities, and therefore hard for the individual practitioner to apply in concrete cases. The emerging profession is also unable to construct the machinery of interpretation and enforcement of its codes that exists in the established professions.

The leaders establish or try to strengthen a professional association. In an established profession, such an association effectively carries on the several functions of self-control, socialization and education of the members, communications with the public, and the defense of professional interest against infringement by the public or other occupational groups.[19] The emerging profession's association seeks to increase its effectiveness in all these functions.

Within their own occupational ranks, the leaders establish measures and titles of more and less professional behavior, hoping, for example, to use such prestigious titles as "fellow" as an incentive for the less professional to become more so. They may also seek legal licensure from the state if it does not already exist. Because their prestige and even their right to work seems to be threatened by such moves, the less professional members of the emerging profession resist these innovations, sometimes violently. To forestall some of this resistance, the elite will provide a "grandfather clause" in all new informal and legal regulations about title and prestige.

The leaders will, of course, seek to establish or strengthen university professional schools. The flexibility of the American university system has permitted even marginal professions to get some kind of connection with some kind of university, thus holding open the door for any further possible development of professionalism. Because marginal professional schools are a threat to the standards of the university, it in turn tries to strengthen such schools out of its own resources. In some cases, thus, a beneficial spiral of progress for the emerging profession is helped along.

Desiring prestige and support from the general public, the leaders will engage in a program of public information about the "professional" services it provides and the "professional" standards of community orientation it maintains. Such campaigns are sometimes dismissed by outsiders as "mere" public relations, that is, an attempt to flimflam the public with half-truths and deceit. There may be such flimflammery in some public information campaigns by emerging professions, though often an aspiring profession is fooling itself as much as the public. Insofar as the public's ignorance is replaced with genuine facts about the emerging profession, facts which the public can test in the actual social reality, such public information campaigns will effectively raise the professional status of an occupational group. Similarly, with regard to professional titles, the public will respect only those titles the emerging profession gives itself which seem to symbolize actually realized standards of performance and morality.

And, finally, the leaders of an emerging profession will have to engage in some conflict with elements both inside and outside their occupational group. We have already seen that they may meet with some opposition from the less professional members within the group. But also, as they make claims to certain levels of technical performance and certain standards of community orientation, they may have to label those outsiders who fall short of these levels and standards as "charlatans," and they may themselves be branded as "encroachers" on other established occupational and professional specialties.[20] In such social situations, competition and conflict often have positive as well as negative functions.

Professional Roles and Organizational Necessities

Modern society is characterized by a multiplicity of specialized goals and specialized, formal organizations, or "bureaucracies," devoted to the realization of such goals. It is this aspect of modern society that Weber had in mind when he spoke of "the bureaucratization of the world." In all kinds of bureaucratically structured organizations (government, business, labor union, philanthropic foundation, university and voluntary welfare association), professionals of many different kinds (lawyers, doctors, scientists, social scientists and publicists) are now indispensable. The sociology of the professions has, therefore, been much interested in the relationships between professional roles and organizational requirements, or necessities.

One of the essential attributes of the professional role, we have seen, is autonomy, or self-control by the professionals themselves with regard to the development and application of the body of generalized knowledge in which they alone are expert. On the other side, it is an essential requirement of an effective formal organization which is devoted to the coordination of a variety of activities necessary for the realization of some specialized goal that the executive maintain adequate control over all those persons in the organization responsible for carrying out these subsidiary activities. Whereas professions find the pattern of "colleague control" most suitable, the required pattern of authority for formal organizations is "superordinate control." The former consists of control by peers, the latter of control by superiors. As a result of these different types of required authority, it is inevitable that there be a certain amount of strain when professional roles confront organizational necessities. For example, professionals in business or government organizations resent being appraised by those who are not their professional peers but only their superiors in office. Or again, professionals in all kinds of formal organizations regard as unnecessary "red tape" all kinds of control procedures—control over time, over the spending of money, over choice of work task—which these organizations impose on all who work in them.

Inevitable strain exists, then, in this situation, but this does not mean inevitable conflict. For where such inevitable strain is created by different social patterns, a variety of accommodative mechanisms can often be created to reduce the strain or to forestall conflict resulting from the strain that remains. Unfortunately, to the detriment of effective cooperation between professionals and the executives of the organizations they work for, there has been a widespread tendency to overlook both the possibility and the actual existence of effectively functioning accommodative mechanisms of this kind.

There has been a tendency to construct a "lo, the poor professional" myth, and to see an irreconcilable conflict between the professional and his employing organization. In this conflict, the professional is seen as inevitably exploited, frustrated and stifled.

We shall describe three types of accommodative mechanism by which the inherent strain between professional roles and organizational necessities can be reduced. They are: differentiated role structures, differentiated authority structures and differentiated reward structures.[21] These accommodative mechanisms help to meet the different and somewhat opposed needs of professions and organizations. The mutual effectiveness of professions and organizations is enhanced when such mechanisms exist and are working well.

Organizations that use professionals can usually create for them specialized roles in partially segregated substructures of the organization so that the professionals may carry on their own activities as they require. Thus in business or in government, special legal or research or medical departments are created for this purpose. Even these professional departments or substructures may be further subdivided according to specialized types of professional roles. Where these different types of professional activities are needed, an organization may create specialized departments for basic professional research, for the development and application of these basic ideas, and for minor professional service activities. For example, in the government there can be separate departments or suborganizations for basic medical research, for the development of medical technology and for day-to-day medical care. This differentiation of roles in a variety of specialized substructures of the organization as a whole helps to preserve professional needs for autonomy.

Such differentiated role structures create some new problems of their own for the professional. He may find it harder, for example, to get other differentiated groups in the organization to use his ideas and skills. These other groups or departments have their own needs and vested interests. Thus, production departments in an industrial organization may ignore or resist the professional research department, or the sales department may dismiss the suggestions of the legal department as professional niggling. Where differentiated role structures exist to protect his own needs, the professional must be all the more active in transmitting his professional knowledge and skills to other differentiated subgroups in his employing organization. He has to be forceful in promoting his ideas, because of lack of knowledge of what he can do and because of structural resistance.

In addition to differentiated roles, organizations that use professionals can also usually create a specialized type of authority structure which is an accommodation between the organization's need for the pattern of superordinate control and the professional's need for the colleague control pattern of authority. The key role in this accommodative and specialized authority structure is played by the "professional-administrator." The occupant of this role must be a professional who can judge and direct another professional but who can also exercise superordinate control when necessary. It is the function of the professional-administrator to grant as much autonomy as possible in the choice and evaluation of professional work, while providing overall direction and coordination with the primary goals of the organization, whether these be to make money or to land a man on the moon. Where many professionals are employed, there may be a hierarchy of professional-administrators. The higher the administrator's position in this hierarchy, the more his concern is with the problems of coordination for the whole organization in which the professionals are employed. The higher the position, moreover, the greater the use of superordinate control. The lower positions in the hierarchy of professional-administrators can use more colleague control. At the actual working level, therefore, in contact with his section administrator, the professional can have the colleague control which he needs and wants.

Specialized professional authority structures of this kind face their own problems. One of these is that it is hard to find professionals who combine the proper mixture of professional and administrative abilities. Also, pressures from both sides make the role of professional-administrator a focus of strain which not all men can handle successfully. Nevertheless, despite some tendency for professionals to disparage the role of professional-administrator, there seems to be increasing prestige for it among them and an increasing willingness on their part to commit themselves to filling it effectively. Even university deans, the oldest of professional-administrators, have this new prestige.

Finally, there is the accommodative mechanism that consists of differentiated reward structures. Organizations that employ professionals can usually create opportunities for them to achieve professional rewards while still serving the primary needs of the organization. Among these professional facilities and rewards are the opportunity to participate in professional association meetings, to publish research, to continue professional training through tuition subsidies and leaves of absence, to be employed full time on strictly professional work, to be a member of a strong professional group on the job itself, and to advance in salary and prestige for continuing in strictly professional work. Organizations that have gone furthest in providing such opportunities have often set up multiple career channels for their employees, one for line executives and other channels for their different sets of professionals. On a "professional ladder," such as exists in many government and business organizations, professionals can improve their prestige, income and facilities without giving up their professional specialty. In some cases they can even continue as full-time working professionals, not even being required to become professional-administrators.

The difficulty in providing this accommodative mechanism for professionals in organizations is that the rewards for achieving the primary organizational goals are always, and probably necessarily, at least a little higher than those for achieving the subsidiary professional goals. There is some pressure, therefore, on professionals to move from their own specialized career ladder to the central executive ladder, where the rewards are greater, certainly in monetary terms. While individual moves to the main executive ladder are in part a loss to the body of professionals, such moves also have advantages. Former professionals, once established in high executive places, are in a better position to understand the specialized needs of their former professional colleagues. A former lawyer or scientist at the head of a business organization will know the needs of the legal and research departments better than a nonprofessional. Former professors make better college and university presidents than businessmen or generals.

Organizations which have successfully set up these accommodative structures for their professional employees would have, as Kornhauser has put it, "a pluralist character," and would tend "toward a balance of freedom and power." [22] In most organizations, of course, there exist only different approximations to success in establishing these differentiated structures required by professionals. With better understanding of them as necessary accommodative mechanisms, however, considerable improvement in the relations between professional roles and organizational necessities could be achieved in many business, government and other formal organizations.

Professionals and Politics

Up to now the sociology of the professions has not produced a general analysis of the subject of professionals and politics. Given the broad scope of the subject, the scarcity of research comparing different professions in this respect, and the considerable diversity of political behavior and ideas among professionals which in fact exists, this is perhaps not surprising. A beginning is possible, however, and that is what we shall present here. There are five generalizations about political behavior that seem to apply to all the professions.

An increasing number of professionals, of both the established and newer types, are being employed directly by governmental departments and agencies. While public employment of professionals has a long history, much of it entirely satisfactory on both sides, there remains a considerable amount of unresolved tension between professional roles and organizational necessities in the government sphere. Improvements in accommodative mechanisms are slowly being worked out.

As their educational, research and other resources and facilities are more and more supplied and affected by governmental actions, professions increasingly find themselves required, usually through their professional associations, to anticipate, respond to, and seek to control these actions. Professions seek to control both the formal governmental legislative processes and also the day-to-day administrative decisions that affect them. In short, professions are included among the ranks of "pressure groups" on the government scene, and often they are very effective ones.[23] Professional as well as other kinds of "pressure groups" are, of course, often entirely legitimate and positively functional in their attempts to control governmental actions.

There seems to be no movement toward either formal or informal integration of the professions into a single power group in modern society. The several professions often compete with one another. They also differ on a variety of social issues where their own competition is not involved. One of the minor bugaboos of a certain group in modern society, the fear that the professionals would take over society and establish a technocracy in the name of their common and esoteric knowledge, is unlikely to be realized.

There is some diversity of patterns of political participation, partisan affiliation and political ideology *within* any given profession. Powerful as it is, the American Medical Association, for example,

29

is not without considerable political opposition from within the medical profession, especially from the better university medical schools. In the American military profession, "a deep split pervades its ranks in respect to its doctrine and viewpoints on foreign affairs," and there is even a small minority that identifies itself as generally "liberal" in opposition to a majority that identifies itself as "conservative" on an anonymous questionnaire.[24] The diversity within a profession results in important international political activity. The politics of professional associations is a subject well worth more research.[25]

In the seeking and giving of expert advice between politicians and civil servants on the one side and professionals on the other, it is sometimes very difficult to know where the technical professional knowledge ends and where the political and moral judgment begins. Politicians and civil servants must, more and more frequently, get advice from professionals; but there are dangers on both sides when it is hard to distinguish between the technical and the moral-political. On their side, the politician and civil servant run the danger of abdicating their duties and responsibilities; on theirs, the professionals run the dangers of intruding their values where they do not belong and of having to pay a heavy price when the client discovers that their advice has been nonprofessional and faulty. Since the war, politicians, civil servants and professional scientists have been keenly aware of these several dangers.[26] But they are dangers that occur for all professionals who give advice to those who make political decisions.

In addition to these five generalizations about some constants in the subject of professionals and politics, there are others that specify the social factors that help to explain the diversity of political behavior and ideology among the professions. The diversity of political behavior among professionals can be accounted for in part in terms of the relative degree of applicability of the professional's knowledge to the political process. In American society, for example, the skills which the lawyer develops in interpersonal mediation, conciliation and verbal persuasion are directly applicable to the political process. Hence despite the fact that lawyers comprise only 0.1 per cent of the American labor force, they have made up about half the membership of the United States Senate in recent years.[27] In contrast, because of the limited applicability of their knowledge, doctors are seldom members of the United States Congress. In the recent Eighty-sixth Congress, for example, there were only four licensed physicians, three of whom no longer practice.[28]

Full-time participation in politics is also dependent on the relative degree of freedom for the professional to absent himself from his regular practice. Here again, lawyers seem to be more dispensable for longer periods of time than, say, doctors, scientists or many kinds of professors.

Related to the degree of dispensability and also influencing the diverse modes of professional participation in politics is the relative rate of obsolescence of professional knowledge. Legal knowledge, for example, changes less rapidly than medical knowledge or scientific knowledge. Lawyers can return to professional practice from full-time political participation more easily than can doctors.

The amount of gain for one's professional career to be derived from political participation also helps to determine diverse patterns of professional behavior in this sphere. Again, the lawyer has the most to gain; he can acquire friends, knowledge, power that will help in his professional practice when he comes back from the political field. The doctor and all kinds of research professionals have little to gain, though many who are in the social sciences feel that the necessity to confront policy situations for at least short periods of time is stimulating to their research when they take it up again.

Finally, the relative amounts of income, prestige and work-satisfactions characterizing the different professions help to determine diverse modes of political participation. In American society, for example, doctors have the highest income, prestige and expressed work-satisfactions among all the professions.[29] There is little incentive for them to seek individual careers in politics. There is a greater variety in these respects among lawyers, many of whom can find higher amounts of income, prestige and work-satisfaction in a political career than in their own professions. Doctors, further, since they are so well rewarded, tend to be well satisfied with the society as it exists; they have the more conservative political affiliations. In contrast, a study of a nationally representative sample of 2451 members of college and university social science departments shows that a disproportionately large number of these professors are more liberal in their political affiliations because they feel dissatisfied with the prestige that the society accords them.[30]

Conclusion

Our society has been seen as a "business society," an "industrial society," a "capitalist society" and a society of many other kinds. It is obviously each and all of these, in some partial sense, just as, obviously, in some equally partial but nonetheless important sense, it is a "professional society." The generalized knowledge and the community orientation characteristic of professional behavior are indispensable in our society as we now know it and as we want it to be. Indeed, our kind of society can now maintain its fundamental character only by enlarging the scope for professional behavior. An important contribution to this enlargement can be made by a better understanding of the nature and actual functioning of professionals of many different kinds. This is a continuing and challenging intellectual task for the sociology of the professions.

REFERENCES

1. For a study containing recent evidence, see Francis X. Sutton, S. E. Harris, Carl Kaysen and James Tobin, *The American Business Creed* (Cambridge, Mass.: Harvard University Press, 1956). See also David Rogers and Ivar E. Berg, Jr., "Occupation and Ideology: The Case of the Small Businessman," *Human Organization*, 20 (1961), pp. 103–111.

2. See Bernard Barber, "Is American Business Becoming Professionalized? Analysis of a Social Ideology," in E. A. Tiryakian (ed.), *Sociocultural Theory, Values, and Sociocultural Change: Essays in Honor of Pitirim A. Sorokin* (New York: The Free Press of Glencoe, 1963).

3. Emile Durkheim, *Professional Ethics and Civic Morals* (Cornelia Brookfield, trans.), (London: Routledge and Kegan Paul, 1957), p. 29.

4. R. H. Tawney, *The Acquisitive Society* (1920), (New York: Harvest Books, 1946), Chapter 7, "Industry as a Profession."

5. Louis D. Brandeis, *Business: A Profession* (1914), (Boston: Hale, Cushman & Flint, 1933), p. 12.

6. *Ibid.*, p. 1.

7. On work in general, see Erwin O. Smigel, "Trends in Occupational Sociology in the United States: a Survey of Postwar Research," *American Sociological Review*, 19 (1954), 398–404. On the professions, see R. K. Merton, "Some Preliminaries to a Sociology of Medical Education," in R. K. Merton, George Reader, M.D., and P. L. Kendall (eds.), *The Student Physician* (Cambridge, Mass.: Harvard University Press, 1957), esp. pp. 36ff. For one teaching professional's view of one aspect of the sociology of the professions, see George Reader, M.D., "Studies in the Evaluation of Hospital Function: Some Examples of the Contribution of the Behavioral Sciences to Medicine," Lowell Lecture, Massachusetts General Hospital, Boston, February, 1963, to be published by the Harvard University Press.

8. See Talcott Parsons, "The Professions and Social Structure," *Social Forces,* 17 (1939), 457–467 (reprinted in Parsons, *Essays in Sociological Theory,* rev. ed., Glencoe, Ill.: The Free Press, 1954); *The Social System,* pp. 343ff. *et passim;* and "Some Trends of Change in American Society: Their Bearing on Medical Education," in Parsons, *Structure and Process in Modern Societies* (Glencoe, Ill.: The Free Press, 1960). As the citations throughout this paper will show, two other sociologists in the Parsons tradition, Robert K. Merton and William J. Goode, have made important and continuing contributions in this specialized field. Important contributions in a different tradition have been made by Everett C. Hughes, who has written a special paper for this issue of *Dædalus.*

9. These facts from U. S. Census data analyzed by Alba M. Edwards can be found in W. J. Goode, "Community Within a Community: the Professions," *American Sociological Review,* 22 (1957), 194–200.

10. W. J. Goode, "Encroachment, Charlatanism, and the Emerging Profession: Psychology, Sociology, and Medicine," *American Sociological Review,* 25 (1960), 902–914.

11. On the professions in one "modernizing" society, see Edward Shils, *The Intellectual Between Tradition and Modernity: The Indian Situation, Comparative Studies in Society and History,* Supp. 1 (The Hague: Mouton and Company, 1961), esp. Chapter I, "Dimensions of an Intellectual Class."

12. One sociologist has gone so far as to say that "labor itself is becoming professionalized." See Nelson Foote, "The Professionalization of Labor in Detroit," *American Journal of Sociology,* 58 (1953), 371–380.

13. Our discussion here follows very closely that in Barber, "Is American Business Becoming Professionalized?" pp. 130–133 (see Reference 2). The essential contributions to the definition offered here can be found in the three Parsons references given above, especially "The Professions and Social Structure." See also A. M. Carr-Saunders and P. A. Wilson, "Professions," *Encyclopedia of the Social Sciences* (New York: Macmillan, 1933); and, R. K. Merton, "Some Thoughts on the Professions in American Society," Brown University Papers, No. XXXVII, 1960.

14. Certain "derivative" attributes follow from these essential attributes. For a list of ten "derivatives," see Goode, "Encroachment, Charlatanism, and the Emerging Profession."

15. On occupational prestige, see Bernard Barber, *Social Stratification* (New York: Harcourt, Brace, 1957), pp. 100–111. On honors in science, see R. K. Merton, "Priorities in Scientific Discovery: A Chapter in the Sociology of Science," *American Sociological Review,* 22 (1957), 642–646.

16. The discussion in this section is much indebted to two papers by W. J. Goode: "Encroachment, Charlatanism, and the Emerging Profession," and "The Librarian: from Occupation to Profession?" *The Library Quarterly,* 31 (1961), 306–320.

17. Even in business, the ideology of professionalism flourishes chiefly among

the managerial elite who are pace-setters in knowledge and practice. See Barber, "Is American Business Becoming Professionalized?" esp. p. 127.

18. *The New York Times,* December 27, 1957.

19. See Robert K. Merton, "The Functions of the Professional Association," *American Journal of Nursing,* 58 (1958), 50–54.

20. For an account of the conflict among the emerging professions of psychology, sociology and psychiatry, see Goode, "Encroachment, Charlatanism, and the Emerging Profession."

21. The discussion in this section is much indebted to that in William Kornhauser, *Scientists in Industry: Conflict and Accommodation* (Berkeley: University of California Press, 1962).

22. *Ibid.*

23. See David R. Hyde and Payson Wolff, "The American Medical Association: Power, Purpose, and Politics in Organized Medicine," *Yale Law Journal,* 63 (1954), 938–1022; William A. Glaser, "Doctors and Politics," *American Journal of Sociology,* 66 (1960), 230–245; and Morris Janowitz, *The Professional Soldier* (New York: The Free Press of Glencoe, 1960).

24. See Janowitz, *op. cit.,* p. viii, and Chapter 12, "Political Beliefs."

25. See Oliver Garceau, *The Political Life of the American Medical Association* (Cambridge, Mass.: Harvard University Press, 1941).

26. For the evidence, see Robert Gilpin, *American Scientists and Nuclear Policy* (Princeton: Princeton University Press, 1962). See also Don Price, "The Scientific Establishment," *Science,* 136 (1962), 1099–1106; Wallace S. Sayre, "Scientists and American science policy," *Science,* 133 (1961), 859–864; and Bernard Barber, *Science and the Social Order* (rev. ed.) (New York: Collier Books, 1962).

27. See Donald Matthews, *U.S. Senators and Their World* (Chapel Hill: University of North Carolina Press, 1960).

28. Glaser, *op. cit.*

29. *Ibid.*

30. Paul F. Lazarsfeld and Wagner Thielens, Jr., *The Academic Mind* (New York: The Free Press of Glencoe, 1958).

PAUL A. FREUND

The Legal Profession

THE LAW, as Frederic William Maitland perceived it, is a seamless web. However apt the metaphor, it would be misleading if transferred to the legal profession itself. The practicing bar, the judiciary and the academic are everywhere distinct segments of the profession; and within the practicing bar there are various models of separation, the *avoué* and *avocat* in the French system, the proctor and advocate in the Scots, the solicitor and barrister in the English. In the United States the formal division among practitioners never became customary, so that a practitioner may serve at once as a solicitor, advising clients and drafting documents, and as a barrister, appearing in the higher courts and rendering opinions on points of law to other lawyers.

The specialization that goes on in American practice is voluntary, a function of the organization of law offices within which partners may specialize and call on one another informally for advice. Although almost 70 per cent of American practicing lawyers are practicing alone, the number is declining and the great bulk of large-scale legal business, as well as the greater number of graduates of the leading law schools, gravitate to the firms.[1] The solo practitioner in the city, with some spectacular exceptions in the field of trial practice, tends to rely on the grubbier aspects of practice, such as bill collecting, and is in many instances identified with his own ethnic group as clients.[2] He is at the opposite pole professionally from the solo practitioner in England, the barrister, who may not enter into partnership, who does not deal directly with clients, who looks to the solicitor as intermediary for his fees, whose earnings at the top are the highest in the profession, from whose ranks exclusively the places on the higher courts are filled, and who in general enjoys a special prestige, even though in the junior ranks it is often the prestige of genteel poverty.[3] It is the business of scholarship,

Justice Holmes remarked, to make poverty respectable. If the United States has not altogether succeeded in that aim, the organized legal profession in England seems to have come closer—indeed to have achieved, as the younger barristers might insist, an excess of virtue.

The relative merits of the modes of professional organization have been debated at length and inconclusively, for the reason primarily that organization is inextricably bound up with larger social patterns. Indeed if there is a seamless web with regard to the legal profession it is just here, in its relationship to the economic, educational and political systems. If the English barrister is subject to a very high degree of professional and ethical discipline, at least part of the explanation lies in numbers: fewer than three thousand members, each attached to one of the four Inns of Court in London. Adding to that figure the number of solicitors, the total is around twenty-five thousand, or twenty thousand in active private practice, a ratio of one lawyer per 2222 of the population, compared with the American total of about one lawyer in private practice per 900 of population. But the numbers, in turn, reflect other differences: a more limited conception in England of the lawyer's function (in relation, for example, to accountants), and a dampener on litigation through the rejection of contingent fees and the high costs of appeals, particularly for the losing party. Again, if the insulation of barrister from client promotes independence in legal advice and the conduct of litigation, it may also tend to a certain aloofness from the actions and passions of the time on the part of those who will mount the bench in the superior courts. An English law professor, who has held judicial office in Germany and who has also taught in the United States, was struck by this detachment. "The English Bench is deliberately insulated from the impact of public opinion— this has its advantages and disadvantages—and the dichotomy of the legal profession has very probably been one of the factors contributing to the intensity with which professional traditions are capable of resisting 'outside' influences. This may be beneficial in that it may keep the law aloof from the hysterias of the political arena. It has also perpetuated long-standing injustices which might have been remedied by a judiciary more apprehensive of a rift between the attitude of the court and the expectations of ordinary people."[4] This detachment, however, reflects a conviction that law reform in response to the felt needs of the public is a concern of the legislature, not of the judges; and there is some institutional basis for this allocation in the fact that the chief judicial officer, in close contact with the doctrinal product of the courts, is the Lord Chancellor, who is also a prominent political figure and whose office is the center of a governmental law reform committee.

Of even greater significance than the question of insulation within the practicing bar is the problem of insulation or mobility among the major branches of the entire profession: the practitioners, the teachers and the judges. On the continent of Europe a law graduate elects quite early the branch in which he will make his career. While mobility is limited, the tradition of the scientific exposition and critique of the law by the academic branch, together with the subordination of judicial opinions, gives the continental law teacher an important role in the development of legal doctrine as well as in the revision of systematic codes. In England the position of the academic lawyer has been more isolated. Strongly case-oriented, English lawyers and judges have been less sensitive to academic commentaries, and indeed some eminent lawyers have had little or no university education in law; the present Lord Chief Justice, for example, read law in London after taking honors at Cambridge in geology. At the 1957 annual meeting of the Society of Public Teachers of Law, at which I happened to be present, there was great excitement over the unprecedented attendance of the Lord Chancellor, and greater excitement over his invitation to the members to volunteer suggestions for law reform to his office. The barriers of communication and consultation are melting, but movement from one branch to another is not as commonplace as in the United States. Where solo practice is required, movement in and out of the active bar is awkward, owing to the necessity of rebuilding a practice. In the United States mobility is fostered by group practice, so that a lawyer may move from practice to corporate employment or government service or teaching on a temporary or an experimental basis. The value of mobility is multifold; it provides a measure of economic choice, and more important, it can fortify independence of spirit and serve to refresh the currents of wider awareness in each of the several branches.

Before turning from these organizational factors to a closer look at the current problems of the profession, perhaps something should be said by way of comparison of the law with other professions. Lawyers, when put beside natural or social scientists, are parochial; their expertness ceases at the water's edge. An anatomist or an economist can move from a German to an American setting (making allowance for differences in professional style and concerns) with unimpaired competence; the flow of blood or of income is no respecter of political boundaries. But a German lawyer would have to be retrained before qualifying in a common-law jurisdiction. Anglo-American law is, to be sure, more parochial than it ought to be; comparative law needs to be more fully exploited. But the point is that law is still a cultural specialization, not directly transferable or assimilable like a scientific theorem. If modern physics is, as a physicist has said, international gossip, modern law is condemned to appear tongue-tied.

Another provincialism in the legal profession is economic in nature. Because men's legal problems, unlike their medical or spiritual ones, tend to differ along with their economic status, legal specialization may result in a stratified clientele. A specialist in workmen's compensation is not likely to deal with the same clients as a specialist in estate planning or corporate securities, even though there are some specialties, like litigation practice, that do cut across economic lines. Without overstressing economic provincialism, there is one aspect of legal practice that differs markedly in comparison with medical practice, and this difference is worth some emphasis. A medical clinic for the poor is valuable for medical education precisely because it presents a wide range of interesting medical problems. In contrast, a legal aid clinic is sharply limited in the scope of the problems that it offers to the lawyer. The problems are important because they are important to the clients, and they may occasionally even be challenging; but they contribute nothing to the legal intern or the teacher whose field is corporate finance or restraint of trade or international law. The provision of legal aid to the indigent is more purely a philanthropic service, less colored by a tint of self-advantage, than is comparable medical aid.

The distinctive role of the legal profession is to serve as the architect of structure and process. To define law, as sociologists frequently do, as rules with sanctions is to obscure the essentially facilitating role of a good deal of law—the law of wills, of contracts, of corporations, of labor organizations, to take examples. Because important sectors of law are of this directional kind, there is a wide area of creativity within them to be exploited by the lawyer. In assessing the creative capacity of the law and its actual fulfillment, it is necessary to examine the products of the lawyer's office more attentively than the decisions of the courts. No Nobel Prize is awarded for the most revolutionary judicial decision of the year.

Judges are circumscribed by rules of evidence, by precedent, by limitations on sanctions, by all the constraints that make it tolerable to sit in judgment on the responsibility of others, that serve to remind the judge, in Holmes's phrase, that he is not God. Consensual arrangements contrived through negotiation and formulated in legal documents are less subject to these constraints and represent a form of law making in which the legal imagination is called upon to devise a viable framework that will provide a modicum of order while respecting the disorder, complexity and spontaneity of men's aspirations. It is the aspect of legal practice that most nearly resembles the enterprise of the artist. Until this side of the lawyer's work can be extricated, re-created and made visible through a sort of *Road to Xanadu* constructed from lawyers' files, the history of the legal profession will remain unwritten.

The shaping of structure and process is performed more obviously in legislation. In the federal House of Representatives lawyers comprise ordinarily a majority of members, and in the Senate close to two thirds. But it is in the administrative agencies that the lawyers carry on functions more akin to those in private practice. The responsibility of representing an agency as an advocate is by no means the most significant function of the legal staff. More significant is the sharing in the development of policies and in the taking of administrative decisions; here the lawyer's professional concern for collaborative procedure and the reaching of shared goals may put him in the role of mediator seeking to synthesize positions within the agency, positions that may reflect a conflict between career experts and men of affairs. In this role the lawyer's hand is strengthened by reason of the fact that his will be the responsibility of defending the agency's position if it is subjected to challenge in the courts. Moreover, because his professional traditions and perhaps his own experience have been directed to the service of diverse points of view, he may be able to comprehend the nature of fidelity to the complex mission of a public agency more realistically than those whose commitments have been to the dogmas of a discipline or the devices of profit making.

Like any profession which considers its function to be that of serving the public, the legal profession must strive for, and will be measured by, three standards: its independence, its availability and its learning. Each of these criteria requires some attention.

The independence of the bar is a concept of many facets. For one thing, it concerns the lawyer's relation to his client, which entails ethical problems that are often subtle and delicate. A lawyer owes complete loyalty to his client, as it is usually put; but it is a loyalty within the bounds of honor and fidelity to the presuppositions of the system itself; and so there is some circularity in any effort at short definition. But a few things can be said by way of explication. The duty of an advocate in court presupposes a framework in which roles are not confused: the judge is entitled to hear the best that can be said for each side, lest his appreciation of the issues be conditioned by a single point of outlook. This procedure is distorted if the advocate essays the role of arbitrator. In counseling, however, where the adversary process does not operate, the lawyer has a wider scope and obligation to see around a problem unconstrained by what may be too parochial concerns of his client, and to advise accordingly. The mobility of the profession, as I have already suggested, can help to foster both a broader view and the courage to maintain it. Insofar as the lawyer is an employee of the client rather than an outside practitioner, this relation may become more difficult to hold, although of course the elements of personal force and respect make generalization hazardous. The risks, at least, were recognized by Justice Brandeis when he advised young men in the profession to have clients rather than to be somebody's lawyer. The lawyer-client relation in counseling has about it something of the attitude of a sympathetic critic to a work of art—immersion and withdrawal: immersion lest he be pedantic and unfeeling, withdrawal lest he become bemused and sentimental.

The independence of the bar concerns also its relations to government. Given the increasingly pervasive impact of government on the citizen, the traditional role of the bar as the citizen's counselor and advocate and the absence of governmental subvention of the bar, there is no reason to fear the subservience of the profession. The problem is rather more like that of the press—not independence in itself but the exercise of responsibility whatever the climate of the day. In the representation of the unpopular client, lawyers can be helped by their professional organizations, both through the education of the public and, if need be, by financial support. Such aid in the case of representation of Communists has been given by the action of several bar associations, but the situation is by no means satisfactory. One complication has been the insistence of certain groups of defendants on controlling the trial tactics and the public statements regarding the trial, conditions which are rightly repugnant to counsel. The organized bar has an obligation, as yet imperfectly discharged, to see that zealous representation is provided, and on terms that do not pervert the litigation process.

A final aspect of the independence of the bar is its authority over professional standards and the discipline of members. This is typically a function of bar associations, at least as screening agencies for the courts that exercise ultimate responsibility in the several states for the admission or suspension of members of the bar. These functions center on the egregious defaults in the profession; the attainment of a generally higher level of competence and vision is a function more intimately committed to the institutions of legal education, including continuing education for practitioners. Apparently in recognition of this, the Association of American Law Schools was established in 1900 as part of the program of the American Bar Association, and it has evolved into an independent society for the elevation of standards of legal education. Both organizations undertake, separately, the accreditation of law schools. Nevertheless a sizeable, though diminishing, number of students are enrolled in nonapproved schools; as late as 1950, eleven thousand of the 57,000 law students were being trained in such institutions.

The oldest of the bar associations, the Association of the Bar of the City of New York, was established in 1870, as a response to the revelations concerning the Tweed ring in that city. The association has had exceptional leadership and continues to be an outstanding professional organization whose studies and recommendations on legislation and law reform are highly respected and influential. The American Bar Association was founded in 1878 and has evolved through three periods of growth: the so-called Saratoga period, to 1902, when it held its meetings usually in that city; a period of expansion to 1936; and finally a period marked by reorganization, the so-called era of federation, in which the governing board has been made up predominantly of delegates from the bar associations of the states and in which the total membership includes about half the lawyers of the country.[5] This reorganization has tended to elevate the organization man in the hierarchy of leadership and to produce certain dilemmas in the formulation of policy on controversial public issues. To escape from a least common denominator position, the association has on occasion resorted to the establishment of two committees in what is actually one field (civil liberties is an instance, foreign relations another), which submit reports that are at odds with each other. On more technical aspects of law the specialized committees have done useful work.

There are those who argue that the standards of the profession will be enhanced through a so-called integrated bar in each state, that is, an association in which membership is obligatory. The movement to this end, begun in the 1920's, has taken hold chiefly in the West and South, where the voluntary associations have been least strong, and about half the states have adopted the integrated system.[6] Certain limitations, some of them with constitutional overtones, are implicit in this form of organization: since membership is compulsory, the association may be circumscribed in taking positions of a political nature that do not reflect the wishes or promote the common interests of all the members. On the score of strengthened public service, as through more ready provision of counsel in unpopular causes, one must register reservations as one notes that among the integrated bars are those of Alabama and Mississippi.

We are brought from a consideration of the independence of the bar to the second of its professional criteria, the availability of its services. The problem is not one of numbers, although the annual admissions to the bar in the past decade have remained stationary in absolute numbers, around eleven thousand, dropping in terms of population from about seventy to less than sixty per million. The relative decline may be attributable to the growing attraction of postgraduate work in arts and sciences both for its own sake and in consequence of more liberal fellowship programs. However, the decline does not appear to have brought with it a depreciation in the quality of law school applicants.

The real problem is one of making legal services available on a wider basis. In the area of the criminal law rapid developments are in process, spurred by the pressure of new constitutional interpretations which give to indigent defendants accused of serious crimes an absolute right in the state as well as the federal courts to the appointment of counsel. Various methods have been in operation on a limited scale to provide such assistance: the designation by the judge of a member of the bar to serve without compensation; financial aid through community charitable funds; bar association support; and public defender offices staffed by publicly paid full-time lawyers. Disagreement over the merits of these plans has tended to obstruct a definitive solution, but a recent federal bill, endorsed by the President, would cut the knot by authorizing the

judges in each district to opt for one or a combination of these
plans. In populous communities the public-defender office, despite
cries of socialization, appears to be a necessary response to the need.
On the civil side a similar need, though not deriving from a constitutional command, has been met in many localities by a legal aid
society, and recently by a referral service for those of limited
means under which the local bar association maintains a panel of
cooperating lawyers.[7]

A more deep-seated, if obscure, need is the provision of legal
advice in advance of trouble and with a view to preventing it. The
infrequency with which lawyers are consulted for this preventive
service is not so much a result of financial inability as of an apprehensive or limited view of the lawyer's role. Yet it is just at the
point of entering on a transaction, be it a lease or installment contract or joint venture, that the person of moderate means can best
protect his interests. Some form of large-scale service for small transactions is called for. A legal office maintained by a labor union for
its members is a possibility, but it would have to meet the canons of
legal ethics that stress the client's personal relation with his lawyer
and freedom from control of the lawyer by other laymen. The
canons should not prove to be insuperable for a resourceful profession bent on filling a void by supplying its services.

The third of the suggested criteria of a practicing profession,
its learning and its advancement of learning, also presents levels of
complexity. At the narrowest there is the problem, which the law
no more than other professions has escaped, of the burgeoning mass
of data to be assimilated. Those who compute such things have
announced that from the year 1658 to 1879 there were about
407,000 reported American cases; from 1879 to 1932, about 1,121,-
000; the latter increment was duplicated in the less than thirty
years to 1961.[8] The statute books and the monographic literature
have more than kept pace. From the pioneer modern law review at
Harvard in 1887, the current Index to Legal Periodicals covers more
than 300 journals published in the United States and the British
Commonwealth. This intimidating bulk reflects as well the creation
and growth of new specialties as law making has coped with and
facilitated the more complex relations in an industrial society; administrative law, labor law, income taxation, securities regulation,
workmen's compensation, social security were all in a primitive
state a generation ago, and many lawyers now at the bar received
no law school instruction in any of them. The same will almost

certainly be said a generation hence of such subjects as comparative and international law.

All of these developments are acute issues for legal education, conceived of both as preparation for the profession and as continuing instruction of the practitioner. At the stage of practice, a number of expedients are being developed. Practicing law institutes are held in the major cities, some in connection with law schools, to acquaint the participants with newer movements in the law, not with a view to creating specialists but to give the general practitioner an insight into some specialties and to broaden the general legal cultivation of the specialist. It is a safe generalization that to be a good patent lawyer or international lawyer one must first be a good lawyer. Judges too are not immune from the necessity to keep their learning active, and small beginnings have been made to that end through summer institutes under law school auspices. This is a development that deserves encouragement. Meanwhile, the institution of the judge's law clerk, engaged annually from the leading graduates of law schools, has spread widely. This practice contributes not only to the legal sophistication of the clerk but to that of the judge as well, by exposing him to the current of contemporary academic thought.

The law schools themselves are struggling to fit the new learning into the traditional three-year curriculum. Occasional voices are heard contending for an additional year, but there is general sentiment that this should be a last resort and that the present challenge is to revise the curriculum. Much has been done in this direction; the issues of the *Journal of Legal Education* and the meetings of the Association of American Law Schools are heavy with reports, programs and exhortations on the subject. Surely no profession is more self-conscious about teaching methods and curricular arrangements. Some of the older subjects have been dropped or streamlined to make way for the new, but this obvious device, it is generally recognized, does not go to the root of the matter. The transitoriness of a large part of the informational content has forced the schools to a sharper appreciation of what they have always professed, that their mission is not to produce lawyers but minds trained for law. More specifically there is an intensified effort to explore fields of law by sinking shafts rather than covering the ground. More basically there is encouragement to seek for common or unifying principles that will help to consolidate and simplify what have been treated as discrete areas: a law of associations, for example, that would comprehend certain features of the law of corporations and of labor unions. There are real dangers here in confusing shallowness with profundity, but there is also a challenge to do for wider areas of the law what the systematic scholars have done for the conventionally demarcated subjects.

Legal development, which is generated by a tension between continuity and change, has proceeded from metaphor through simile to overarching concepts: witness Brandeis' invention of the category of a right to privacy, based on seemingly diverse and discrete legal rules. What is called for is this kind of imaginative learning; the occasion is the crisis in legal education, but the significance for a principled body of learning will be much deeper. In such an enterprise the three branches of the profession, the academic, the practicing and the judicial, should be represented. Just this sort of collaboration has marked the work of the American Law Institute, an association of about fifteen hundred selected members, which has produced Restatements of the principal conventional subjects as well as model legislative proposals, most recently a model penal code. The basic thinking is likely to be done in the solitude of an academic study, where, as Percy Bridgman put it, ideas can saunter through the mind; but the ideas and their formulation will be strengthened when rubbed against the minds of those who will be called upon to translate them into the living law.

Along with this systematic work there will be an increasingly urgent call for research on distinct problems, all the way from legal procedures to simplify and expedite litigation to legal inventions for dealing with displaced labor or international wrongs. Hopefully such research could release some of the time of legislators now consumed on investigating committees. The law schools will have a role in these projects, along with other professions; what institutional form such collaboration should assume would take us afield. But there are manifest implications for legal education itself, which must take responsibility not to train students in the social sciences, but to prepare them for collaborative enterprise by seeing that they acquire some insight into the methods and concepts of those disciplines. One form of program to this end, which has had a limited trial, deserves more attention: an optional seven-year college-and-law school program, as at present, but with entry to law school after the third year and the final two years an admixture of law school courses and related courses in the social science departments. There are administrative difficulties, particularly in the case of students entering law school from another university; nevertheless a plan with so much promise ought not to be thwarted by unsympathetic administration.

One last observation, which may seem irrelevant: law is probably the most neglected phase of our culture in the liberal arts curriculum. Yet the legal profession, no less than the scientific, functions in a lay society that does, and should, judge its performance. If this judgment is to be effective, it must be based on knowledge of the role of the profession and the character of its thinking. General education requires that somehow a view from the inside should be provided of this profession as of other learned disciplines.

REFERENCES

1. C. Ray Jeffery, "The Legal Profession," in *Society and the Law* (New York: The Free Press of Glencoe, 1962) pp. 329-330; see generally Albert P. Blaustein and Charles O. Porter, *The American Lawyer* (Chicago: University of Chicago, 1954).

2. Jerome E. Carlin, *Lawyers on Their Own* (New Brunswick, N.J.: Rutgers University Press, 1962).

3. L. C. B. Gower and Leolin Price, "The Profession and Practice of the Law in England and America," *Modern Law Review,* XX (July, 1957), 317.

4. Otto Kahn-Freund, "English and American Law—Some Comparative Reflections," in *Essays in Jurisprudence in Honor of Roscoe Pound* (Indianapolis: Bobbs-Merrill, 1962) pp. 362, 383.

5. Edson R. Sunderland, *History of the American Bar Association and Its Work* (privately published, 1953).

6. Roscoe Pound, *The Lawyer From Antiquity to Modern Times* (St. Paul: West, 1953) pp. 272–275; William A. Glaser, *Three Papers on the Integrated Bar* (New York: Columbia University, 1960).

7. Emery A. Brownell, *Supplement* to *Legal Aid in the United States* (Rochester, N. Y.: Lawyers Co-operative Publishing Co., 1961). It is stated (p. 10) that in 1960 there were 132 legal aid offices on a salaried basis in cities having a total population of 16 million, and volunteer panels of lawyers in 128 communities with a population of 23 million. Since the present paper was written, a valuable study has appeared: Elliott Evans Chatham, *A Lawyer When Needed* (New York: Columbia University, 1963).

8. F. Reed Dickerson, "Electronic Computers and the Practical Lawyer," *Journal of Legal Education,* XIV, No. 4 (1962), pp. 485, 486.

JAMES HOWARD MEANS

Homo Medicus Americanus

THE CHARACTER which the doctor of medicine has assumed in the United States today is the subject of our inquiry. The behavior pattern of any profession does not develop overnight; it takes time to evolve. Its characteristics and configuration are formed by its environment and its heritage, as are those of a species in the course of its evolution.

To understand fully the doctor in the United States today, we must know something of his past. How did he get to be the way he is? He and his medicine, of course, came first from Europe. Medicine of the sixteenth and seventeenth centuries was rather medieval in character. Authoritarian since the time of Hippocrates (460-377 B.C.), it had finally run into scholasticism and intellectual stagnation. In addition, it had probably declined somewhat in quality in the process of exportation from the Old to the New Worlds. It is unlikely that those doctors who were well established in the Old World would have left their comfortable practices to settle in an unknown wilderness.

Those intrepid medical souls who did venture to cross a dangerous ocean and invade a hostile continent, accompanying other pioneers and settling where they pleased, probably got distributed fairly adequately with respect to need. In New England, at least, some of these men were members of the Puritan clergy who, having resolved to migrate to America, took the precaution of also obtaining a medical education before embarking, thus equipping themselves to care for the bodies as well as the souls of their flocks in the wilderness. All of these doctors had their heritage of Old World medicine to guide them, but what had that to offer them in their new circumstances? Some elementary knowledge of anatomy, physiology and materia medica, a bag of drugs and a few technical gadgets of one sort or another were their equipment. Their method of practice was highly empirical. They purged, they puked, they sweat and they bled, especially the last, all on the basis of tradition rather than of

47

experience or of scientifically proven fact. Their drugs were chiefly medicinal herbs, generically called "simples," which they also used in accordance with accepted custom. They could do very little for their patients beyond relieving certain symptoms and bestowing comfort and moral support.

In the early days, the colonies were swept by one deadly epidemic after another, all imported, in the face of which the doctors were helpless: smallpox, measles—very deadly in those days—scarlet fever, plague, typhus, diphtheria and many others. These epidemics at least left behind a considerable number of immune survivors, whose presence in the community tended to slow up the rate of spread in subsequent epidemics. Until 1800, when vaccination to prevent smallpox was introduced by Dr. Benjamin Waterhouse, who got his vaccine directly from Edward Jenner, there was no specific way of controlling these pestilences. However, attempts to block their importation by the establishment of quarantines at the ports began as early as 1648. These restrictions were perforce imposed by government, and thus we may say that the principle of governmental responsibility for the safeguarding of health was established.

European-trained doctors of medicine were few and far between in the early settlements, and as the population in the new country expanded, they became in short supply. It is said that between 1620 and 1650 about 25,000 English settlers arrived in New England, after which they largely stopped coming. Probably the doctors stopped as well as the rest, yet the population doubled every twenty-five years from its own growth potential. For a continuing supply of doctors the colonists were obliged to train their own by the apprentice system or to send some of their young men of promise to Europe to obtain proper medical education in the great centers of learning. Increasing numbers of the more gifted and privileged of these students followed the latter course, or perhaps a combination of both courses: first an apprenticeship at home followed by a visit abroad for truly learned instruction, or vice versa. This pattern continued to be followed until well into the nineteenth century. To walk the wards of the great European hospitals afforded an opportunity to see and learn about all manner of diseases and the treatment thereof, a practical clinical* experience obtainable at that time nowhere else in the world.

* The words "clinic" and "clinical" can be confusing to the nonmedical person. Derived from the Greek word meaning "bed," they came to be applied to

One cannot say that any real progress in the theory or practice of medicine was made in seventeenth-century America. There were as yet no medical schools. Doctors, however, were going abroad to study in ever increasing numbers, and some of these on returning gave up-to-date instruction to their apprentices. A few were teaching anatomy by dissection of the human body—in those days anatomy was basic to nearly everything in medicine. We can picture the evolution of our own doctors of today from the autobiographical material from their colonial predecessors which is still extant. They were in the early days for the most part general practitioners who, as population increased, acquired large and far-flung practices. They became the classic horse and buggy doctors, or in the more sparsely settled areas, doctors on horseback.

With the arrival of the eighteenth century, progress in American medicine became more perceptible. Practitioners of considerable distinction began to appear, most of them, but not all, settled in the larger cities and towns. The wars which beset America in the eighteenth century, the old French and Indian Wars and the first war with England, called forth a flock of surgeons to attend the wounded and thus gave a great impetus to surgery in America.

American medicine, however, could not have survived indefinitely on the momentum imparted by Europe. It had to develop its own medical institutions on this side of the Atlantic before a truly indigenous medical profession could come into being. Medical schools were the prime necessity, for without them no physicians or surgeons could be adequately qualified. The first of these was established in Philadelphia by the University of Pennsylvania in 1765; in New York City, King's College (later Columbia University) founded one in 1767. Harvard University founded a medical school in Cambridge, Massachusetts, in 1783, and the College of Philadelphia did likewise in Philadelphia, Pennsylvania, in 1790. Dartmouth College started a two-year school in Hanover, New Hampshire, in 1798, and Yale University started its medical school in 1813 in New Haven, Connecticut.

But medical schools alone, in which instruction is given largely by lectures, are far from sufficient for the education of good practi-

---

a patient in a bed, and finally to anything having to do with patients whether in bed or out of it. Thus "clinical" means having to do with patients, and "clinic" denotes a place where patients are cared for. We speak of clinical medicine to mean practical medicine—diagnosis and treatment of patients—in contrast, for example, to laboratory medicine or public health medicine.

cal physicians and surgeons. Hippocrates himself insisted that the training of the physician should be primarily through personal observation of patients. It is in hospitals that patients can be had for teaching purposes in the greatest abundance and variety. In the English colonies in North America, no hospital was available for such a purpose until the Pennsylvania Hospital in Philadelphia, of which Benjamin Franklin was one of the founders, opened its doors in 1756.* A teaching hospital was set up in New York (the New York Hospital) in 1791, and another in Boston (the Massachusetts General Hospital) in 1821. These were the first of the so-called voluntary hospitals in the United States, and with their establishment American medical education can be said to have been launched.

In a learned profession, if it is to remain learned, there must be free interchange of ideas among its members. All knowledge must be shared. Agencies for the diffusion of professional knowledge beyond the medical school level become indispensable. The facilities needed to meet these requirements are chiefly medical societies, medical journals and medical libraries. In the latter part of the eighteenth century, there was a great burgeoning of medical societies in North America—state societies, county societies and societies for various local and special types of medicine. These societies were where doctors gathered to exchange experiences, to argue things out with one another. They provided a form of intellectual sharpening which Sir William Osler called "brain dusting"—not to be confused with the present-day term "brain washing"—without which the attainment of professional excellence is impossible. Doctors took to it with avidity and gusto. Finally in 1848 a national medical society emerged, which was the creation of a congress called together for that purpose by the Medical Society of the State of New York. All medical societies and schools of medicine in the country were invited to send delegates. This national body took the form of a superstructure federating the state medical societies, and chose the name of American Medical Association—the A.M.A. The original intent was that it should be democratic in character, patterned somewhat after the nation itself. In the beginning the A.M.A.'s avowed purpose was "to initiate reforms to correct the deplorable condition of medical education which then prevailed." Its establishment was a very important event in the history of American medicine, for it

---

* Both French and Latin American colonies were ahead of us in establishing hospitals. For example, Cortez founded a hospital in Mexico City in 1524, and the Hôtel Dieu was founded in Montreal in 1644.

was the beginning of "organized medicine," so-called, and it made the American doctor an organization man. We cannot, therefore, understand him without knowing something of his societies, which determine much of his behavior. They have made him a conformist and a conservative to a considerable extent. Through the years, the A.M.A. has gained steadily in political power. It has learned that through collective action it can exert great political pressure effectively to further the ends favored by its leadership. It has become oligarchic rather than democratic in character.

The establishment of native medical schools and teaching hospitals inevitably had a profound effect upon the nature and quality of American medicine and on the direction and speed of its progress. In the beginning the schools were flimsy affairs and a very far cry from the multimillion-dollar university medical centers of today. They were nonetheless their precursors. The facts that these schools required faculties, and that these must needs for the most part be trained in Europe, provided a strong stimulus to the improvement of medical scholarship in the United States. A great many of these early professors were actually trained in Edinburgh, some in London, and a bit later, many in Paris.

The nineteenth century saw many scientific discoveries and technological advances in the practice of medicine. It was the time, especially in France, of the great clinicians. It also saw the beginnings of our principal preclinical sciences of today: physiology, biochemistry, histology, pathology, bacteriology, immunology and pharmacology. These subjects, which constitute the usual first and second year subjects of the modern American medical school, had their initial greatest effulgence in Germany, and also to a considerable degree in Britain. Even the United States at this time had its William Beaumont, a great pioneer in the physiology of digestion. Also, although there has been much controversy as to who discovered ether anesthesia, no one can contradict the fact that it was an American contribution. About this time another discovery was made by an American doctor, that by Oliver Wendell Holmes of the infectious nature of puerperal or childbed fever. Thus the United States began to contribute on its own account to the progress of scientific medicine and was no longer solely dependent on Europe for advancement in the basic sciences.

The last two decades of the nineteenth century were the time in American medicine when the great clinicians were paramount. In the United States they reached their ascendency before the medical scientists reached theirs. It was also a time when the private practitioner was in his glory. The vast majority of doctors of medicine in the United States in the nineteenth century and into the twentieth derived their livelihoods exclusively from fees received from private patients for services rendered. They became segregated into categories in accordance with their aptitudes and preferences. In rural areas there were the country doctors, who were general practitioners and family doctors. They had immense self-reliance and would undertake to do nearly anything. When they ran into problems they could not handle, they called in consultation doctors better equipped than they were themselves. The education of these men was usually inadequate. To a considerable extent they got their training on the job, in their own practices. Many of them were products of proprietary medical schools, of which there were many in the nineteenth century. The faculties of these proprietary schools were practitioners who voluntarily banded together, called themselves a faculty, offered instruction consisting largely of lectures, and financed the affair by the tuition fees they collected. Rather inferior medical education it was, which perforce had to be supplemented by apprenticeships, but in a country as widespread and growing as fast as ours was then, such medical schools were probably unavoidable. Even the schools set up by universities were not much better at this time.

These general practitioners and family doctors worked hard and developed wonderfully good relations with their patients and families of patients. They made endless house calls, day or night, driving long distances over the countryside in their horse-drawn vehicles, and saw many patients in their offices, which were usually located in their own homes.* When patients required bed care, the doctor usually looked after them in their homes. Only rarely did he

---

* I have the following statement from the daughter of such a doctor, Frank B. Adams of Plymouth, Michigan: "The life of a country doctor of the late 19th century presented facilities and relationships almost the exact opposite of those of a general practitioner of today. His office was in his home, his family supplied the kind of assistance given by secretaries and office nurses today. Telephone service was primitive, and, therefore, there was a merging of family and professional life which worked to the advantage of the patient. The physician was either immediately available or his whereabouts could be discovered without delay. He was ready to respond to a call at any time of day or night, and night calls to travel several miles into the country in darkness were frequent. I can remember no feeling on father's part that such calls were made for any illness not serious."

send them to a hospital, of which there were very few. Such care, if rather primitive medically, was a humane service of inestimable value. The doctor's availability gave the patient a feeling of confidence and security which is by no means always to be had today.

In urban areas the situation was similar, but on a somewhat more exalted level. The doctors, again almost entirely in private practice, were for the most part unspecialized, but it was during the mid-nineteenth century that specialization began to appear. To get training in a clinical specialty one was practically obliged to study abroad, preferably in Vienna. Then one came home, hung up the certificate of his specialty training in his waiting room, and went to work on much the same basis as the general practitioners, except that much more of the work would be done in the office than in the home. It was from all these practitioners that the faculties of medicine in the clinical subjects were recruited.

Those physicians and surgeons in each field who had the most acclaim in their communities, who were most highly thought of by their fellows, and who had had the most distinguished educations were likely to be made professors and chiefs of service in hospitals. These doctors were usually unpaid. They were happy to serve for nothing on the staffs of the teaching hospitals because of the acclaim to be gained and because of the experience in both the care of patients and the teaching of students which was to be had there. These great clinicians became the idols of the medical students. To walk through a hospital ward to the wake of such a one was as stimulating an experience as they could have. Much of the diagnostic technology of today was still undreamed of. Far more dependence was placed on direct observation, history taking and physical examination than today. The teacher who could discover a great deal about the patient and his disease by the power of his own unaided senses was greatly revered.

One very important difference between those days and today lay in the matter of hospital care for private patients. The great voluntary hospitals and the municipal and county hospitals did not ordinarily admit to their wards the wealthy or well to do. If the doctor wanted to hospitalize a private patient and care for him himself, he had to send him to a private hospital of one sort or another, and these were few and far between before 1900. But he was not likely to seek hospitalization if he could possibly manage in the patient's home. With the much greater availability of good private-duty nurses in those days, this was usually possible. Surgeons did even major surgery in homes, usually on the kitchen table. I can recall vividly how in 1897 my younger brother was cared for quite successfully in our home through typhoid fever with two relapses. Everything that was available in a hospital was made available at home.

With the arrival of the automobile, the practicing medical profession very rapidly became motorized and it was possible for physicians to cover much wider areas than their horse-drawn predecessors. Surgeons often traveled through several counties in a morning, doing three or four major operations at widely scattered points and instructing the local family doctor on subsequent treatment. One of Boston's leading surgeons in my boyhood lived a few doors away from where my family did. Often I saw him taking off early on a winter's morning in a huge open touring car. Surgeon, chauffeur, assistants, nurse, and maybe a medical student or two, all in great coonskin coats, made a very impressive sight.

But even this sort of care was on the way out. Gone are the days when the doctor went to the patient. Now the patient usually must go to the doctor. In those days, too, there were consulting physicians who would answer calls by motor up to 100 miles or so. In some cases such work constituted the major part of a doctor's practice. The memory of this style of practice remains vivid in the minds of some people, who long for its return. Doctors who remember this era may also regret that today's civilization no longer permits them to practice in this manner.

Such briefly is the background and evolutionary heritage of the American doctor of today. We must now investigate what use he is making of his inheritance. Before doing that, however, let us take note of three momentous events which stirred American medicine around the turn of the present century.

The first of these was the opening of the Johns Hopkins Hospital in 1889, in which four men played vital roles. There was Mr. Johns Hopkins himself, who had the vision of a new kind of higher education for the United States and who gave the money to found a university to implement it. Next was Dr. John Shaw Billings, who planned and built the Johns Hopkins Hospital and participated in the selection of its staff. The third, William Henry Welch, was selected by the university's President Daniel Coit Gilman—who in turn had been proposed for the Johns Hopkins presidency by

President Charles William Eliot of Harvard University—to be the first professor of pathology. Welch had been thoroughly trained in Germany at the time when the basic scientific disciplines were blossoming in almost explosive fashion. France had had its Claude Bernard and Louis Pasteur, but it was in Germany that scientific medicine had its first most vigorous growth. Welch was thoroughly cognizant of this new knowledge and transplanted it to Baltimore for the benefit of American medicine.

The fourth, William Osler, who came to Baltimore from Canada via Philadelphia to be the first medical chief at Hopkins, revolutionized the clinical training of the medical student. He got him to the bedside and gave him a responsible role under guidance in the care of the patient, as Robert Graves had done in Dublin a half century earlier. This system of teaching, which Osler imported from Britain, represented a great advance in clinical instruction in the United States. Indeed, what Osler and Welch accomplished between them was the fusion of Germany's best in basic medical science with Britain's best in clinical teaching. The blend was better than the sum of the ingredients, and it constituted an uplifting force in American medical education which has been felt ever since. It was really the birth of scientific medicine in the United States. I interpret "scientific medicine" to signify the making available in the care of the patient all that basic medical science has to offer which may benefit him; in other words, putting the great corpus of medical knowledge at the patient's service.

The second of the great events which I mentioned was the founding in 1903 of the Rockefeller Institute for Medical Research. The chief significance of this event was that it pointed up the facts that without research there is no progress, and that effective research requires specially skilled people abundantly supported in all their basic needs, scientific and otherwise. It was a first step in the chain of events, continuing to the present time, which led to the stupendous expansion of medical research facilities and activities which we see all about us today, and which constitute a large segment of the total medical establishment.

Finally, the third event, the publication of the Flexner Report in 1910, rocked medical education in the United States to its roots. Abraham Flexner, an educator and a brother of the famous Dr. Simon Flexner, made for the Carnegie Foundation for the Advancement of Teaching a survey beginning in 1908 of nearly every medical school in the United States. His findings were shocking. Nearly everywhere he found grossly inadequate teaching facilities. Faculties "consisted of busy practitioners with no time for teaching and no thought of research." After the publication of the Flexner Report many medical schools were closed and many others were reformed and upgraded to meet certain set standards. The only school which Flexner found completely satisfactory was at Johns Hopkins University.

These three great events at the turn of the century brought about a change in the course of American medicine which, with only minor deflections, has been held firmly ever since. There can be no doubt that without them we should not have reached the position we hold today. The most conspicuous results are the great and growing commitment to research and the development of full time university medicine.

Full time university medicine came into being because of the dawning realization that the teaching of medicine required as much pedagogic skill as the teaching of anything else at the university level. It could not be left to amateurs. The fact that a doctor was a superb clinician did not imply that he was *ipso facto* a competent teacher nor that he had the requisite ability to organize and administer the various activities of a teaching clinic in a way to make them effective. For some years before the clinicians, the basic science members of the medical faculties had been on a full time salaried basis. Osler, perhaps earlier and more clearly than anyone else, perceived the necessity that there be on faculties of medicine a certain number of salaried teaching clinicians. As early as 1911 he wrote: "The professor [that is to say of a clinical subject] has three duties—to see that patients are well treated, to investigate disease, and to teach students and nurses. He should be a man of wide sympathies and of trinocular vision. He should have a comprehensive and thoroughly scientific training, and should enter clinical medicine through one of three portals—physiology, chemistry, or bacteriology and pathology. He must be keenly practical, keenly scientific, fond of his patients, fond of his work, and devoted to his students. He should live as much in his wards and laboratories as do his [preclinical] colleagues in their laboratories of anatomy, physiology, or physics." How one finds such paragons has become the number-one question for faculties of medicine today.*

With Osler this kind of medicine began germinating, and after

* See W. Osler, "The Hospital Unit in University Work," *Lancet* 1191, i, 211.

the Flexner Report, its growth and spread through the United States were greatly accelerated. An educational revolution it truly was, and its effects have been felt by nearly all of our present day medical doctors. Although relatively few of them have gone into full time university medicine themselves, at least most of them will at some point in their education have come under the influence of full time clinical teachers who will have left some mark on them. They will be better educated than they otherwise would have been, and they will have a broader understanding of the nature of medicine, in consequence, than did their predecessors.

Let us now attempt to delineate the American practitioner of medicine as he is in 1963. Certainly he is different in many respects from his predecessors of 1900 or even of 1930. He has changed because his social environment has changed. There has been an enormous increase in population, and in its concentration in cities, together with a vast increase in the moving about of people. There has also been an extraordinary extension of technology in many directions. All these changes impose new problems on the medical profession. Moreover, what people think and expect of their doctors, and what their doctors think of them, have been greatly altered, particularly in the years since World War I. Up to the beginning of World War I, the leisurely type of medical practice still prevailed. The doctor was respected and revered; his status in society was high.

Since the last war, there has been, also, a growing public interest in health matters engendered by innumerable articles on health in newspapers and periodicals, and by advertising of the drug industry. All this printed matter has created in the people a greater concern about their health than had ever entered their minds before. In consequence they have developed notions about how they should be treated, and sometimes they have even told their doctors what to do for them. Very often in the early antibiotic days, a patient entered a doctor's office and said, "I have a cold, doc, and I want a shot of penicillin." If the doctor refused to give it, the patient went off and found another doctor who would. This sort of thing is detrimental to the doctor-patient relationship, which to be good requires confidence on the part of the patient in the doctor. With irritation on both sides, the gap between doctor and patient is widened. There are other factors which tend to widen this gap.

For one thing, so much of the diagnostic process is now done through technological procedures that the doctor has lost some of his apparent omniscience, prestige and mystique. For another, along with the development of the affluent society and the increasing demand for medical services, the incomes of doctors and people in allied professions and occupations have risen to incredibly high levels, which did not drop off much even in the depression years, thus causing some resentment among people who were having financial difficulties, often very severe.

The most conspicuous change in the behavior of the doctor is that nowadays he is usually in such a hurry that he is less accessible and less communicative. This also widens the gap. He is usually in a hurry because he is overworked: too many people need medical care, people demand more medical care; and there are not enough doctors to supply it. The doctor is busier than he wants to be or than is good for him. I also suspect that at times his devotion to his patients is lessened and the quality of medical care which he provides is impaired. Moreover, owing to the advance of medical science and technology, the care he is expected to supply becomes ever more complicated. A greatly increased burden of work is thrown upon him. No wonder he is in a hurry. He is desperately trying to catch up, and despite the longest working hours of any of the professions, he can never quite do it. This is veritably a doctor's dilemma. Will the doctor inevitably have to confine himself to strictly medical matters, or can he continue to be the family friend and counselor?

An outstanding example of a corner cut is the disappearance of the home visit, especially the night call, which has been supplanted by the telephone. Something essential can be lost when the home visit is not made. Seeing the patient in a relaxed and leisurely manner in his customary setting and in contact with his family can be very important to the doctor in developing a complete understanding of the case. In the old days the doctor was the intimate friend of the family, almost a member of it. He was the family counselor for all sorts of things other than medical. The family was usually devoted to him, and he to them, for his relation with the family was an endearing experience. Occasionally such a relationship persists today, but the practice of home visitation is waning in the United States, although it is still going strong and likely to survive in Britain.

Actually, under present-day working conditions in medical practice, home visits have become so difficult for the doctor that he cannot be blamed very much for not wanting to make them. If he has a waiting room full of patients eager to be seen and very likely there by appointment, or if he is conducting a ward round or holding a clinic in a hospital, how can he rush off to pay a home visit? Traffic jams and parking difficulties are also inimical to house visiting. Another change in today's way of life which impairs the quality and continuity of medical care is the greatly increased moving about of individuals and families, induced by the exigencies of the giant industries. Continuity of care becomes difficult—sometimes impossible.

One of the greatest responsibilities of the practitioner of medicine is to be available to his patients. As time goes on, he is less and less likely to be so. He will accept, for example, the care of a patient with a prolonged illness for whom curative medicine has nothing to offer, but who for psychological reasons needs frequently to be visited. The doctor may get more and more irked by having to make such visits; he regards them as a waste of his precious time, which he would rather spend on patients he thinks he can help specifically. The element of compassion ceases to count very much. Of course there is a solution for a problem of this nature. The doctor can, and should, withdraw from the case and turn it over to another doctor who is competent and willing to accept full responsibility in his place. The official code of medical ethics prescribes just such a procedure.

Our doctor's professional forebears of the nineteenth century, and earlier, practiced medicine in a serenely individualistic and leisurely manner, not permitted by our present society. Now the doctor is inevitably part of a great social structure which we may call "American medicine," or the "health forces of the nation." In these forces the doctor of medicine, together with his counterparts in public health, may be said to constitute the top echelon. He is also surrounded by, and dependent upon, a host of other professional people known as paramedical—nurses, social workers, therapists of many kinds, administrators and technicians of endless variety. Without access to this great array of skills, our doctor could not make available to serve sick people the vast stockpile of medical knowledge which exists. Nor can the doctor who does have access to them utilize them for the people's benefit without organization for medical care, of which we shall have more to say later.

There are other evidences of a declining sense of responsibility among doctors. For example, we have recently seen doctors walking out on strike, quite like labor union members, in Saskatchewan, and threatening to do so in New Jersey. This would have been unthinkable a few decades ago. The increasing willingness to practice medicine by telephone and the custom of giving patients appointments weeks in advance, during which time their illness may become seriously aggravated, seems to me to fall short of the ideal doctor-patient relationship. The growing gap between patient and doctor—the poorer communication between them—should indeed give the profession some uneasiness.

Another feature which characterizes the medical practice of today is the great increase in specialists. Nearly everyone in medicine nowadays seems to wish to be a specialist. Even the most bona fide generalist * will find some little area in which he seeks to acquire some touch of authority or expertise. Very disruptive to the old patterns is this great expansion of specialism. It is disturbing that so many of our medical graduates are determined to become specialists, disturbing because it leaves us short of generalists, of whom we have great need. Specialization is favored by doctors because it is easier to know a great deal about a little than the reverse. The specialist, moreover, makes a better income and enjoys a somewhat higher status in the public mind. It is interesting and perhaps significant that figures show that the abler medical graduates prefer to go into specialties. It is generally the scholastically lower standing men who go into general practice.

In medicine the diseases of most of the organs or systems of the body are regarded as fit subjects for specialization: neurology, hematology, gastro-enterology, dermatology, ophthalmology, as well as many others. Sometimes a specialty is built up around a technology, such as radiology and endoscopy—of course, surgery actually is in this group. These are clinical specialties, the older of which are

---

* By generalist, I mean that which is left of the general practitioner of an earlier day, the opposite of the specialist. He is a nonspecialized physician with a broad spectrum of competence. He is the one to whom the patient ideally goes first and who very likely becomes the patient's regular personal physician. His first duty is to make a diagnosis and then secure for the patient whatever treatment this diagnosis calls for. Usually nowadays he is an "internist." This classification is essentially confusing and useful only to indicate the kind of training the doctor has had.

now being further split up into splinter specialties. To practice any of them exclusively and with expert skill, the doctor must first have become a well trained general physician or surgeon, and upon these qualifications superimpose his training as a specialist. In order that the public can be assured that a doctor is a properly qualified specialist, a flock of so-called specialty boards has been established to define training requirements and conduct examinations which, if passed, permit the doctor to be declared a certified specialist in his particular field. These boards are voluntary, not official; nevertheless, they have with the passage of time acquired sufficient prestige so that their accreditation is as good as official. A specialty may be said to have reached full maturity when it gets its board. This process can easily be carried *ad absurdum*.

It is not usually best that patients go directly to specialists since they may choose the wrong ones. Their generalist should refer them to appropriate specialists. Sometimes patients engage in what we call medical shopping; that is to say, they make their own list of specialists on the basis of information picked up by hearsay. This is bad because no competent person correlates the information thus gathered or makes any well ordered plan for the patient to follow. However, the general practitioner or family doctor today is not quite what he used to be. In my youth he was expected to do nearly anything, and to accept a very broad responsibility. Now the public has been educated to the point of demanding specialty services for many of their problems. Contrariwise, specialists should not undertake the general care of patients without the collaboration of generalists. They are too sharply focused on one aspect of the patient's care to be well balanced and reliable in the care of the whole of him. We hear much these days about comprehensive medical care, which everyone wants for himself and for his family. This means the making available to him of up-to-date and good quality medical care—diagnostic, therapeutic and preventive—for any sort of illness that may afflict him. Ideally, it means also that measures have been taken to protect him against preventable disease and to safeguard his health generally, as for example through periodic health examinations. The idea is to keep the patient well, not merely cure his ills. Obviously, medical service of this degree of comprehensiveness cannot be provided by any single doctor; modern medicine is too complex to permit that. A group of professional people is required —very likely some paramedical as well as medical—who must integrate their efforts and cooperate as a team in the care of each individual patient. Such a team must have a leader who takes the final responsibility for the operation of the total program of care and for making the final decisions. This leader normally should be a generalist.

Consultative activities have also changed a great deal within my memory. In the Victorian spirit, the consultation used to be a formal affair. If the attending physician reached an impasse, he asked to be allowed a consultation; or if the family were concerned about his capacity to deal with the case, they could ask for one. Under these circumstances the ethical code required that the attending physician call in a consultant. Consultations, then, were personal meetings; a date was set and the doctors—sometimes several of them who had been called—gathered at the bedside. After observing the patient as much as they liked, they adjourned until they had arrived at a consensus of opinion. This manner of procedure is probably nearly extinct. There is no longer time for such formalities. Now the attending physician refers the patient to such specialists as he deems necessary, and the patient must go to all their offices to see them. In due course he goes back to his personal physician, who will have heard from the several consultants and digested their separate opinions to form a final one of his own, on the basis of which he instructs the patient, or should instruct the patient. This type of procedure is, I think, inferior to the older one. There is no direct meeting of minds. In contrast to the old "live" consultations, it is, we may say, epistolary consultation. If the patient is in hospital, which he is more likely to be than formerly, consultants can be mobilized to see him more easily and effectively.

It has seemed to me that in recent years, doctors have become increasingly reluctant to call for consultations, especially in smaller towns and rural areas. One reason given is that they wish to save their patients expense, but a more likely reason is that they fear some loss of face if they ask frequently for consultations. They fear the implication may be drawn that they lack professional self-confidence or skill; they may be fearful of losing a patient to a consultant or of having the embarrassment of being proven wrong.

In a profession such as medicine, which deals with the lives and health both of individuals and of communities, recognition, definition and acceptance of responsibility by doctors are of the essence. The changes which have taken place so cataclysmically of recent years in our society have made this more difficult. Society is becoming ever more complex. Self-sufficiency has declined in the individual, as well as in the family and in business; politically it has shifted from town to state to nation. Under such circumstances, and in view of the fragmentation of his own responsibility because of specialization, the generalist finds it increasingly difficult to identify the skills and services offered by the various specializations, some of which may be indicated in a given case; nor does he always recognize his own responsibility to bring these skills to bear or to integrate their contributions to the benefit of his patient. When the doctor, therefore, does not recognize his responsibility in all these directions, the whole medical effort may come to naught.

Let us take the example of psychiatry. This specialization has grown prodigiously in importance and capacity in the last generation or two. Deterioration in interpersonal and intercommunal relations has created mounting tensions which constitute probably the biggest barrier to health that we have in our society today. The immediate prescription of tranquilizing drugs is no adequate solution to these problems, but many generalists or other types of specialists never think of using psychiatrists instead. Indeed many of them seem even a bit hostile to psychiatrists. This is unfortunate, because there are in our society an increasing number of people who are made ill by emotional conflicts and who could be greatly helped by skillful psychotherapy.

In similar fashion many doctors seem to be reluctant to call in paramedical people, such as social workers, visiting nurses or occupational therapists, when they could render important benefits to patients. Doctors even seem to be ignorant of what resources of this kind are available in their communities, or how to call them into action. Medical social service was originally designed to help impecunious patients find the ways and means to carry out the therapeutic program which the doctor had ordered. Nowadays, however, it has been found that nearly any sick person, regardless of economic status, may need the services of a social worker. The social information which this worker brings in may contribute directly to the making of diagnoses and certainly to the planning of treatment. It may help particularly in the planning for convalescent or chronic care in finding resources in some new place to which a patient is obliged to move, or in informing and organizing the family to withstand the impact of a sick member and educating them to adjust to the conditions imposed by illness with least disturbance to themselves or to the patient. In all these activities, which so often are necessary, the social worker is usually much more adept than is the doctor. They should work together.

The ethical standards of the doctor today form an essential part of our characterization of him. Have they been maintained at the highest level ever achieved by the profession, or have they deteriorated? The code of ethics to which the profession has at least given lip service through some twenty-three centuries is embodied in the Oath of Hippocrates. It is completely valid and appropriate today, but there are certain very urgent ethical problems which bedevil the modern doctor about which the Oath gives but limited help. The most important of these are birth control and euthanasia. It is for society, not for the medical profession, to solve both of these problems. Both birth control and euthanasia involve the taking of human life and are therefore repugnant, but the former need not do so. It may rest upon measures designed merely to prevent conception, not to abort life already started. I believe that the problem it poses will be solved by society as soon as population density gets so high that the people living at the time can no longer tolerate it. Then the medical profession, with the measures it has already developed, can step in and reduce the rate of population increase to whatever seems to be the desirable level.

Euthanasia by definition involves the taking of life, but nowadays it often takes the form of merely permitting nature to end life for us. The questions may well be asked: How long are we justified in prolonging life by artificial means in the person who has no prospect of recovery? Are we justified in curing pneumonia with penicillin in the old or chronically ill person who has nothing but a life of misery to look forward to? How long are we obligated to maintain life by mechanical artificial respiration when there is evidently no chance whatever of the patient's being able to live without it? May we turn it off and let nature take its course? The humane answer would seem to be yes, but we have, inadvertently, trained our young doctors to consider it a virtue to prolong life for the sole purpose of prolonging it.

> Thou shalt not kill but needst not strive
> Officiously to keep alive.*

It is necessary that we consider how doctors behave when organized as well as how they act as individuals. The founding of the A.M.A. in 1848, which to all intents and purposes was the begin-

* Arthur Hugh Clough, "The Latest Decalogue."

ning of so-called organized medicine in the United States, has already been mentioned. In seeking to identify the role played by organized medicine in the progress of medicine in the United States, it will best serve our purpose, I believe, to consider the whole establishment of national, state and county medical societies as constituting, from the sociological and political points of view, a single great apparatus. This is organized medicine or the doctors' guild. Its ideology is very like that of the big labor unions. It is out to improve medical education and medical care, but in its own way; and it has done much to accomplish these ends. But what it does is always done in such a way that the best interests of the doctors are never contravened. Thus in 115 years the A.M.A. has stood steadfastly against any extension of government participation in medical affairs. "Keep the government out of medicine," is its primary slogan. To that end it has spent huge sums of money on lobbying and propagandizing the public and on other pressurizing tactics, and it has now set up a continuing political action committee quite like those of the fighting labor unions. Every attempt that has been made by liberally minded groups to improve medical care and make it more accessible—and there have been a succession of such attempts since 1932—the A.M.A. has attacked with ever increasing truculence. The most recent example is their blocking of the Kennedy health program in 1962. It will keep coming up, however, until passed.*

When organized groups become truculent, it is usually because they feel threatened or insecure in some way. Just how do the organized doctors feel threatened? Presumably they are fearful that any further extension of government into medicine (we already have considerable) would sabotage certain prerequisites of practice which they cherish or would diminish their power in the community. They wish to be the sole arbiters of their own professional affairs. They wish to maintain a monopoly in medical practice. They forget perhaps that medicine is for the people, not for the doctors. They need some enlightenment on this point.

Not only is the doctor of today under constant pressure from his guild to conform to its tenets and ideology, but also various other socio-economic forces peculiar to our times bear down upon him and condition his behavior to some degree. He is in and of his culture, and like all other members thereof he must adjust to the

* In February, 1963, an announcement was made that a medical care bill would be reintroduced, and the A.M.A. has already attacked it.

conditions it imposes. One very characteristic problem of the doctor today is the constant and growing pressure that he is under from the drug industry. Of course, our whole society during most of its waking hours is under constant bombardment by Madison Avenue through all the mass media, but the technique used with the general public is a bit different. In the case of the doctor, it includes a daily deluge of advertising material by mail, invitations to try out new drugs on unsuspecting patients, and free samples left by detail men on the doctor's desk. The effort is to make the doctor "beholden" to a drug company and thus oblige him to prescribe its products. And consider the increasing amount of iatrogenic disease —disease produced by the doctor. Many of the new drugs can produce very serious untoward side effects, which are worse from the patient's point of view than the malady for the treatment of which they were prescribed. One of my teachers once said, very wisely, "Gentlemen, in the practice of medicine, for God's sake at least do as little harm as possible."

And now one may ask what is to be done to make the situation better. If the primary trouble is the shortage of medical manpower, more effective recruitment would seem to be one way. Medicine must be made to appear more attractive to our young people seeking professional careers, for it requires the longest and most difficult of all professional education programs in the United States today. It is especially arduous for married couples, among whom it sometimes creates very difficult emotional problems. The wives of medical students and house staff members are left alone a great deal, so long are their husbands' hours of work. Medical education is also the most costly. The situation is much worse in these respects than it was a decade or so ago. And to cap it all, there is the threat of military service always in the background.

A good suggestion for increasing recruitment of medical personnel is to entice more women into medicine. Some countries, notably Russia, have a very much higher percentage of women in medicine than we do. From my own experience in this matter, which goes back at least to the middle 'twenties, when we began taking women interns and residents on the medical services of the Massachusetts General Hospital, I have formed the opinion that women are as capable of becoming fine physicians as are men, and that we should welcome as many well qualified ones as we can get. It should be pointed out, however, that women who raise families may not be able to give enough time to medicine to justify the costly education which they have received. This presents a dilemma which I will not attempt to resolve. However, if these recruitment difficulties could be overcome, and a great increase in medical enrollment should result, then we would be short of teachers and of teaching facilities. To many educators and others it seems that these difficulties can only be overcome by government aid, but organized medicine always has and may be counted on to continue to oppose such aid.

Another important way in which medical care can be made more available is through increased efficiency in the use of the doctor's time by organization for medical care. Since one doctor can himself no longer provide all a patient may need, doctors will have to work in well integrated groups in which the various members play individual roles, the sum of which will add up to a good medical care program—group practice. Group medicine is, actually, the multiple representative of the single practitioner of earlier days. There is nothing particularly new in the concept of group medicine or group practice. Every hospital with a closed visiting staff and an organized house staff is, in effect, practicing group medicine. There is now throughout the country a growing interest in group medicine, and a steadily increasing proportion of doctors in the country are practicing as members of organized groups. There is now even a national society working vigorously to promote group health plans (G.H.A.A., or Group Health Association of America). The existing groups run all the way from small ones with less than twenty doctors to great chains of such facilities as in the Health Insurance Plan of Greater New York or Permanente in California. The Mayo Clinic is certainly a group medical unit of a sort. In well arranged groups much time is saved by staggering the load and keeping all doctors busy during their working hours, and by avoiding duplications and eliminating lost motion.

In group practice at its best, the doctors are paid by salary, and patients pay for services on prepayment plans of some sort. As such medical groups proliferate and especially as they become arranged in chains and networks, they well may be expected to cover the country and afford what amounts to a national health program on a private enterprise basis. Under the challenge of group practice, the presently prevailing system of solo practice for a fee for service may be expected in time to disappear, to be replaced by the prepayment group system. Under these circumstances a given number of doctors should be able to bring better medicine to more people than under the present system. Then indeed we could have prepaid comprehensive medical care for all, which this writer would regard as the ideal.

Such then in very broad outline is a representation of the practitioner of medicine in the United States today. Whether he likes it or not he is inevitably a functional unit in a vast network of services which collectively have the overall function of preserving, promoting and restoring the health of the American people. He is a very far cry from his horse and buggy professional ancestor, but it is very surprising that he is not as aware of this fact as he ought to be. He clings to that rugged individualism of the colonial doctors. As indicated earlier, he is very well organized for political action, both at the national and at local levels; he has his own professional politics conducted within the framework of the medical societies, often by professional medical politicians. But within the realm of providing medical care, which after all is his *raison d'être*, the doctor is hardly organized at all. For the most part he is hostile to organization at this level; he calls it socialized medicine if and when government has any part in it, and he may even occasionally brand private efforts to achieve the purpose "socialized medicine." The public should be aware of this animus.*

Allotted space does not permit discussion of some other large and important aspects of today's medicine in the United States, which are as much the doctor's concern as is the practice of medicine itself. Medical education has been touched upon and closely related to the practice of medicine. Medical research, which has undergone an incredible expansion since World War II and which has absorbed the interest of thousands of doctors, I have not been able even to touch upon. I can only record in this context that it is a very large and essential part of the total medical establishment of our time. Its growth began explosively during World War II as an essential ingredient of the total war effort (OSRD); after the war and continuing to date, legislators have been induced to appropriate ever larger amounts of money for medical research. The National Insti-

* For a good description of group practice and what it has to offer the patient, see E. P. Dearing, "The Challenge of Comprehensive Health Care," *American Journal of Public Health* (1962), p. 2071.

tute of Health with its far flung programs, both intramural and extramural, came into being and has provided careers in research medicine for young doctors and others, in tremendous numbers.

Public health medicine is also growing apace and finding new avenues for work. Originally thought of as having to do solely with communities as patients, so to speak, it now is beginning to regard medical care as part of its bailiwick. The elevation of standards of medical care inevitably improves the health of the community, which is the direct objective of the public health forces. The American Public Health Association has lately created within its organizational pattern a section on Medical Care. This, indeed, betokens an expanding horizon and community of interest on the part of public health forces and the rest of medicine which are very commendable. Many other new areas of medicine are also opening up: some closely related to the practice of medicine; others quite remote from it, for example, industrial medicine and aviation and space medicine.

Thus the functions and character of *Homo medicus americanus* are extraordinarily diverse and far flung. Yet the basic principles of Hippocrates still apply to them all, and bind them together into one great profession.

In conclusion, we can say that the doctor of today is hard pressed from many points of view. He is to a considerable degree a harassed person. He is engulfed by a deluge of new scientific knowledge, which his conscience tells him he is obligated to grasp and apply to his patients' betterment, but which his education has not prepared him always to understand easily. He finds in a sorry state of chaos the organizational machinery which is necessary to make the medical care he can provide easily available to any or all people, and finds very little good will or intent to set it aright. If he tries to find a better way by experiment, he is chastised by his powerful union. He is under constant pressure to conform. At a time when he is hard pushed to get his work done, he sees recruitment to his profession slowing up while the total professional work load is increasing. He sees a steadily increasing number of his fellow professionals being siphoned off into research or other full time medical occupations and thus rendered unavailable to help him meet the total medical care problem. He has every right to feel frustrated, but the amazing thing is that he rarely if ever shows any outward or visible evidence of it.

JAMES M. GUSTAFSON

The Clergy in the United States

THE AMERICAN CLERGY is as heterogeneous a group as exists within
any of the professions in our society. The general title "the Reverend" says very little about the man who has it. He may be a
Roman Catholic, a Protestant, a Jew or an Eastern Orthodox. He
may have a high school education, or he may hold a Ph.D. degree.
He may be an administrator in an ecclesiastical bureaucracy, or a
professor in a theological faculty, or a pastor responsible for work
with young people within a "staff ministry." Since the diversity
among the clergy is as great as the diversity in religious life in the
United States, the risks of generalizing about the clergy are patently
clear and appalling. But an essay which seeks to interpret the situation of a profession must be more than an account of endless variety.

It is the thesis of this essay that the activities of the clergy in
the United States are increasing in number and in variety, and that
the conditions for this reside primarily in three areas. The first is
the voluntary character of religion in the United States, which in
its various dimensions makes the clergy unusually responsive to the
desires and needs of the laity and to changes in the culture. The
second is the breakdown of a sense of independent authority in the
clergy; in the absence of wide acceptance of the traditional bases of
their authority, clergymen seek substitute ways to make themselves
legitimate. The third is the effort of the clergy to find new ways to
make religious faith relevant to changing social and cultural patterns. The net effect is a profession undergoing change, but with
grave doubts about whether the changes are viable in the light of
its historical traditions.

Proliferation of Activities

For what is the clergyman responsible? The traditional answers are rather clear. He is responsible for the religious life of the members of his congregation or parish, for the preservation and propagation of his religious tradition, for the administration of the means of grace, for the application of moral and religious law, for the maintenance and growth of religious organizations, for the moral well-being of the society and for the spiritual needs of individual persons. These responsibilities are exercised in traditional roles of the clergyman. He is the preacher, the scholar and teacher, the priest at the altar, the moral and spiritual counselor. But the American clergyman is also responsible for many other things: the behavior of his youth group on a bowling party, the conduct of a financial campaign for a building fund, the public relations of the parish church, the effectiveness of the local council of churches or ministerial association, mitigating tensions between conflicting groups in the community, saying the blessing at the service club luncheon, the sex education of adolescents, premarital counseling, and many more.

Roman Catholic priest, Jewish rabbi and Protestant minister tend to function in similar ways in American religious life. They extend their traditional activities into the same general areas and require the same skills to pursue them. Indeed, recent assessments of the "roles" of priests, rabbis and ministers list activities and skills which are virtually interchangeable among the major traditions.

Jewish commentators write about the "Protestantism of rabbinic functions." [1] The phrase suggests that the traditional orthodox rabbi, who understood himself to be the "scholar-saint," no longer functions well in American society. The rabbi who was the expert in Talmudic scholarship and in the history and practices of Judaism has become, like his Protestant colleague, the leader of public worship, the director of educational and social activities, the one who spearheads the promotional activities of his congregation in its competition with other synagogues and temples. He becomes the active representative of Judaism in the religious and social affairs of his community. He is the pastoral counselor in personal and family crises. He no longer speaks exclusively the language of the Jewish tradition, but he preaches also about social problems, the latest important novel or play, psychiatry, philosophy and the care and feeding of children. He is often actively concerned with issues of civil

71

liberties, civil rights, delinquency, politics and international relations. In order to fulfill these various functions he prizes his ability to be a "friendly person who is able to relate easily to others." However, Jews expect their rabbis to remain the scholars of Judaism; the new activities are added to the old.

The Roman Catholic priest in the United States maintains his basic theological and canonical functions at the center of his activities, but he adds to them other responsibilities.[2] He is primarily the mediator between God and man, "a kind of channel through whom supernatural life flows to the laity, a sort of distribution center for sanctifying grace." And he is the father, the shepherd of the flock, the confessor, the spiritual and moral guide. But the American parish requires more of the priest. It demands "a simultaneous co-ordination of multiple roles."

The number of functions that the priest must officially perform are increasing. He participates in many social relationships with his parishoners, informally as well as formally. The Reverend Joseph Fichter calls this his "communal role." He is the administrator and organizer of a great variety of activities of the laity. He is a businessman who spends much time and energy raising and administering funds. He is the symbol and interpreter of Roman Catholicism to various civic and nonsectarian groups in his community. He organizes and directs the free-time activities of the youth of his parish in his recreational role. He dispenses clothing and food to those in the parish who are too poor to meet their bodily needs. He is the instructor in Roman Catholicism, not only through the catechetical classes and parochial school, but to individuals as well. The organization of lay groups in the parish adds to his liturgical duties. His activities proliferate, for "the priest must conform to the needs of the parish rather than insist upon doing only that for which he is best trained or in which he has the greatest talent and interest. It is a striking anomaly in an age of specialization that the parish priest (unlike trained personnel in other professions and occupations) is forced to maintain an adaptive readiness to be 'all things to all men.'"[3]

Within Protestantism the adaptation and proliferation of activities takes place in two ways: there are new forms of specialized ministries for which particular skill or training is required, and there are changes in and additions to the functions of the local parish parson. The multiple forms of "chaplaincy" which Protestantism shares with other faiths suggest some of the developments in the

72

profession over the past decades: college chaplains, chaplains for mental hospitals, prisons, military forces and industry. "Staff ministries" are coming into being in large urban and suburban congregations which might consist of a "youth minister," educational minister, counseling minister, minister of music, minister of administration and, in a Florida Methodist congregation, even a "minister of world peace"! Denominational and interdenominational bureaucracies demonstrate the extension of specialized activities in the churches. Administration has become a skill in itself in the institutional life of churches just as it has in science and technology. Local councils of churches have executive officers who seek to engender cooperative planning and activity among the Protestant churches in a metropolitan area. In denominational and interdenominational agencies one finds executive experts on college education who are likely to run a teacher placement agency, to counsel on curriculum developments, to conduct study programs for religious faculty members and to administer the allocation of funds to church-related institutions. One finds experts in parish education who write books on family life and on teaching procedures for various age levels, and who act as architectural advisers for additions to the church school buildings. In "social action" agencies there are experts on race relations, international affairs, labor relations, economic policy and politics. There are specialists in social welfare, in urban and rural church problems, in social research, in fund-raising, in planning church buildings, in financial affairs, in public relations and mass communications and even in "creative ideas" to submit to other executives. The department that is responsible for the overseas work of the church may have experts on the Peace Corps, on refugee problems, and may, like the State Department, have an Africa desk, a Near East desk, an India desk, and a Southeast Asia desk. In the vast metropolitan areas of the nation, Protestants have been engaged in physical education and recreation programs, language classes, vocational training, and political activity. The extension of institutional forms is one of the means for the extension of the activity of the Protestant clergy.

The local congregation with a single minister remains, however, the dominant form of ministerial office. Like the Roman Catholic priest and the Jewish rabbi, the minister feels the weight of the "simultaneous co-ordination of multiple roles." The traditional functions of preaching, leading in public worship, pastoral care and teaching remain, but new activities have been added, and there is evidence of a reordering of the relative importance of activities. Samuel Blizzard's extensive research gives evidence of the shifts. The representative Protestant clergy that he studied gave as the normative ordering of their activities the following: preacher, pastor, priest (worship leader), teacher, organizer and administrator. Their personal assessment of effectiveness in these roles ranked them: preacher, pastor, teacher, priest, administrator and organizer. They enjoyed their roles in the following order: pastor, preacher, teacher, priest, organizer and administrator. The amount of time spent in each of these activities, however, shows a distinctly different order: administrator, pastor, preacher and priest (including the time spent in preparation), organizer and teacher. Blizzard found no important differences between rural and urban ministers. Administration, a new activity which is peripheral to what pastors are called and trained to do, takes the greatest proportion of their time and energy.[4]

Other studies have revised Blizzard's list and added to it. Some have suggested that the minister spends a significant amount of his time as the representative of religion in civic affairs and on boards of various social agencies. He is expected to be the expert on religious knowledge, able to answer all questions about religion. He has a social reformer role, as was seen in the Depression, and is seen occasionally now in the racial crisis. His pastoral activities have become more complex with the extension of knowledge of human behavior, so that often the minister becomes a psychotherapist.

Roman Catholics are not satisfied to have a "rectory priest" or a "sacristy priest." They want priests who can be "all things to all men." Jews want their rabbis to be learned in Judaism, but the rabbi is most important to them in his "Protestantized" roles. Protestants proliferate the activities of the clergy until the minister is "macerated," to use Joseph Sittler's expression. Is this proliferation a distinctly American phenomenon? Changing clerical activity is not unique to North America, but it is certainly more striking here than elsewhere. Father Walter J. Ong has noted that the French Roman Catholic priests are "inner-directed" and the Americans are "other-directed."[5] This other-directedness results in the extension of clerical activities, and adds a distinctly American shape to Roman Catholicism. Marshall Sklare and others indicate that orthodox Judaism with its traditional conceptions of the rabbinate has been transformed to a great extent with the Americanization of Jewish immigrants and their children. The Swedish Lutheran pastor who visits a daughter denomination in the United States is overawed by the scope of program and activity that he witnesses. There appears to be an element of the total American phenomenon that deeply affects the profession of the clergy.

Religious Voluntarism and the Clergy

The voluntary character of religion in the United States makes the clergy responsive to the desires and needs of the laity and to changes in the culture. It makes adaptation and proliferation in the activities of the clergy a virtue and a necessity. Traditional functions must be adapted to be accepted by the laity, and new functions must be created to win their continuing support.

What is meant by the "voluntary character of religion"? The phrase points to several dimensions of religious life in the United States. The most obvious is the absence of legally established and preferred religious institutions. The First Amendment to the Constitution insures this. But what historians identify as voluntarism was present in colonial American religious life long before the First Amendment was in effect, and even longer before Congregationalism was legally disestablished in Connecticut and Massachusetts. Its keystone is *consent;* religious activities are consented to by the members of the community. Thus the clergy always have in view the consensus of particular groups on questions of religious belief, institutional authority and practical activities. The voluntary system is the basis of the rise of denominationalism and the diversification of Protestantism and Judaism in the United States; it is the ground for the influence of the laity in all forms of American religions; and it creates the conditions under which the clergy have to be engaged in activities that are "useful" to the laity and the society if they are to be considered legitimate or effective.

In contrast with the clergy of established national churches in Europe, the American clergy cannot rely upon preferred legal and institutional status to authorize and sustain their work. Legal establishment, by and large, lends its weight to traditionalism and conservatism rather than adaptability and creativity in church life. The fact that there are still nations in which a major revision of a prayer book requires authorization by a parliament appears incomprehensible to Americans. A debate on the floor of the United States Senate on the question of the ordination of women for the ministry is unthinkable. Changes in the patterns and activities of the American

75

clergy need not clear extensive legal and bureaucratic obstacles in the government. Furthermore, the financial support that is given to churches from tax funds in some countries creates an institutional security that tends to isolate the clergy from vulnerability to the critical responses of the laity. They are sustained even if the consensus of a secularized nation is that the traditional functions of the clergy are largely irrelevant to modern life. In the United States, the absence of government financial and legal support makes the clergy more susceptible to the voluntary support and consent of the laity. The actual social authority of the clergy is radically altered by the fact that it is not a status in the civil service and cannot rely upon legalized tradition to support customary patterns of professional activity. Legal freedom of religion requires that the clergy attend to the will of the laity and engage in those works which win its support.

Denominationalism is one of the effects of the voluntary system, and it in turn deeply conditions the status and activities of the clergy in the United States. Denominationalism is characterized by the fact that "no denomination claims that all other churches are false churches." [6] Winthrop Hudson suggests that the case for denominational pluralism rests on principles generally accepted before the Revolution. Differences of opinion about the implications of the Christian faith for church life are inevitable, considering differences in human needs. Yet it is believed that the discourse between differentiated groups is more profitable than destructive, for a fuller apprehension of the truth emerges from it. The denominated groups share a wider unity, and they are divided only as voluntary societies, not as schismatic groups from the Church. Protestantism is most obviously denominational, but the divisions between Orthodox, Conservative, and Reform groups in Judaism is part of the same phenomenon. And, if Will Herberg's well-known thesis is accurate,[7] the triple designation of Protestant, Catholic and Jew might well be a newly denominated form of a general American religious faith.

Denominationalism deeply affects the status and activity of the American clergy. For the most part, they are not representatives of exclusive institutions with clearly differentiated beliefs and practices. The Methodist clergyman cannot assume that Methodism makes him unique within the denominational spectrum. Rather, the clergy are engaged in a common enterprise, with many areas of common concern, as the existence of clergy associations in most

76

American communities indicates. Sometimes the activities of particular groups of clergy are related to particular groups in the society: an intellectually oriented Presbyterian has difficulty in "reaching" the Negro migrant from Mississippi to Chicago, and the aesthetically barren worship of a Baptist church is not so attractive to an artist as is the richness of Roman Catholic liturgy. In the main, however, denominational differences are not clear cut. In many communities the clergy are in competition with each other for the loyalties of people. This situation induces adaptation and extension of activities in order to win consent and support. The laity have a buyer's market in religion, and the clergy find those ways which will gain for their church a fair share of the market. The denominational system places a heavy premium on the ability of churches and individual clergy to establish those practices which will attract a maximum audience. The clergy become public relations men, provide expert youth ministries, stress their amiability in personal relations and maximize what their church program can do for the laity in the free market economy of American religious life.

Absence of government support and denominationalism both point to the importance of the laity in American religion. Indeed, the voluntary system creates religious groups dominated by the laity in a way that does not exist in much of Europe. The laity, especially in Protestantism and Judaism, believe that the churches belong to them. This is especially true in churches that have a congregational pattern of church government, where the locus of authority rests in the vote of the membership of a local church. But even in instances where church government is episcopal or presbyterian in character, the clergy work with a strong sense of dependence upon the consent of the laity; this is part of the American religious tradition. Sidney Mead indicates that it was present in the eighteenth century. "In this situation the laity, in the absence of any visible and present reminders of ecclesiastical ubiquity and power to awe and influence them, tasted and relished the possibilities of control to such an extent that later they only grudgingly could be induced to surrender a part—and among Protestants they never surrendered all of it." [8] In his study *Conservative Judaism*, Marshall Sklare notes that "the influence of paid officials and of functionaries [the rabbis of local synagogues] on high policy has been minimal. . . . Historically, Conservatism has been a movement led by *laymen* rather than by rabbis. . . . One additional consideration—the existence of extreme congregationalism among Jewry—helps explain why rabbinical influence has been so small." In American history, even Roman Catholicism had a controversy over efforts of the laity to control the churches to the extent of seeking to take over from the bishops the right to appoint and dismiss pastors.

Laicism has had a double effect on the American clergy. First, it has made them willing to accept new responsibility and to reorder the importance of old ones in order to win the favor of the people. Voluntarism has promoted an instrumentalism, a functionalism in the American clergy. The clergy need to be engaged in activity that is useful in the eyes of the laity if they are to be maintained in their positions. The praise of God for his goodness and power does not legitimate a clergyman in the United States. He is expected to be engaged in practical activities that affect the lives of the people in his community or congregation. Thus he becomes the psychotherapist, the family counselor, the director of recreation for adolescents, the administrator of multiple organizations in a local congregation. The laity exercise great influence and, in some instances, decisive control over the clergy. The laity view the religious enterprise as an instrument for human, earthly good. The clergy by necessity fall into line with this instrumental view of religion and engage in those activities that are "useful" in the eyes of the laity. If the traditional responsibilities are no longer as meaningful as they were in a less secular age, the clergy must add to them new responsibilities.

Not all bending to win the consent of the laity, however, is due to the need for their financial and moral support. Lay domination provides opportunities for the clergy which also tax their inventiveness and adaptability. Thus the second effect of laicism is to engender in the clergy the motive to affect as cogently and powerfully as possible the personalities and secular activities of the people in their care. The clergy seek out ways to influence the opinions and convictions of the laity about matters concerning life in the church and life in the world. If the traditional functions of preaching and daily prayer services do not "reach" the laymen, new activities are invented. "Men's clubs" are formed; the clergyman meets with laymen for lunch; he creates as many occasions and activities as he can to gain access to the laity in order to influence and educate them. If adolescents will not come to a worship service and Bible study program, the clergyman believes he ought to meet them in their own world. He may learn to call folk dances or join them in a baseball game or take them on a tour somewhere. In effect, if the laity take themselves seriously as a source of control in the voluntary system of religion, the clergy take them seriously as well, and participate in those activities that make for maximum contact and influence.

Religious voluntarism calls for the relevance of religion to the centers of interest that dominate the life of the laity. The American clergy have traditionally chosen to enlarge their responsibilities and activities rather than run the risk of irrelevance. If the traditional functions of the clergy make them appear anachronistic, they are prepared to adapt themselves so that they remain in touch with the laity and with the main currents of cultural life. Versatility and adaptation are the very life and virtue of the clergy in a voluntary system of religious life. But obvious difficulties are raised for the clergy. They are responsible for many things, but *to whom* are they responsible? They are responsible not only to the laity, but to ecclesiastical officials and, though it is often forgotten, to God.

Loss of Authority

The American clergy extend their areas of responsibility in part because they are no longer certain what their unique function is. To be sure, they maintain the traditional religious activities, but in the secularization of modern life God is very remote to most men. Indeed, it is difficult to be a clergyman in an age in which the death of God is one of the basic principles of life. The psalmist could write about God, "He covers the heavens with clouds, he prepares rain for the earth, he makes grass grow upon the hills." But every schoolboy in our time knows that the clouds, the rain and the grass can be explained by a scientific understanding of nature and that God is superfluous in this regard. The Protestant preacher for several centuries could assume that a strong sense of guilt was the result of human sin, and that faith in God was the only possible relief. But contemporary psychology offers several alternative explanations for guilt, and the minister as counselor is more likely to act in accord with one of them than in accord with a traditional theological conviction. The dilemma of the modern clergyman is that he represents a historical tradition which in many respects is dissonant with contemporary knowledge and with the principles of practical life in the age of technology. He is no longer clear about his authority. In this uncertainty he seeks out those activities which secure for his profession some legitimacy. In his self-image the clergyman still represents a largely viable tradition; he still speaks for God, though in a qualified way. He has authority which is not dependent upon the consent of the laity, or upon the contemporary state of knowledge and values in the culture. But he also stands as a modern man of the world, and he is faced with uncertainty because of this. He is responsible *to* God, but he is unsure about how this defines what he is responsible *for*. On this issue, however, there are important differences among American clergy.

The Roman Catholic priest has engaged in less adaptation of his roles than have his counterparts in most of Judaism and Protestantism. This is the case in large measure because he is more certain of what his authority is. He knows that he is responsible to his ecclesiastical superiors, and his tradition defines for him what his authority is under God. His authority is adequately institutionalized: there are stated canonical expectations of proper definitions of the Christian faith and of proper clerical practices. His ordination places him in the office of the priest; and in the sacramental act of ordination he is given the divine grace to act as a person in that office. His actions as a priest have efficacy regardless of the immediate state of his intellectual, moral and spiritual life. As a pastor in a local parish he does not derive his authority from the consent of the laity; he is appointed by his bishop, and he is responsible to his bishop. To use the well-known typology of Max Weber, the Roman Catholic priest has traditional authority in that the laity accept his functions without radical question pertaining to their propriety, and he has rational authority in that canon law and dogma define for him both *to whom* he is responsible and *for what* he is responsible. Any addition of activities is marginal to the basic definitions of his person and his work; any adaptation of his function occurs slowly and carefully within a clearly stated set of expectations. Thus, in contrast to many ministers and rabbis, the Roman Catholic priest knows what he is doing and why he is doing it.

The rabbi might appear to be in a more fortunate position than the Protestant minister in regard to his authority. There is a long tradition of proper rabbinic functions: he is to be the scholar who knows the law and its historical interpretations; he is to be a saintly man of prayer. Jews have turned to their rabbis for authoritative judgments on questions of religious and moral behavior for many centuries. The orthodox rabbi in enclosed Jewish communities continues to function in the traditional manner. But large numbers of American Jews no longer accept the traditional authority of the rabbi, and consequently the rabbi is forced to find those activities which give him a legitimate place in the modern Jewish community. The rabbi has always been responsible to the laity, but the laity's changed expectations of rabbinical functions leaves the rabbi in doubt. He is responsible to his tradition: he is still the expert on Judaism and does not take kindly to the loss of its identity. He is also responsible to a laity acculturated to American life, and he seeks to make an ancient religious culture acceptable and relevant to them. Thus he often finds himself a man of compromise. Indeed, his effectiveness depends in part upon his personal ability to represent both Judaism and modernity in his many activities. Traditional authority is displaced by personal authority and by the rabbi's ability to be rationally pragmatic in the determination of his activities.

Protestant ministers present no single case of the problem of authority. There are Protestant traditionalists who live and work in religious cultures that do not demand many new responsibilities. The Bible Belt Protestants are often satisfied to have the minister confine his activities to preaching and praying. A few can live by the dictum, "Where the Bible speaks I speak; where the Bible is silent I am silent." Such a clergyman's responsibility to God is defined by his literal understanding of the Scriptures, and this in turn defines what he is responsible for. But Protestant traditionalists are not confined to sectarians; within the ethnic churches one also finds a great conservatism about the clergy. A German-American Missouri Synod Lutheran pastor is quite secure in his religious culture. He is loyal to the Word of God found in the Bible and defined by the Lutheran confessions. His congregation expects those activities which clearly are shaped by this loyalty, that is, the traditional activities of preaching, leading public worship, teaching the catechism and pastoral care. The bulk of the Protestant clergy in the United States, however, suffer from acute *anomie*.

The *anomie* of the Protestant clergy takes a fairly typical shape. The minister is responsible to the laity in very immediate ways; but he also is responsible to God and to his denominational officials. He lacks a clear delineation, however, of the relation of these authorities to each other. He knows that the voice of the congregation is not the voice of God; but he has little to support him if he chooses to speak for God against the will of the people. He may have no clear canonical definitions of his office, and if such do exist the statements are abstract and general. He has no dependable support from ecclesiastical superiors. In congregational polities, he is

81

literally on his own, for the contract for his services is between the laity and him alone. In presbyterian and episcopal polities, where there is a structure of church government to which he is responsible, it often fails in its responsibility to him. The presbytery and the bishops, he quickly finds out, are also dependent upon the laity. Traditional authority has eroded, and institutional authority is very weak. Thus he is left to find new devices to maintain the necessary political support for his ministry. He relies all too often, in the sardonic words of a cynical theological student, on "his smiling, smiling face."

The Protestant minister's normlessness is not merely institutional; it exists for many ministers in the realm of belief as well. In some denominations there are no authoritative statements of belief which set the intellectual framework for his ministry; and where such statements exist, as in the Presbyterian church, they have often been so reinterpreted in the light of critical scholarship that their force is gone. Thus there is no accepted set of principles in the light of which the minister makes his judgments or directs his activities. His ordination vows pledge him to preach the word of God faithfully, to care for his flock, to be loyal to his denomination and to tend to his own spiritual nurture. But often the church and the minister are unclear what the authority of ordination is. In the absence of clear authority grounded in a theological tradition, two substitutes are found. One is the individual conscience of the minister, who directs his activities in the light of his personal beliefs, which may or may not ring true to traditional ones. The other is the intellectual and religious climate that prevails. He may demonstrate his skills as a therapist or as a commentator on literature, or he may become an efficient promoter of the denominational program.

The normlessness of the Protestant ministry tends to place a heavy burden on the individual minister. He is left to his own resources in shaping many aspects of his professional life. Often this leads to reliance upon the minister's own personality and political skills as the actual basis of his authority. He is expected by the laity to be the friendly man, the person skilled in interpersonal relations, the representation of a state of concord above the struggles of life, the creator of zest and enthusiasm for life. None of these expectations can be found in the Protestant theological and churchly tradition; all of them place the man with "personality" at a professional advantage. The Protestant minister is free to find those new patterns of activity which will win the support of the laity. Indeed, in the absence of traditional and institutional norms he must be versatile, adaptive and creative in order to be successful.

No matter what his faith and tradition are, the American clergyman stands between an ancient tradition and a culture in which God is remote, if not dead. This situation is felt to be a deep and agonizing crisis for many of the most sensitive and educated clergy. Consequently they are seeking those ways of work which will overcome the radical separation of religious life from the mainstream of the culture.

Overcoming the Irrelevance of Religion to Life

A third force that revises clerical activities and expands them is the honest effort of anguished clergy to break out of the isolation of religious faith and of professional life. Alert Protestant ministers particularly are ready to share in the jeremiads that are directed against the superficiality of religious life in American society, against its confinement to children, women and family life, against its preoccupation with increasing memberships, budgets and size of church buildings. They sense their guilt when they are accused of running the new children's crusade in the child-centered program of the suburban church. They are painfully aware that the prophetic dimensions of Christian and Jewish faith are blunted in the contemporary church. They know that 11:00 A.M. on Sunday mornings is the most segregated hour of the week. They accept the sociological observation that men are oriented toward their professions and women toward the home, and they are restless in being the chaplains only to family life. Some young clergymen are "pro-Christ" and "anti-church"; they view the denominational bureaucracies and congregational organizations as major impediments to the cause of religious faith. They strive to speak the religious message in the idiom of the arts or in the language of politics on the assumption that the traditional religious language is no longer meaningful. Books entitled *Noise of Solemn Assemblies* and *The Suburban Captivity of the Church* [9] evoke personal crises in the clergy. They see themselves merely as adding to the useless noise, or as confined within the captivity of their churches.

Under the conviction that much of the activity of the churches is without theological justification or moral purpose, and indeed that it is an expression of the faithlessness of the church, many younger clergymen are seeking to break from the stereotyped roles and activities to find those patterns through which religion can be more influential in shaping cultural life, social and political policy, and the secular activity of the laity. The more conservative among the guilt-stricken clergy seek to "renew parish life." They rely less upon preaching and more upon gathering people into small groups for discussion. They may address themselves to the laity first in the language of a drama such as *Death of a Salesman,* or of popular sociology such as *White Collar* or *The Organization Man.* Some ride the commuter trains to engage the laymen in the issues of his forthcoming day. No end of ingenuity is applied to bring the life of man in the world into the discourse of men together in the congregation or to bring the essential message of religious faith into the world in nonreligious language.

The more radical of the disenchanted clergy believe that the normal activities of the traditional church have outlived their usefulness. The church must scatter; the real ministry is that of the laity in the world of their vocations rather than that of the clergy before the altar and in the pulpit. To overcome the distance between church and world some have taken jobs in factories; others have affiliated with experimental ventures such as "Faith and Life Communities" in which the usual marks of the clergy are suppressed and the minister joins a seeking, working laity as one among them.

Not all the changes in the activities of the clergy are defensive, or merely substitutions for the lack of traditional authority. Protestantism particularly is in a state of ecclesiastical ferment, confined to a large extent to a deeply conscientious minority of the younger clergy. But these versatile and creative clergy wield powerful pens and make effective speeches and demonstrate in their own novel ways that ministry is not confined to the symbols of a Gothic age. If they should win the day, American religious life might well take shapes that are externally secular but inwardly religious.

Adaptation in Theological Education

The theological schools that train men for the ministry reflect the same tensions that occur in the ministry and in church life in the United States. On the one hand they perpetuate and develop religious traditions with their sacred books and the centuries of interpretation and commentary on them. On the other hand they train men for religious leadership in the decades that lie ahead for very American congregations and other ecclesiastical institutions.

Roman Catholic training for the priesthood has clearly been more faithful to the traditional modes than is the case for Conservative and Reformed Judaism or Protestantism. With Protestantism the variations are great: Lutheran schools have been less adaptive than Protestant Episcopal and Presbyterian schools; Methodist and Congregational schools have been more concerned with "relevance" than any of these others.

The recent trends in curriculum changes in Protestant seminaries indicate the double loyalty of the ministry. During the decade of the 1920's under the impact of "liberal" theology and the movements for social action and a progressive Christian education in the parishes, the traditional Biblical and theological disciplines were somewhat neglected in favor of more purely vocational and practical courses. In response to the revival of interest in Biblical and theological studies, and to the sense of loss of religious identity in Protestant churches, "biblical, church-historical and theological studies have been re-established or re-emphasized as the stable but not static basis of theological education." [10] In the past three decades, many nontheological subjects have been added to the curriculum, especially sociology and psychology. The main intention in this seems to be to provide the background knowledge needed for the practical work of the ministry.

The most extensive addition to theological curriculum in recent years has been in the area of psychology and pastoral counseling. In addition to course work, seminarians are trained in large numbers during the summer months in mental hospitals under the guidance of supervising chaplains. There is also a perceptible increase in interest in the Biblical languages. Greek was never as neglected as Hebrew in American theological schools, but both are enjoying a new status because of increased interest in Biblical theology. Social ethics has been generally holding its own in recent years, though it is not an expanding field. In the past decade, the interpretation of art and literature has become more popular than social ethics as a bridge discipline between the tradition and the contemporary world.

A tension continues to exist within most theological schools between the "content" disciplines and the "practical" disciplines. Although this is almost universally deplored, no widely effective resolution has been found. Students continue to be engaged in some "field work," either in conjunction with their residence in the school or during an "internship" year away from the school. Various programs have been used to give men experience not only in the actual responsibilities of church life but in the "lay" world as well, such as "seminarians in industry" programs. Responses of alumni to their schools indicate that many of them feel inadequately trained for their "practical" and, particularly, their administrative responsibilities. Others, however, desire more work in the Biblical, theological and historical disciplines in order to be grounded in the religious faith and knowledge that ought to give purpose and direction to their work.

The seminaries persistently operate with a different conception of the ministry than the one which actually exists in ecclesiastical life. Sklare's observations about the discontinuities between professors at Jewish Theological Seminary and the "functionaries" in the congregations has a parallel in Protestant circles. "As functionaries gradually lose interest in rabbinical learning, they cannot help but earn the disapproval of the schoolmen." [11] A Protestant theologian significantly quipped, "The task of the seminary is to unfit men for the ministry as the churches define it today."

Within parts of Protestantism, there are many persons who enter the ministry without the standard B.A. and B.D. degree preparation. This is the case for many sect groups who accept "called" laymen or who accept men trained at one of the many "Bible Institutes" in the country. Many of these institutions are upgrading their academic work, and some encourage their graduates to pursue further academic work. There are approximately 20,000 Protestant students in theological schools belonging to the American Association of Theological Schools; approximately one fourth of these are enrolled in Southern Baptist Seminaries. The most rapid growth in theological education in recent years has come from denominations that formerly were satisfied with a less educated clergy.

The Negro Protestant ministry and their education present one of the least satisfactory pictures when standards for ministerial training are brought into view. While the number of Negro students who graduate from accredited theological seminaries is steadily increasing, there are probably nine or ten times as many who are ordained or become lay preachers without this academic training.[12] Some observers believe that the ministry has gained a higher status in the eyes of the generation of young Negroes who are leading the desegregation movements because of the effective leadership being given by Martin Luther King and others. In the main, however, the religious life of Negro churches is closely bound to the social and

The Clergy in the United States

cultural status of the Negro community; the higher education of Negroes for the ministry often has the effect of separating them culturally from the mass of Negro Protestant laity.[13]

Continuing education programs for the Protestant clergy are expanding under the auspices of both theological schools and church agencies. The intention in all of them is to keep the parish ministers abreast of the latest developments in Biblical research, in theology and in practical church affairs, and to stimulate their continued study in the parish. Some of these programs are conducted during the summer months; some seminaries have pastors in residence for a period of time during the course of a semester.[14]

The adaptations of the seminary occur both to meet the felt needs of the men in the ministry and to initiate new ideas and practices for ministers. In the work of theology and Biblical research, the teaching of the faculties is always ahead of the consensus that exists in the ministry. In the practical fields the seminaries often tag behind the most progressive developments in church life. Experimentation in new forms of effective ministry are occurring continuously, for example the Detroit Industrial Mission, which seeks to work with industrial workers and management through their occupations. Seminaries are, however, largely geared in their practical training to the traditional forms of parish ministry—the forms which exist in the bulk of the denominations and congregations.

Recruitment

Judgments about the quality of men who enter the ministry are difficult to make. Many unfounded assertions are made about both a decline in quality and a continuation of high quality. Protestants and Roman Catholics are actively engaged in the recruitment of religious professional workers. "There is probably no other occupation or profession in the American society that has a more intense recruitment system than that of the religious and ecclesiastical vocation of the Catholic Church."[15] Among Protestants the recruitment is rather unorganized and competitive. Denominations have programs which begin at the high school level, since it is known that the first serious consideration of the ministry usually occurs between the ages of sixteen and eighteen. Seminaries are engaged in programs at the college level. The Rockefeller Brothers Fund has for ten years sponsored a program of fellowships for able persons who are considering the ministry as a vocation. The men selected attend a theological school for one year; 60 per cent of them continue, and 60 per cent of these have thus far found their way into the parish ministry. The Conservative Jews have traditionally recruited a large number of men from Orthodox families that are being acculturated. Sklare reports that the rabbinate is not regarded as highly as other professions in the Conservative families, and that the early preparation in Hebrew studies is declining among them as well.

Among Protestants there are two notable trends in recent years among students who enroll as seminarians. One is the increase in the number of students who are vocationally uncertain at the time of admission. Indeed, many of them are uncertain about their religious convictions and commitment. The seminary, then, functions not only as a professional school training men for an occupation, but as a center for the cultivation of religious life. A second trend is for men who have established themselves in other occupations to engage in theological study and to become ministers. The Protestant Episcopal Church seems to draw more of these men than other churches, but they are found in other denominational schools and university divinity schools as well.[16]

A relatively small number of women have been trained for Protestant church professions over the past four decades. Unlike Roman Catholicism, which has institutionalized the status of women in religious vocations, Protestantism has no clarity or consensus on their place in the church. Relatively few women seek ordination, partly because relatively few denominations ordain them. The United Presbyterian Church in the United States recently joined the group of churches who ordain women: the Methodist Church, the United Church of Christ, the Disciples of Christ, Baptist churches, and smaller groups presently do. The Protestant Episcopal Church, the Lutheran churches, and many other groups do not. The most available opportunities for women in professional religious work are service as directors of church school programs, in youth programs and in college work. As with other areas of graduate professional education for women, however, many of the students are diverted from their professional intentions by marriage. It is notable that the Rockefeller Brothers Fund program recently dropped the recruitment of women for the ministry because so few engage in professional work.

Protestant theological school enrollment has maintained itself at approximately the same level for more than a decade. A decline of

5 per cent occurred several years ago, but this numerical loss has been made up. There is a considerable amount of anxiety, however, about recruitment. Within the next decade a more systematic effort than has occurred heretofore to encourage young people to enroll in the seminaries will probably take place.

Adaptation—The Story of the Clergy in America

Adaptation is obviously not unique to the religious professions. Engineers, medical doctors and others are involved in a more rapidly changing professional situation than are the clergy. But their situation is significantly different, for they are in professions in which the latest is usually the best, in which modernity is a virtue. Perhaps the most unique aspect of the clergy's situation is that it retains a loyalty to ancient traditions in thought, in institutional life and in practice. Yet it cannot simply rest its case for contemporary validity in its faithfulness to the ancient and honorable paths of the fathers. The overused phrase "the problem of relevance" points to the reality of its dilemma. The ancient must function under the conditions of modernity, and under the conditions of a voluntary system. Yet the clergy cannot simply seek modernity or be functional with reference to pragmatic criteria of judgment, for in so doing it loses its identity as the representative of a tradition that still has validity for religious men. "Adaptation was thrust upon the ministers from the beginning," wrote Sidney Mead of the American clergy. Adaptation will be thrust upon them until the end.

REFERENCES

1. Jerome E. Carlin and Saul H. Mendlowitz, "The American Rabbi: A Religious Specialist Responds to the Loss of Authority," in Marshall Sklare (ed.), *The Jews* (Glencoe, Ill.: The Free Press, 1958), pp. 377–414; and Marshall Sklare, *Conservative Judaism* (Glencoe, Ill.: The Free Press, 1955), chapter 6.

2. Joseph Fichter, S.J., *Social Relations in the Urban Parish* (Chicago: University of Chicago Press, 1954), chapter 10; and *Religion as an Occupation* (South Bend, Ind.: University of Notre Dame Press, 1961).

3. Fichter, *Social Relations,* p. 137.

4. Samuel W. Blizzard, "The Minister's Dilemma," *The Christian Century* (April 25, 1956), pp. 508–510. This article provoked widespread comment and has been followed by many articles in the popular press. Robert

Michaelsen in "The Protestant Ministry in America, 1850 to the Present," in H. R. Niebuhr and D. D. Williams (eds.), *The Ministry in Historical Perspectives* (New York: Harper, 1956), pp. 250–287, describes many of the recent activities of Protestant clergy.

5. Walter J. Ong, S.J., *Frontiers in American Catholicism* (New York: Macmillan, 1957), chapter 3.

6. Winthrop Hudson, *American Protestantism* (Chicago: University of Chicago Press, 1961), p. 34. For a brilliant account of the Protestant clergy in the United States that stresses the theme of their adaptability under the conditions of voluntarism, see Sidney Mead, "The Rise of the Evangelical Conception of the Ministry in America (1607–1850)," in Niebuhr and Williams, *op. cit.*, pp. 207–249.

7. Will Herberg, *Protestant—Catholic—Jew* (Garden City, N.Y.: Doubleday, 1955), especially chapter 10.

8. Mead, in *op. cit.*, pp. 212–213.

9. Peter Berger is the author of the first, Gibson Winter of the second.

10. H. R. Niebuhr, D. D. Williams and J. M. Gustafson, *The Advancement of Theological Education* (New York: Harper, 1957), p. 21.

11. Sklare, *op. cit.*, p. 190.

12. Niebuhr, Williams and Gustafson, *op. cit.*, Appendix, "The Theological Education of Negro Ministers," pp. 226–236.

13. The activity of Negro ministers in a Northern urban community is graphically portrayed in St. Clair Drake and Horace Cayton, *Black Metropolis* (New York: Harcourt, Brace, 1945). Ira Reid of Haverford College prepared the most comprehensive report of the Negro ministry in recent years, *The Negro Baptist Ministry, An Analysis of Its Profession, Preparation and Practices* (Philadelphia, 1951, mimeographed).

14. A survey of these programs was recently published in mimeographed form: Connolly C. Gamble, Jr., *The Continuing Education of the American Minister* (Richmond, Va.: Union Theological Seminary, 1960).

15. Joseph Fichter, S.J., *Religion as an Occupation* (South Bend, Ind.: University of Notre Dame Press, 1961), pp. 9–10. This book is as complete a study of a religious profession from a sociological point of view as we have. It gives accurate information about the source of recruits, their motivations for entering the priesthood, their training and status, etc. Information is included about both men and women in the orders as well.

16. For an overview of Protestant theological students, see the author's chapter, "Theological Students: Varieties of Types and Experience," in Niebuhr, Williams and Gustafson, *op. cit.*, pp. 145–173.

ALMA S. WITTLIN

The Teacher

EDUCATION may be defined as a process of shaping behavior. In a general sense every waking moment of life from birth to death is an educational experience, for better or for worse. The function of the educator is to effect behavioral changes in specified groups of people, and to do so in a planned and goal-directed manner.

Storage and dissemination of knowledge are among the great energy-saving devices of mankind. The teacher is one of the foremost guardians and transmitters of knowledge. He occupies a shunting point between generations: he may reinforce the continuation of traditions; or he may be a factor in unsettling or in reshaping them. And he may perform either of these functions with a greater or lesser consciousness of his role. Directly or circuitously he may be a powerful force molding society. A single teacher may accelerate the fruition of talent in hundreds of individuals, neglect or warp it; he may further or stifle potentials for creativity or waywardness. A teacher's trade is concerned with the human condition, with human promise and destiny.

The teacher claims to be a *professional*. Contrary to an amateur, a professional person assumedly possesses a body of knowledge and of skills, and he uses them with confidence. It would not befit him to skip from dabbling in one thing to trifling with another; he is to be earnest, persistent and accurate in his work. A dilettante may engage in a pursuit for the built-in recompense of doing or toying, but a professional person is entitled to a monetary reward. Certain professional people, however, are expected to put service to others before personal profit. In this respect, the image of the educator has common traits with that of the healer of the sick.

According to dictionary lore the terms "vocation" and "profession" are to some degree interchangeable, but while a vocation often

91

presupposes routine jobs, a profession enshrines the meaning of a calling and an avowal to a higher purpose. In logical conclusion the respect of his fellow men would seem to be due the teacher, as well as a wide scope in decision-making that would be commensurate with his status. The setting of special standards and their enforcement are among the privileges of a professional group and of its members.

In Martin Luther's judgment the teacher's vocation was next to that of the ministry. In *Sartor Resartus*, Thomas Carlyle referred to teachers as to "fashioners of souls," who ought to be "world-honored dignitaries" like generals and field marshals. Notables of England, Sweden and Hungary vied for the counsel of the seventeenth-century schoolmaster and writer on education John Amos Comenius, the son of a Czech miller. Johann Pestalozzi's schools in Switzerland were places of pilgrimage in the early nineteenth century. The philosopher Johann Herbart was among the visitors, and Johann Fichte referred to the educator in his "Addresses to the German Nation." Later in the century Friedrich Froebel's Kindergarten was a subject of international admiration, in which Charles Dickens joined with the French historian Jules Michelet and with Giuseppe Garibaldi, the leader of the newly unified Italy.

In a period of accelerated change the teacher's function acquires special significance. The era of automated industry, of computors performing operations hitherto reserved to the human brain, of global intercourse and of space exploration demands a quickened pace in lifting increasing numbers of people to higher levels of education. ". . . never before were men and nations compelled, by inescapable challenge, to learn so much, so fast, so well." "Indeed, this is a revolutionary era . . . calling for a new and better life. But I wonder if it is not true to say that there has been no comparable revolution—and perhaps no revolution at all—in the realm of edution?" These two statements were made at the International Centennial Conference at Vassar College in 1962, by Emmet John Hughes and Ralph J. Bunche respectively.

In the course of the last decade teachers have been severely criticized for failing in their tasks. There is young Johnny who after several years of schooling cannot read. There are the dropouts from high school, estimated to be 4 out of 10 students, and referred to by Dr. James Conant as social dynamite. There are the graduates of an education known as liberal or liberalizing who show little sensitive regard for humane values in their daily lives and who remain stubbornly immature in spite of their credits for courses in Greek history or in literature. Teachers are often accused of incompetence in the subject matter they teach. To make up for the omissions of science teachers, scientists feel challenged to take time off from their research and college teaching to act as school reformers from the high school down to the grades. Scholars, businessmen and union leaders are demanding that students receive instruction in economics and other significant aspects of their present environment. The ratio of private to public schools rose from 10.9 per cent to 14 per cent between 1950 and 1960, and is an index of the dissatisfaction of parents with public schools.

One of the contributors to the first symposium on "Automation and the Challenge to Education," held in Washington, D.C. in 1961, the economist Dr. Walter Buckingham, Director of the School of Industrial Management at the Georgia Institute of Technology, Atlanta, called for teachers of ". . . higher quality . . . who are creative, courageous, imaginative, intelligent, sensitive, personable." He expressed his conviction that "teachers of this caliber are capable of stirring a student's imagination so that he can develop his own potentialities. Dull, uninspiring teachers may well force students into the ranks of those who are indifferent, even hostile, to knowledge and reason."[1]

Public schools are accused of anti-intellectualism and of offering cafeteria-style curricula, superficial and discontinuous, requiring neither concentration nor precision. Teachers are blamed for being popularity seekers instead of representing legitimate authority. The question is raised, what function does a school teacher first and foremost fulfill—that of an instructor, of a custodian or of a social worker? The professional status of the school teacher is altogether questioned on the grounds of his limited autonomy, of his restrictions in decision-making concerning what and how he teaches, and of his position as a strictly supervised employee.

Any attempt at a judicious and constructive evaluation of criticisms and of their causes must begin with an analysis in which each symptom of a complex syndrome would appear in isolation, with the help of which the hierarchy of the symptoms and their possible relations to each other could be better understood. Both the teacher and his habitat require examination: the school, the society, and the legacies of the past which live on in the minds of men. If teachers are accused of being supervisees, to what extent and in what respect are they responsible for shortcomings in education? Who is the master-mind behind them who carries the main burden of responsibility? Or is it a group-mind, and if so, what is its composition? Does society wish the teacher to be in this position, does it tolerate such circumstances, or is there an insufficient general awareness of the situation?

The number of elementary and secondary teachers in the United States may approach one million and a half. How can such a large contingent of human beings be uniformly assessed and judged— like a homogenized mass? There are men and women among them, people from 22 to 65 years of age, and representatives of a variety of religious and political persuasions. There are natives of all states and graduates of a wide range of colleges and universities; people without any academic degree and holders of advanced degrees. There are grade-school teachers who take care of all subjects, instructors of physics or of literature for advanced high school students, and teachers of driving an automobile. What may be the specific traits characterizing so many people of such heterogeneous backgrounds?

The place of direct impact of formal education on the pupil is in the classroom, and in considerable measure in the interaction between teacher and pupil. As I. L. Kandel said, "To erect fine buildings and to seek to meet the needs and abilities of all individuals who desire to avail themselves of the opportunity so generously offered without providing teachers with qualifications commensurate with the ideal is a sham." Yet the teacher in the American classroom has only a very limited power of decision-making. In their book *The Role of Schools in Mental Health,* W. Allinsmith and G. W. Goethals listed among the main functions of a teacher's immediate superior, as item number one, "to make decisions"[2] and they note: "Teachers have unclear perceptions of the policy-making processes and practices in the school system." In a publication of the U.S. Office of Education, *Elementary School Administration and Organization,* of 1960, by Stuart E. Dean, the main role of the school principal is described as that of a supervisor of instruction. In fact, the principal's autonomy is bridled by the central office of his school system. If he retains 41.8 per cent authority in assigning pupils to classes and 23 per cent authority in matters of pupils' promotion, little is left of important decisions to the classroom teacher. Lack of democratic administration procedures and of a share in policy-making were among the main causes of poor teacher morale recorded in a survey made by the George Peabody College for Teachers in Nashville, Tennessee.

Owing to the increasing pressure of public demand for better academic standards in the schools, the scholastic achievements of an elementary teacher may currently serve as a recommendation for a post, contrary to a previously prevailing .distrust on the part of administrators of overqualified teachers. The physical appearance of a candidate for a teaching position is, however, still receiving considerable attention; it is questionable whether any very able teacher with some physical disability or deformity would be hired. Of primary importance is the teacher's conformity with existing standards. The code of ethics of the National Education Association demands that a teacher accept the community's pattern of behavior.

Parents, members of the P.T.A., and other citizens are vociferous in expressing their views on school matters. They criticize, advise, and demand the institution of certain courses and the abolition of others; they argue in favor of or against strict discipline or children's right to creative self-expression, though they would hardly take it upon themselves to compete with their physician or with their legal adviser in matters which require professional expertise. As Sterling M. McMurrin, former U.S. Commissioner of Education, pointed out in his introduction to J. D. Koerner's *Miseducation of American Teachers*, the average citizen has taken it for granted that teaching is a profession appropriate for persons of second- or third-rate ability.[3] The public's attitude toward the teachers of the growing generations is, however, rarely based on solid facts. As Mr. Devereux Josephs, chairman of President Eisenhower's Committee on Education Beyond High School, said, "The public knows more about potato prices, the number of hogs slaughtered, and the status of bank loans than it knows about its schools."

If salaries are to be considered as an index of status, teachers rank lower than members of other professions. After considerable improvement in the last few years, the average yearly salary of a public school teacher has risen to a little more than $5000. About 15 per cent of teachers earn less than $3500, although according to the U.S. Department of Labor's estimate the average city worker needs more than $6200 per year to maintain an accepted standard of living. There may be a few hundred high school teachers who earn about $10,000 yearly, a paltry sum for similarly successful physicians or attorneys.

The present status of the teacher is the result of conditions reaching back into a distant past. There is a plurality of antecedents rather than a single step-by-step sequence of cause and effect—economic and political determinants together with ambivalent human attitudes which obfuscated and distorted the rational perception of a changing environment. In ancient Greece philosophers were highly honored teachers, and fees were deemed acceptable only among Sophists. The men who taught children to read, to write and to memorize passages from poetic history accepted a meager pay and enjoyed little respect. The original *paidagogos* was a servant whose function was literally implied in his title—he had to lead the boy to and from school. In the traditional Chinese school for young pupils the schoolmaster was by definition a man who had failed intellectually. Having fallen short of the requirements at a civil service examination he stooped to the job of compelling boys to the confrontation of ideographs and to the memorization of hardly understood texts. To meet the unprecedented demand for teachers on an elementary level misfits and invalids were sometimes considered equal to the task of teaching. Russian theological seminaries disposed of some of their undesirable students by turning them over to the new common schools under Peter the Great. In Frederick the Great's Prussia invalids of the army were promoted, or demoted, to teachers.

The low opinion of the rank-and-file schoolmaster in Europe spread to the New World, and a seventeenth-century Rector of Annapolis recorded that on the arrival of every ship containing bondservants or convicts, schoolmasters were offered for sale but that they did not fetch as good prices as weavers, tailors and other tradesmen. Eighteenth-century rural families in America often had tutors in their houses who lived like people "on alms." When the instruction of "petties," or young children, became necessary in great numbers, instructors were sometimes "poor women or others whose necessities compelled them to undertake it as a mere shelter from beggary." In referring to conditions in 1823, Arthur Bestor quoted a previous author: "The common schools are, in not a few instances, conducted by individuals who do not possess one of the qualifications of an instructor; and in very many cases, there is barely knowledge enough to keep the teacher at a decent distance from the scholars."[4] In his Annual Report of 1842 the state superintendent of public instruction of Michigan wrote that "an elementary school, where the rudiments of an English education only are taught . . . requires a female of practical common sense, with amiable and winning manners, a patient spirit, and a tolerable knowledge of the springs of human action."

The monitorial schools of the early nineteenth century seemed ideally to fit the early state of industrial civilization. Pupils were cheaply mass produced, down to $1 per year. The scholars, who first learned their lessons from the teacher, conveyed exactly the same lesson to other children, ten to every monitor. The financial expenditure was limited to a wage for a single teacher and to the maintenance of a single hall. Western man was under the spell of an unprecedented experience: of the realization of abundance produced by the inanimate power of machines. Since the dawn of memory human fate had been identified with toil in striving for the bare necessities of life, except for the conspicuous consumption indulged in by small elites. The harnessing of the wind and of the muscle power of animals had eased the grind, but millennia had to pass before energy became plentiful with James Watts' steam engine and with the use of electric power transmitted over distances. The increasing demands of industry on labor and the extension of the ballot made improved general education imperative. Large-scale mechanisms were needed for education, mind-factories comparable to those factories used in the manufacture of goods. In the 'thirties of the nineteenth century a superintendent in Chicago became known for his motto: "Organize, deputize, supervise," which he recommended to schools in imitation of big business. The analogy of the industrial plant, of assembly lines and of speed was haunting human minds (and may still have a grip on them). In 1916 a book appeared in Boston on *Public School Administration*, by E. P. Cubberly, in which it was stated that ". . . the schools are, in a sense, factories in which the raw materials are to be shaped into products to meet the various demands of life." According to this philosophy the educator was alloted the modest role of a copyist of patterns.

The United States was the first country in the world to provide free public schooling beyond the elementary level, and American education was becoming a colossal enterprise. In 1900, 17 million students went to school; their present number is close to 50 million. As Paul Woodring wrote, "Many people seem satisfied merely to have more schools, bigger schools, and to keep children in them for a longer period of time."[5] It is in the nature of any large enterprise involving many people and masses of materials to crystallize into a corporate structure. Big business followed the example of governments and of armies, and was in its turn followed by big-scale education. But for all the bureaucracy and hierarchy, for all the chains of command and delays of action which are entailed in corporate structure, business in competitive society could hardly have survived without remaining flexible, without retaining scope for autonomy and spontaneity in its strategic managerial posts where a salaried person had to have something of the character of an entrepreneur, of a risk-taking innovator. In the schools, however, where products do not lend themselves to the same quick evaluation as marketable merchandise, the figure occupying the strategically most significant post, the teacher in the classroom, was deprived of most of his opportunities for decision-making, for spontaneous and original action. He was demoted to an employee on the bottom link of a long chain of command which winds its way from the state governor's office and the chambers of the state legislature to state boards and state education departments, further down to local school boards and offices of superintendents, and from them to the principals of individual schools. A host of statisticians, supervisors, guidance officers, counselors, testing experts and other specialists supply a supporting cast which in Myron Lieberman's terms leads "to a splitting, not a fusion of power and technical competence" and to "a power structure which is inconsistent with the professional status of the teacher." [6]

All these educator figures may have their relevance, but as in any interaction among human beings their roles have to be subtly defined and teamwork has to replace hierarchy to make each individual productive without debilitating others. It has been shown, for example, that the presence of guidance officers may deprive some teachers of a sense of individual responsibility needed by an adult for successful performance. The school superintendent may feel somewhat akin to a corporation executive, he may receive the highest salary in his occupational group and appear in the beam of publicity as the authoritative representative of the school system; yet in fact he is a short-term employee of the local school board, which is mainly composed of laymen, if he is not occupying an elective office of partisan-political denomination. When Abraham Flexner in 1908 wrote his historical report on "Medical Education in the United States and Canada," which was based on extensive studies made under the sponsorship of the Carnegie Foundation, he recommended that all state medical boards which judged on such matters as the accreditation of medical schools and the licensing of doctors should be composed of doctors and not of laymen. A publication of the Council of State Governments, "Occupational Licensing in the States," recorded in 1952 that all or the majority of members of professional boards of dentists and of attorneys had to be practicioners of the profession in all the states of the union. A similar ruling existed in 42 states with regard to barbers, in 41 states with regard to beauticians, and in 5 states with regard to teachers.

Even now, in the 'sixties, educational boards in many states are still largely or exclusively composed of laymen. They exercise authority over teacher accreditation, salaries and tenure, the selection of courses, the adoption or rejection of textbooks or the keeping of deviant pupils in ordinary classrooms, sometimes in opposition to a superintendent's request for special classes for such students. No lay adviser would defy a hospital administrator or doctor with the immoral request of accommodating in a general ward patients suffering from an infectious or mental disease.

Two specific examples will illustrate actions of lay boards or ignorant citizens. The community of Levittown, New York, is the topic of a report of an investigation conducted in 1962 under the auspices of the National Education Association and the New York State Teachers Association. One of the numerous controversies between the community and the schools was centered on the letter of a housewife to the superintendent of the local schools, in which she protested the use of the cantata "The Lonesome Train" which describes the journey of the train bearing Lincoln's body from Washington, D. C. to Springfield, Illinois, for burial, and which was allegedly written and scored by "known communists" and therefore communist propaganda. This happened in 1955, but the temper of the community has not subsided, as could be witnessed recently when the Levittown school board voted 5 to 2 to ban a textbook, *Subcontinent of India,* by an established author of history books and professor at Fairleigh Dickinson University on the grounds that the author, Emil Lengyel, had sometime in the past been a member of objectionable organizations. The trustee who made the motion had read the book and did not object to its contents. These are merely two of the numerous happenings at Levittown which hamper the education of children.

When Gordon Lish, a teacher of English at Mills High School in Burlingame, California, was dismissed by the school board but was offered help in finding another school job, he answered: "I don't want one . . . teaching is not a man's job. They won't let you be one and they don't pay a man's salary. I used to think teaching was the most rewarding thing you could do, but I have begun to care less and less. Yet just walking away from this seems like an immoral decision." Mr. Lish was fired for spending time on the editing of a literary quarterly, *Genesis West,* among whose contributors were Stephen Spender, Kenneth Rexroth and Mark Harris. He was also blamed for reciting the Allegiance to the Flag too rapidly and for telling his students that they were free not to crouch beneath their desks during nuclear attack drills.

It is encouraging to learn that the new superintendent of the New York City schools, Dr. Calvin E. Gross, hopes to establish "administrative control points" manned "by individuals, not committees." In his opinion decentralization of authority in schools is needed, and a wider margin for the delegation of responsibility.

Why do people choose teaching as a career? There is a preponderance of teachers from the lower or lower middle socio-economic groups of the population. To them teaching means advancement in social status. In the case of women it is one of the traditional occupations, and there are in the public schools of the United States 73 women teachers to 27 men. Up to about 1939, teachers' salaries were higher than the wages of employees in industry, and this served as an additional inducement. The financial picture changed, however. In 1952 a classroom teacher's average annual salary was 1.4 per cent below the average annual income of all employed persons, while that of industrial employees was 12.9 per cent above it. [It ought to be noted that from 1952 to the present, teachers' salaries have gained in momentum.] Between 1904 and 1953 the purchasing power of the income of a coal miner and of a railroad switchtender increased by 163 per cent and 134 per cent respectively, while the elementary school teacher's purchasing power rose by 60 per cent, and that of a high school teacher and a college professor by even less. The disparity between white and blue collar incomes lessened. Furthermore, teacher training extended over a longer period of time, and so did the school year. While industrial and office work decreased from a six-day work week of at least 48 hours to a five-day work week of not more than 40 hours between 1904 and 1953, children's school terms increased in length by about 23 per cent.

In spite of the lengthening period of teacher training, it is still short if compared with the preparation for other professions such as medicine or law, and this aspect in itself may encourage some people to choose education as a career. Secondary school teachers receive a much more thorough training in a specific subject matter than teachers for elementary schools, but are at present required to show credit in such courses as Educational Psychology, Educational Measurement or School Procedure.

"When national samples of education students are compared with comparable samples of students in other curricular areas, they consistently fall below the liberal arts, science and engineering groups. . . . Under conditions now prevailing in the country as a whole . . . the field of education is not competing successfully with other professions in drawing the high-caliber personnel that it so urgently needs," wrote Robert D. North in *Education of Teachers: New Perspectives* in 1958.[7] In a Selective Service Qualification Test of 1955, the I.Q.'s of students majoring in nine different areas were compared. Engineers scored highest; physical scientists and mathematicians came next, with students of humanities following them; students of education appeared at the bottom of the list. In another study, made in Philadelphia, high school students scored higher than students in a teacher training college. The image of the prospective school teacher might look brighter if such comparisons were repeated at present, after several years of increasing demand by critics for better teachers; but these and similar often-quoted statistics still leave a very incomplete image of the prospective teacher. Supposing that the student of education of 1963 compares more favorably with his counterpart in economics or in physics than he did five years ago, how will he compare after several years of teaching? Furthermore, is the "I.Q." the most relevant characteristic of people? Or are there other "queues"—such as for example an A.Q., a C.Q. and a F.Q.—measures for ambiguity tolerance, for adaptation to change, for flexibility? And which endowments, or lack of them, may motivate people to choose teaching as a career? So far we have invested our faith in the I.Q.

What discourages people from teaching? The attitudes of families and of friends act in varying degrees as deterrents, especially if the candidate for the teaching career is a male. As Allinsmith and Goethals reported, he is told, "You can do better than that." The neutral attitude toward the girl who intends to teach may acquire an acid tone if she wants to teach in the elementary school. A liberal arts student will consider elementary school teaching as an acceptable female occupation but as an undesirable way of living for a man.

There is a strange contradiction between the prestige in which students of "Ivy League" colleges or liberal arts colleges hold teaching and their rating of the contribution the teacher makes to society. In terms of social prestige a secondary teacher may rank at the bottom of twelve occupations, on a par with salesmen and small-business proprietors, even though above elementary school teachers. As a contributor to society he rises to the fourth rank from the top, above lawyers, engineers and business executives, and below medical doctors and ministers of religion.

"A continuing hardship under which public schools operate is the annual loss of a substantial number of their experienced teachers. Each year many thousands leave the profession permanently. . . ."—"The public school . . . is not only unable to hold experienced teachers . . . but it does not attract enough of the able young men and women of each new generation. . . . In the elementary schools where the total need is the greatest, the annual supply of new teachers is least adequate in numbers. Why do one-fourth of the young people who go to the effort and expense of completing teacher education turn away at the point of employment?" These are statements and questions of the authors of *Conditions of Work for Quality Teaching*, published under the auspices of the Department of Classroom Teachers, N.E.A. in 1959. One of the answers, found by a touring investigator of Ohio State University, is that "able teachers are deeply dissatisfied; many are leaving the schools because of working conditions . . ." Teaching loads are too heavy, pupils too numerous, clerical routines and community projects too distracting from the professional purpose. Salaries are inadequate, buildings and equipment are unsatisfactory.

There are beginnings of changes to the better, even though insular and unevenly distributed throughout the country, and often as yet in the preparatory phase of discussion and experiment. There is a growing awareness of the need for a teacher's competence in subject matter. A questionnaire on this aspect issued in 1959 to secondary teachers elicited from two thirds of them the answer that a thorough familiarity with subject matter is "very important" or "important." More than one fourth of the responding teachers were at least part of the time working outside their field of major preparation. A recently released study of the National Science Foundation, *Secondary School Science and Mathematics Teachers, Characteristics and Service Loads,* stresses the problems arising in schools owing to the wrong teacher assignment pattern. With comparatively few students requiring courses in physics or chemistry, specialists teach only one or two courses in their discipline and spend the rest of their time on subjects in which they have no formally acquired competence. A no more desirable alternative is the teacher of physics who had a single one-year college course in the subject, or none at all.

The specialized teacher in the elementary school is gaining ground in the face of still considerable opposition. There is no evidence in support of the old wives' tale of children being in need of a single teacher as a substitute mother, and of their experiencing insecurity when changing teachers or rooms. Children, like people of all ages, are profitably stimulated by a change of environment, in the form of both things and people. The elementary school curriculum having proliferated greatly from its original narrow task of teaching the rudiments of the three R's, no single person can be competent to teach it adequately. It may be that the reading difficulties of children are to a considerable measure due to the incompetence of instructors in this difficult skill, whatever the method of teaching may be. The growing acceptance of Team Teaching may not yet have defeated the prejudice against specialist teachers in grade schools, but it serves as a serious challenge.

Team Teaching incorporates several budding new approaches to teaching as well as to learning. Ideally, school time is divided into three parts—into large assemblies, small discussion groups, and children's individual work combined with consultations with teachers. An assembly for 150 children frees two or three teachers for preparation and evaluation of lessons; teachers gain opportunities to teach the subjects in which they feel competent. Children learn to use time on independent study and to avail themselves of the facilities of the library and of mechanical aids. Theoretically, this approach tends to make for a higher ratio of school staff to pupils, but a constant awareness of pitfalls is needed to make the principles come alive in daily practice. A fine exposition of developed Team Teaching on the secondary level is offered in the publication *Images of the Future,* by J. Lloyd Trump, sponsored by the National Association of Secondary School Principals of the N.E.A. in 1958. Instructional staff is divided into full-time professional or career teachers, who may be specialists or general teachers; instructional assistants who may work part time; clerks; general aides; community consultants and staff specialists. The customary sixteen teachers working together some 150 hours weekly are replaced by five full-time teacher specialists and five full-time generalists, by 200 hours of instructional assistance, 100 hours of clerking, and 50 hours of miscellaneous help. The annual cost is over $2000.00 less than the expenditure for traditional staffing.

The consultation between an individual pupil or a few pupils with a teacher in the quiet of his study is a modern adaptation of a teaching situation which has proved effective over thousands of years. The original was, and still is, the parent who interacts with his child or children. "And thou shalt teach [the Laws] diligently unto thy children, and shalt talk of them when thou sittest in thine house and when thou walkest by the way," is a command of the Bible, in the sixth chapter of Deuteronomy, to the father of the family in ancient Israel. It was no doubt taken for granted that both parents trained their children in the traditional skills of simple farming, husbandry and domestic arts. Variations of the theme were still common in rural parts of Europe in the nineteenth century. The master-craftsman and the private tutor were substitute figures of the parent-educator. There is again the personal relationship, the bond between an elder and one or a few disciples. There is mutual trust, intimacy and spontaneity. The apprentice is an heir of the master-craftsman, and a tutor spiritually fathers his disciple. In medieval, feudal society the son of a noble spent fourteen years as a page and a squire to a knight. In ancient Egypt governmental officials started their careers as apprentices. In Athens a youth received his education by watching men in public places and listening to their speeches.

Another new venue is opened up by the ungraded elementary school, in which pupils of different ages are grouped together during lessons in which they show comparable ability. Not only the pupils gain in this manner, both the fast and the slow, but teachers are faced by fewer obstacles. Since every fifth American is supposed to change his residence every year, classes have to shelter many transients from different states whose scholastic equipment varies greatly. On the occasion of a test given to registrants for Selective Service every other Mississippian failed, while the men from Montana did best, with only 2.5 per cent failures. If students of comparable ability are grouped together, learning acquires a new quality. They have an opportunity not only to absorb facts and postulates but to engage in inquiry and to learn how to learn—which may be the most important basic skill in the preparation for an unknown future.

How do we get better teachers in greater numbers? Obviously an extended period of study will be of help, but in my personal opinion it will not necessarily give us the benefit of teachers of a greater intellectual power than we have now. The longer and better courses will benefit only those who are fit to study any subject at any depth and who continue to study while they teach; who are inquisitive, who have a scholarly bent of mind, and who realize the complexities of a teacher's task, be it in a physics laboratory, with a group of fourth graders, or in a kindergarten. Students of this caliber would hardly be content with the sterile atmosphere in some of the teacher training institutions. If college instructors do not continue some scholarly pursuit themselves, they can hardly elicit curiousity and intellectual delight in their students. Both teachers of children and their teachers in colleges and universities must, indeed, have scholarly interests in two domains: in a subject matter and in child development. Another currently advocated reform, extended internship, should provide good results. Yet all approaches ultimately depend on the quality of the people who go into the teaching profession and on their working conditions in schools—on their chances to maintain such good mental health as would allow them to use their talents and their training. No teacher should be allowed to spend more than three lesson-sessions daily in a group-teaching situation with students, and least of all with children. Every school teacher should have a daily period for quiet study—like his colleague in colleges and universities. There is concern in schools over "the sheer constancy of teacher contacts with children" and that teachers might be "taxed to the point of fatigue and diminishing returns," as Stuart Dean put it.

Mental health problems among teachers have not gone unobserved, but they are an unpopular topic. Dr. Clarence O. Senior, a professor of sociology at Brooklyn College and a member of the board of the New York City schools, referred, according to reports, to "mentally-disturbed teachers" in the city's schools, who "hate children." In 1962 a pamphlet entitled "Mental Health" appeared in a series, *What Research Says to the Teacher*, by R. V. Peck and

J. V. Mitchell, under the auspices of the American Education Research Association and the Department of Classroom Teachers of the N.E.A. They pointed out: "If the research on the mental health of school children is still incomplete, it is vast by comparison with studies on the mental health of members of the school staff."

Peck and Mitchell's publication lists some of the tasks a teacher has to fulfill: He has to make careful observations of a child's developing abilities and skills; provide the appropriate experiences just at the right time; be on hand with exciting and worthwhile experiences when the time is ripe; provide opportunities for self-esteem and the utilization of unique abilities; encourage the child's creativity at every turn; help the child to discover and understand himself as a person; understand the defense mechanisms of anxious children who without such understanding may become poor learners and aggressive, antisocial citizens; and create a desire for learning and an eagerness for life in the minds of the students because he himself feels that way about learning and life. . . . This list of tasks and roles is far from being complete.

No human being remains free of anxieties when teaching subjects in which he has no competence. Nobody can enjoy good mental health—a combination of stability and flexibility, of self-confidence and self-criticism, of vigorous curiosity and subtle sensitivity—while spending his working hours without interruption with children; with other adults issuing orders and acting as superiors; trying to play diverse and incompatible roles; in constant noise and under pressure which lead either to the disintegration of personality or to the numbing of the mind. The effectiveness of our teachers is as much a problem of good mental health as of numbers of academic credits. As the late Dr. T. A. C. Rennie of Cornell University wrote in his prologue to *Mental Health in the Metropolis*, by Leo Srole, published in 1962: "We have reached the point in psychiatric development where many psychiatrists feel deeply impelled to turn their interest outward from the individual . . . to the community, to the total cultural scene."[8] The cultural scenes of the school and the classroom are awaiting multidisciplinary research in which the psychiatrist would join with the specialist in psychosomatic medicine, with the clinical psychologist and with the behavorial scientist. In this way we may get definite evidence of the superhuman performance society is expecting of the school teacher. Efforts connected with space medicine are supplying us with a most valuable tool, with a miniaturized transmitter, no larger than a pack of cigarettes, which can be attached to the teacher's body or clothing while he works in the classroom and goes about his business in school. The pupils would be unaware of its presence, and the teacher would hardly remain conscious of it after an initial trial. In this manner several physical modalities of a person can be recorded simultaneously—heartbeat and respiration, skin temperature and blood pressure, possibly the electrical action of the brain. The apparatus is being used in other group-action situations; why not in schools? Psychological tests alone would bring evidence of many of these aspects, but their combination with tests of physiological conditions holds the promise of a far greater convincing power.

The future of a nation may be affected by the acceptance of a new teacher concept in the schools below college level, and especially in the elementary school. A single teacher deals with at least fifteen hundred children during his career. An inquiry of the proposed kind might defeat objections to the employment of part-time teachers in elementary schools: the ones who are there full time physically are not always mentally present. Under stress and fatigue they turn into husks in human shape and react no longer to all signals of inquiry or of distress which come from their pupils.

According to forecasts we shall need an increase of 160 per cent in teachers by 1966. To reach the quota every other college graduate would have to become a teacher instead of every twentieth as at present. How then can we cut down on the teaching time of elementary and secondary school teachers? The answer seems simple: the occupation must not be allowed to remain a drudgery, a series of frustrations, a condition of constant fatigue and of too little autonomy in the classroom. Under changed conditions we shall not only get greater numbers of teachers, but greater numbers of better teachers, and we shall keep them. The improvement will begin with a new self-selection fitting new standards and new expectations.

There is a considerable pool of fine potential teachers among the married women who want to work and who are prepared to spend time and money on training, provided that it will lead to a satisfactory occupation. There are women in their thirties who as young girls may have raised their sights to careers as medical doctors, scholars or lawyers, had they not married and raised a family. Deriving satisfaction from their home life and hesitating to embark on a training of five or more years, many of them would probably be interested in being trained as specialized elementary school teachers. We need suitable training opportunities for such women, first of all on the undergraduate level, and partly based on self-study and examination. This in itself would provide a needed pilot project, in preparation of the years of acute shortage of college instructors. There ought to be part-time positions for these women, or for any specialized school teacher who wishes to spend only two hours in the classroom and to do his preparation and continuous further study at home, in libraries, or in laboratories at any time of the day or of the evening.

Lieberman considers a change in the power structure of the public school, in the layman-administrator-teacher relationship, as need number one. Bestor demands that an end be put to the "interlocking directorate" of education departments and administrators; he would like to see the entire university shaping a new breed of teachers. Rickover points out that homogenized education does justice to no one. These and other recommendations are facets of the same problem. And so is the one that is here proposed.

The concept of education as investment in human beings has for a long time been familiar among economists from Adam Smith to Alfred Marshall, but the consciousness of people in general has only slightly been touched by the call for "investment in human resources," imperative as it is. We have too long been conditioned to investment in durable things, in inanimate objects and materials. Accordingly vast sums are spent on research and development of goods in industry in contrast to trifling sums of money for research on learning and teaching; and what there is of it has in fact very little to say to the teacher. Our current national expenditure on public education in the United States is $25 billion, about 5 per cent of the gross national product. Five per cent of the total expenditure on education would seem to be an adequate figure to begin research on education, about $1,250,000,000. In actual practice we are spending no more than 0.1 per cent on this type of research. The U.S. Office of Education often received less for research grants than the Department of Agriculture or the Department of the Interior.[9]

Dollar figures reflect human attitudes. It is estimated that we are spending from $15 to $20 billion every year on the leisure-time use of automobiles, rather close to the sum devoted to public education. We are supposedly spending more money on alcohol, tobacco and cosmetics than on public education, although the percentage of personal income spent on education has been rising, from 2.1 per cent in 1950 to an estimated 5.5 per cent in 1970. Our personal incomes are two to twenty times as high as the incomes of people in other countries, and we are the consumers of almost half of all goods produced on this planet. Changes in the education of future generations are hinged on our values, on our choices and on our courage rather than on the availability of funds.

REFERENCES

1. Evans, L. H. and Arnstein, G. E. (eds.), *Automation and the Challenge to Education,* Proceedings of a Symposium (Washington, D.C.: National Education Association of the United States, 1962).

2. Allinsmith, W. and Goethals, G. W., *The Role of Schools in Mental Health,* Monograph Series No. 7, Joint Commission on Mental Health (New York: Basic Books, 1962).

3. Koerner, James D., *The Miseducation of American Teachers* (Boston: Houghton Mifflin, 1963).

4. Bestor, Arthur, *The Restoration of Learning* (New York: Knopf, 1955).

5. Woodring, Paul, *New Directions in Teacher Education* (New York: The Fund for the Advancement of Education, 1957).

6. Lieberman, Myron, *Education as a Profession* (Englewood Cliffs, N.J.: Prentice-Hall, 1956); *The Future of Public Education* (Chicago: University of Chicago Press, 1960).

7. North, Robert D., "The Teacher Education Student: How Does He Compare Academically with Other College Students?" *The Education of Teachers: New Perspectives* (Washington, D.C.: The National Commission on Teacher Education and Professional Standards, N.E.A., 1958).

8. Srole, Leo, et al., *Mental Health in the Metropolis,* Series in Social Psychiatry (New York: McGraw-Hill, 1962), Vol. I.

9. Federal Obligations for Research and Development for 1961–63 as cited in the National Science Foundation, *Federal Funds for Science XI,* Table C–7 were estimated to be:

17.6 millions for the U.S. Office of Education
16.3 millions for the Bureau of Commercial Fisheries
23.2 millions for the Forest Service
92.4 millions for Agricultural Research Service
660.6 millions for the Public Health Service
7,371,3 millions for the Department of Defense

One might suggest that if the funds for deepening our knowledge of processes of learning from kindergarten onward as well as of means of facilitating such processes at different ages were more generous, we might be better equipped to get new insights into the growing of trees and of fishes, of preventing and of curing diseases, and of course, of inventing more effective weapons at a much lower direct cost than we do now.

JOHN J. BEER and W. DAVID LEWIS

Aspects of the Professionalization of Science

THE INSTITUTIONALIZATION and professionalization of science that has taken place in the past century has justly been called the second scientific revolution. Seen historically, this revolution has resulted from the fusion of rapidly maturing scientific disciplines with western organizational and administrative techniques, enabling large numbers of scientists with varying interests and abilities to be marshaled for massive projects of research and development. In the process, the separation which once existed between science and technology has been narrowed and bridged, and science has come to exert a major influence upon economic growth. At the same time, the very methods and objectives of science have been deeply affected, for they are no longer primarily private or personal but have a large social component.

The first scientific revolution introduced to the western world a new way of looking at phenomena, with an emphasis upon accuracy of observation, quantification of data, verification of results, and useful prediction. Although many of these values were shared by those who took part in the technological revolution which laid the foundation for the modern industrial age, the scientist and the engineer or mechanic proceeded along parallel rather than convergent paths. Only when the full utility of science became evident to capitalistic promoters or state officials were the two streams of development combined.

The consequences of this mutual interaction upon society in general have been both numerous and momentous, and they need not be described here. With regard to science and its practitioners, however, two results should be recalled. First, because of the way in which advances in scientific knowledge can be transmuted into tangible and even awesome results, the professional scientist today enjoys financial support and public recognition in high degree.

110

Since World War II, he has gained considerable influence with regard to the formulation and execution of public policy and a strong voice in the councils of many large industrial corporations. Second, as science and technology are drawn into ever closer cooperation, the chief types of institution in which professional scientists are employed—colleges or universities and industrial or governmental laboratories—share an increasing number of common characteristics. The researcher who is employed in the one may be engaged in work which is quite similar to that performed by a scientist in the other.

This situation differs greatly from that which prevailed only a century ago, for professionalized science manifested itself first in educational institutions and only somewhat later in private and state laboratories devoted to increasing agricultural or industrial productivity and efficiency. Before 1900, most professional scientists were teachers in universities, technical institutes and trade or secondary schools. Relatively few were employed in industry, with the major exceptions of the dyestuffs and electrical fields. In some countries, such as Great Britain and France, there was an aristocratic prejudice against abandoning the quest of pure truth for the pursuit of financial gain, stemming in part from a tradition of scientific research conducted by amateur gentlemen of private means. For the scientist unlucky enough to have to work for a living, the main alternative to teaching was government service. Even here jobs were difficult to secure, there being few if any government research laboratories and only a handful of technical or supervisory jobs available in arsenals, mines, observatories, public health services, geodetic surveys or civil engineering projects.

If many scientists looked with disfavor upon industrial employment, manufacturers often had serious misgivings about establishing close relationships with scientists. Although some academically trained researchers had well-developed business instincts—for example, Charles Martin Hall and William Henry Perkin—the entrepreneur typically thought of the scientist as a person too committed to abstract scholarship to be directly useful in a profit-seeking enterprise. In addition, the tradition of trade secrecy which existed in many factories clashed with the desire of scholars to disseminate the results of their research. To those who managed industries based upon empirical methods and employed artisans imbued with a craft viewpoint, the scientist might also appear as a menace to established routine and job classification, and hence as a potentially antagonizing influence with regard to the working force.

111

Finally, and perhaps most important, academic science had only begun to be translated into practical terms so clear cut and potentially lucrative as to entice business interest. More often the non-academic inventor, with largely commercial motives, managed to produce significant innovations by making empirical use of scientific principles already fifty or more years old. In the absence of theoretically trained industrial scientists ever ready to pounce upon new academic discoveries, the lag between initial advance and ultimate application thus remained large.

Although most technical and industrial innovation was still in the hands of empirical inventors during the late nineteenth century, several of the academic sciences, such as thermodynamics, electromagnetism, optics, chemistry, bacteriology and biology, had now reached a point of development at which the existence of large and well-classified accumulations of data permitted the formulation of highly useful and comprehensive theoretical systems which could be exploited in a commercial and technological sense. As the practical and pecuniary potential of these new syntheses and advances came more clearly into view, particularly in the dyestuffs and electrical industries, the purse strings of private donors and governmental bodies were opened to finance improved scientific education and to establish well-equipped research laboratories.

These developments ultimately produced more and more trained researchers and a steadily growing number of positions for which they could be hired. There was an initial tendency for most scientifically trained university graduates to be brought back into expanding programs of technical education, but the proportion gradually decreased as those who entered industry demonstrated their value—indeed their indispensibility—to formerly skeptical entrepreneurs. Although the timing and rate of scientific professionalization differed from one industrial nation to another, similar trends were taking place throughout the world. The nearly complete displacement of the amateur scientist by his teaching colleague was ultimately followed by a sharp growth in the number of industrial researchers, who displaced the empirical inventors and who in time came to outnumber the academic scientists.[1]

It is of interest to note that as science became professionalized late in the nineteenth century, the division between basic and applied research became institutionalized. Basic science remained almost exclusively the province of the university. In industrial laboratories, entrepreneurs seized upon scientific processes or techniques which could lead swiftly to profitable results. Product testing, for example, was one of the first ways in which science demonstrated its utility to the manufacturer, thanks to the proliferation of ingenious analytical instruments and to the need of the industrialist for precise measurements and specifications in the volume production of goods made with interchangeable parts or standardized ingredients. The application of science to improving efficiency, eliminating unnecessary steps, conserving raw materials and finding various uses for by-products was also of great benefit to entrepreneurs who were trying to cut costs in the face of competition and declining price levels. By serving in such capacities, scientists could bring quick and tangible returns at a relatively small financial outlay to a great number of industries.

Positions involving mere testing and analysis had a tendency to become stultifyingly routine, and they were consequently unattractive to scientists with first rate capabilities. Other circumstances also created nagging annoyances which many professionally trained men found difficult to tolerate. Although eager to derive profit from science, most industrialists wanted to keep research budgets as low as possible. In addition, as we have previously mentioned, they wanted to guard against antagonizing craft-oriented employees, to preserve factory stability and to keep knowledge of certain processes from leaking out to potential competitors. It was not uncommon, therefore, for an industrial scientist to be consigned to a poorly equipped back room or an out-of-the-way corner of a plant and strictly forbidden to trespass in other departments. In some cases, manufacturers found it possible to train raw factory hands to make simple tests and routine analyses, and so to limit their scientific staffs to a few professionals who could be counted on absolutely to preserve trade secrets.[2] To such entrepreneurs, it seemed cheaper and less dangerous to buy patents from the outside than to run the risk and expense of large and continuous development programs of their own.

Because of this cautious approach, much applied research had to be done outside the factory if it was to be carried on at all. One type of institution which sprang up partly in response to this situation was the independent commercial research laboratory, typified by the firm of Arthur D. Little, founded in 1886. In addition, certain universities and academic scholars, while retaining a primary emphasis upon basic inquiries, became engaged in applied research. Such faculty members as Michael Pupin of Columbia University,

who devised a loading coil for the effective transmission of impulses
in long-range telephony, found it profitable to invent as well as to
theorize.[3] Professors more and more frequently entered into formal
consulting arrangements with manufacturing concerns, served as
expert witnesses in patent litigation, and steered their students into
research projects having a bearing upon industrial problems. In
time, universities themselves established institutional ties with industry, thanks to the efforts of such men as Robert Kennedy Duncan,
a chemistry professor at the University of Kansas. Believing that the
research chemist was placed in a stultifying position in industrial
employment, where he was likely to do one routine testing operation over and over, Duncan came to the conclusion that most manufacturers had neither the background nor the education to direct
the efforts of scientists. The solution was for the scientist to remain
at the university and to have the industrialist come there for help.
Duncan persuaded academic officials at Kansas to start a program
of industrial fellowships under which graduate students could work
at the university on projects suggested and financed by businessmen.
He later moved to the University of Pittsburgh, where his ideas were
implemented at the Mellon Institute. By 1917, the industrial fellowship idea, which had also been put into effect in Germany in the late
nineteenth century, had spread to universities and technical institutes in such countries as Canada, Great Britain, Australia, Finland
and Japan.[4]

Although their ideas about the undesirability of placing scientists
in factories thus led to the establishment of an important type of institution, the industry-oriented university research institute, such
men as Duncan failed to realize that the condition of the scientist in
a nonacademic habitat did not necessarily have to be as stultifying
as they depicted it. The small manufacturing concern, highly competitive and cost-conscious, continued to rely on routine testing, and
farmed more demanding projects out to other institutions. On the
other hand, a large industrial organization, heavily capitalized and
holding a dominant market position under cartel or oligopoly conditions, could provide a reasonably satisfying atmosphere for the
creative researcher under wise and percipient executive leadership.
This type of situation, lacking in most manufacturing plants, eventually came to exist in such fields as the dyestuffs and electrical industries. In Germany, for example, such firms as Meister, Lucius &
Brüning and the Badische Anilin- und Soda-Fabrik established
genuine research organizations clearly distinguishable from the one-

or two-man operation or from the mere testing division.[5] Similar developments occurred in the German and English electrical industries as new leaders succeeded men like Werner Siemens, who had retarded his company's development by rejecting the alternating current system as unworkable, by insisting that the laboratory work mainly on his own pet problems, and by manifesting an excessive skepticism toward academic theoreticians.

In the United States, where the emergence of large chemical empires was delayed until World War I, the electrical industry had the distinction of bringing the first really modern industrial laboratory into existence. After Thomas A. Edison had relinquished control of the electrical enterprise associated with his name, and Charles Coffin became the dominant figure in the newly constituted General Electric Corporation, conditions were brought about under which such academically trained theorists as Charles P. Steinmetz could make outstanding careers within the confines of an industrial organization. Furthermore, the exploitation of alternating current phenomena and the need to develop highly complex equipment for electrical transmission and use made it absolutely necessary for the industry to hire the best men available for research work. In 1900, the General Electric Laboratory was established at Schenectady, New York, under the direction of Willis R. Whitney, and an outstanding program of experimentation and creative effort was begun. Other large American firms followed in short order as Du Pont established explosives laboratories in Wilmington, Delaware and Gibbstown, New Jersey; Eastman-Kodak set up a research program in photography under C. E. K. Mees at Rochester, New York; and A.T.&T. began a centralized laboratory in New York City through the efforts of John J. Carty.

At such laboratories, both in Europe and in the United States, research work was placed under the direction of men who were purely scientific in their interests and who managed to introduce much of the university atmosphere into the industrial situation. Under such scientists as Carl Duisberg in Germany and Whitney in the United States, academically trained personnel were encouraged to undertake basic research projects, to participate in conferences modeled upon university seminars, to maintain regular contact with academic consultants, to write papers for professional journals and to attend scholarly meetings. In laboratories of this type advanced research was clearly distinguished from development; extensive libraries were provided; up-to-date equipment was made available;

115

auxiliary specialists were hired; and well-organized programs of recruitment and training were undertaken. With respect to the last, industrial laboratories began to exert effective influence upon the curricula of universities and technical institutes to obtain the types of staff members which they desired.

Thus, through the efforts of men like Duncan on the one hand and various industrial laboratory officials on the other, and despite obvious differences in motivation, manufacturing organizations and universities were brought into a mutually helpful relationship. Basic science remained the chief concern of academic institutions, but many industrial researchers, like Irving Langmuir of General Electric, carried on fundamental explorations of their own. Applied research and development predominated in the activities of industrial laboratories, but some university scholars and students also worked on projects of this type. In either case a direct link was provided between science and technology as basic discoveries were systematically explored at the higher theoretical levels of applied research, adapted to industrial use in pilot plants and ultimately exploited commercially. In addition to serving as the source of most of the fundamental achievements and a considerable number of practical applications, the university also provided virtually all of the scientific personnel of the laboratories, thus heavily influencing the quality of work which would be done in such institutions. In turn, industrial organizations endowed professorial chairs; financed university facilities; established scholarships, prizes and loan funds; and placed representatives on academic boards of trustees. As a result of this interaction, educational and business institutions have become parts of a continuous spectrum of scientific effort.

The closeness of this relationship has given rise to a number of problems affecting professional scientists in both the academic and the industrial fields. Fears are frequently expressed that the capacity of the university to advance human knowledge is being impaired by an undue emphasis upon explorations in areas of immediate usefulness. While some educational institutions have not hesitated to seek financial reward by engaging in applied research on toothpaste additives, rodent killers and vitamin compounds,[6] others have made earnest attempts to confine the efforts of faculty scientists to investigations of a fundamental nature. This, however, is not easy at a time in which more and more research at the academic level is being financed through grants from private organizations or governmental agencies. There is no doubt that many basic projects are promoted in this manner, because of an awareness on the part of the donors that serendipity does occur and that fundamental advances can lead to profitable results in unsuspected fields. But the faculty member often still finds that support for research comes more readily if, when writing his proposal, he is careful to stress the potential practical applications of his ideas and does not propose to explore too far beyond the existing frontiers of science. Thus a subtle pressure is detected which could, if unchecked, pose a danger to progress in fundamental science itself.

Of more immediate concern to many professional scientists, however, is the problem of fitting vocational hopes and aspirations into the spectrum of effort just described. One of the most powerful traditions established in the first scientific revolution was that of the liberty of the scientist to pursue truth according to the dictates of his curiosity. Because professionalized science first arose in an academic environment, this tradition was reinforced by the university scholar's desire for academic freedom in teaching and research. In addition, as a member of a profession the scientist shares with physicians, lawyers and other practitioners of specialized knowledge the desire to have the standards of his work set by his peers rather than by persons outside his field of competence. In short, he wants to be a colleague, not an employee. In this respect, the vocational choices available to him frequently fall short of his desires.

Although the sociologist Simon Marcson in particular has emphasized the degree to which the university scientist of today is caught up in an employee situation,[7] the professional who desires a maximum of freedom in his work and an opportunity to expand basic knowledge will normally realize these objectives more readily in an academic position than in an industrial laboratory. Evidence gathered by such analysts as Francis Bello indicates that the most gifted and creative young scientists usually gravitate to the universities or toward employment with a very few business corporations noted for allowing great latitude to talented research personnel. As enrollments burgeon at institutions of higher learning, more and more academic positions are becoming available; but it is obvious that colleges and universities could not begin to absorb all the products of graduate training, let alone the great numbers of those gaining baccalaureate degrees. Most scientists, therefore, must find employment in other fields. The popular stereotype of the scientist as a professor thus fails to correspond with actual facts; he is more likely to be a researcher with an industrial firm or a government agency. If one wishes to understand the pressures and problems facing the typical scientist today, one must examine the conditions that exist in such types of environment.

Despite the many ways in which the industrial laboratory has come to resemble the university situation in the twentieth century, the fledgling researcher may find in this area of employment conditions for which he may have been unprepared by his academic training. Like any business organization, the manufacturing firm exists in order to make a profitable return on the investments of its owners, and its research efforts are conducted with this aim in mind. As we have seen, this does not mean that fundamental research will be entirely neglected in favor of applied science, nor that the industrial laboratory will be subjected to the same type of efficiency analysis and cost accounting used with relation to other departments of the same firm. It does mean that the thought of ultimate application can never be wholly absent from any investigator's mind, and that some basic advances will have to lead to profitable results if a basic research program is to justify itself to management. It also means that most of the scientists employed in industry and most of the money spent for their work will be channeled into the development of applications for known principles.

The industrial research director is well aware that he is dealing with scarce and highly trained manpower imbued with professional aspirations and unwilling to settle for the status of the ordinary employee. As a man of scientific training himself, he also knows that genuine creativity can exist only in a situation in which staff members are impelled by inner drives, rather than by exterior compulsion, to penetrate the unknown. Top management too is normally cognizant of such special circumstances, so that in most large firms the laboratory divisions are allowed a considerable degree of autonomy. However, there are limits beyond which permissiveness cannot go, as the engineer C. E. Skinner learned in the period 1916–1921, when as first director of the Westinghouse research organization, he tried to establish a laboratory in which there was little or no pressure for immediate or short-range results.[8] Far more percipient in this regard was Willis Whitney of General Electric, who unfailingly gave priority to requests for help on problems submitted by the corporation's various operating departments.[9] The successful research director therefore plays a mediatory role between the executive echelons of the company and the professional staff, reconciling if possible the expectations and viewpoints of each.

This far from easy task is usually accomplished by a slow process of suggestion and persuasion through which the scientist is motivated in a relatively indirect manner to carry out company wishes. In at least one contemporary American laboratory analyzed by Simon Marcson, the similarities between university and industrial practices are stressed when a prospective staff member is interviewed. Most new Ph.D.'s in science are imbued at least in some measure with the academic ideal of pursuing knowledge for its own sake, and they express a desire to be permitted to do some independent research. Industrial recruiters are usually able to assure the prospective staff member that facilities and some time are available for this purpose, and they point with pride to the laboratory's discoveries, the articles published in professional journals and the national reputation of the staff. But after the young man is hired, a period of adjustment occurs in which he gradually becomes aware of what his superiors expect of him. In Marcson's words, "Acculturation takes place as the laboratory and the recruited scientist learn from each other and change each other." However, "The laboratory . . . effects more changes in the scientist than vice versa."[10] The very atmosphere and work load of most industrial laboratories are so strongly weighted toward obtaining prompt, tangible and profitable results that the recruit's ideal of independent, basic research is put to a severe test.

At this point the majority of the new men abandon or modify their earlier values and ambitions. They do so for a number of reasons. They may discover that the pressure of assigned projects is so great or the effort to please superiors so consuming that insufficient time is left in the 8:30 to 5:00 day to pursue individual research interests. Staying beyond 5:00 P.M., although perhaps officially encouraged by the company, is generally not practiced by the staff, and hence only the most strongly motivated will stay to work overtime on pet projects. Or, as happens frequently, the new researcher may discover that assigned research is equally taxing and fascinating, and fully as satisfying, as his thesis research had been. Incidentally, that thesis topic is likely to have been suggested by his professor. Hence at this point in his career the young scientist, his idealistic commitment to scientific self-direction notwithstanding, has possibly never initiated a research project of his own, and thus finds industrial research not so different from what he knew at the university as he might originally have thought. Further, he may discover that a considerable amount of self-reliance and ingenious initiative is required in solving assigned problems, and that his work for industry often requires greater tenacity and elegance of execution than were needed in academic research. For at the university virtually any result represents a publishable article, which is the tangible product and measure of academic productivity; but in many industrial laboratories the only acceptable result is one which works, and works simply and well enough to be commercially feasible.

In fact, many of the new staff soon become so absorbed by the challenge of rendering an idea commercially feasible that they forget all about their one-time ambition of making some great contribution to basic science. All too often we hear only of scientists leaving industry for freer research environments elsewhere, when there are probably at least as many or more who leave large laboratories to develop on their own the practical potential of ideas which they obtained while working for industry or government.

Those among the new staff who persevere in their determination to contribute to basic science can usually find some time (one fifth or more in some industrial laboratories) for this purpose; but initially they may need to work overtime on such projects if these are to move along satisfactorily. Should the results prove of interest to the company, the researcher may obtain permission to devote more, or possibly all of his time to his project. Beyond that always exists the chance of being given the support of an entire research team. If, on the other hand, such a scientist fails to convince his superiors of the commercial potential of his personal project, he may feel sufficiently restricted in his effort to quit the company for the academic world or for another research organization more favorably inclined toward his own field of interest. This, however, does not seem to happen too often. Most scientists in industry learn to live with the frustrations and opportunities of their jobs. They usually understand the business framework within which decisions concerning industrial research must be made, and they are aware of the fact that other research environments, including universities, are no less free of tensions and disadvantages.

Aside from the usually superior monetary rewards proffered by industry, many scientists find satisfactions in industrial research which may be lacking in university life. Some, who have little interest in or aptitude for teaching, may welcome freedom from lecture preparation and working with students. Others find the auxiliary services available in industrial laboratories superior to those afforded by graduate assistants and other personnel on the academic scene. Some large companies may be better able to provide expensive equipment than any but the most well-endowed educational institutions. According to at least one laboratory director, it may actually be possible for a manufacturing firm to provide a scientist having marked personality idiosyncracies with a more congenial setting than would be attainable in an academic institution, where such a person would have frequent contacts with students and be obliged to take part in committee meetings or other functions.

Here again must be emphasized the wide variety of objectives and opportunities which exist at some industrial laboratories, particularly the three hundred largest ones which together perform 80 per cent of all American industrial research. Even though the industrial laboratory can make more effective use than the universities of scientists whose talents are rather ordinary, industry is no haven for scientific mediocrity, for it must also attract highly imaginative and superior persons who are among the best that the graduate schools can offer, and retain their services if at all possible. Thus when one examines the techniques used in managing research personnel one encounters a wide variety of administrative practices, *ad hoc* relationships, written and unwritten rules of behavior and informal, but none the less real, channels of influence. The highly structured chain of command which typifies the industrial enterprise is present, but it is considerably modified in practice because of the special problems which are encountered in operating a hybrid organization staffed by specialized individuals who are both self-motivated and disciplined, professionals and employees.

It is difficult to generalize in the face of such a situation as this, but two scientists connected with the Bell Telephone Laboratories have presented a cogent analysis of three basic relationships which develop between staff members of a research department and the management under which they work.[11] At the lowest level is the *artisan-master* relationship. Here the employer knows exactly what he wants and has a concrete idea of how this can be obtained. The scientist engaged in routine testing and analysis fits into this pattern, which exists at any large laboratory and may still be the dominant type of situation prevailing in a small research department run by a highly cost-conscious company which farms out most projects of a higher order, if indeed it has any. At the next level is the *professional-client* relationship. Here the autonomy of management is abridged because those who hire the services of specialists do not really know how a given project is to be consummated, how much time it will take, how much equipment will be needed and how the results will affect the market strategy of the company. Presumably most industrial scientists with advanced credentials—master's or doctor's degrees—will fall into this category. Finally, there is the *protégé-patron* relationship similar to that which once existed between members of the nobility and artists like Michaelangelo, musicians like Haydn, and scientists like Galileo. Perhaps the earliest example of such a person in American industrial research was Charles P. Steinmetz; at a later date, Irving Langmuir filled such a role at General Electric. Working under minimal supervision, protégés may discover basic phenomena of great potential profitability and considerably enhance the growth possibilities of the corporations which employ them. They may also bring the firm great prestige, some of which can be transmuted into advertising value. Langmuir, for example, won a Nobel Prize in 1932 for his studies in the behavior of surface films. Steinmetz brought General Electric such renown that a company official once estimated his advertising value alone at $1,000,000.[12] Thus even the highest form of brilliance does not escape the commercializing tendency in the industrial situation.

The rewards for proficiency and achievement in industrial research are substantial, but often for the professionally minded scientist they are too exclusively monetary and unaccompanied by honorific titles which denote changes in status. There is a tendency in the business world to bestow new job titles only when persons are given new responsibilities or elevated to positions of increasing power, and not merely for growth in capability within the same type of work. Even when industrial scientists are put in charge of group projects, this is frequently done on an informal basis and with no titular change. This is justified by laboratory officials on two grounds: first, that research groupings are only temporary and that flexibility must be preserved if personnel are to be shifted about as the needs of the company dictate; second, that the spirit of teamwork in a laboratory may be impaired if too many distinctions are made. Plausible though these reasons may be, they fail to satisfy the status aspirations of persons whose thinking is heavily imbued with academic standards of recognition.

Cognizant of these circumstances, some industrial corporations have begun to experiment with ranking systems which demonstrate particularly well the manner in which university science departments and company laboratories are becoming more and more alike in certain respects. One leading American chemical firm, for example, has established two scales of titles—two ladders of achievement —one for scientists who remain in actual research and the other for those who go into administrative positions. The recruit is normally classed as a "Research Chemist," corresponding roughly with the grade of "Instructor" in the academic world. If he stays in research work, he may rise to "Senior Research Chemist," "Research Associate," and ultimately "Research Fellow," the pinnacle of recognition on this ladder. If on the other hand he becomes a research administrator, he advances through such grades as "Supervisor," "Senior Supervisor," and "Manager." If his executive abilities are particularly marked, he may eventually become a "Laboratory Director" or proceed into the highest managerial ranks of the company. The obvious distinction between the two ladders, of course, is that the one is almost purely honorific while the other involves formally recognized progress in power.

In order to hold its most creative researchers, the government too has found it necessary since World War II to create civil service classifications that reward the research scientist at a rate parallel and commensurate with the scientist-administrator.[13] Government, however, has found it difficult to make such changes in personnel policy as quickly as has industry, so that it has tended to lag behind in its capacity to attract and retain scientists. Despite vigorous action by the research agencies and the Civil Service to extend the salary scale, particularly at the top, to expedite hiring procedures and to maximize the researcher's freedom of action and communication, many scientists still leave or refuse government employment because they consider the salaries and the opportunities for advancement inferior to those of industry.[14] Less often than formerly, however, are they quitting because of unsympathetic management practices and red tape. Job security, superior research facilities, and fringe benefits which in former times tended to offset the disadvantages of government employment are on the whole no longer superior to what industry now offers, though they remain better than what academic institutions can manage to hold out. The fact that much governmental research is contracted out to private industry on a cost-plus-fixed-fee basis has often permitted industry to outbid government laboratories for scientific personnel, and hence has added to the government's recruitment difficulties.[15]

Yet, despite all these handicaps, the government has managed to diminish or offset them so as to increase appreciably the fraction of the nation's scientific manpower which it employs. It has been particularly successful in attracting and holding biological and social scientists, for whom there is a less desperate demand than for mathematicians and physical scientists. In mathematics, the physical sciences and engineering the government has competed effectively with industry for recent university graduates, but less successfully at higher levels. Indeed in many cases government laboratories have acted as training centers for industry, which lures away promising scientists just as they reach full productivity. When an agency loses such an individual, it often raids other government laboratories to fill the vacancy.

Clearly the point is at hand when the government must re-evaluate its manpower policy and scientific priority system if it is to maintain any kind of order and balance in its research activities, particularly as it plunges deeper and deeper into the gigantic space programs now underway. Furthermore, since governmental science by its very size now vitally affects the direction of all scientific activity in the country, such a manpower policy must be conceived within the framework of a plan encompassing the whole nation's scientific endeavors. Thus far, no such plan is in the making. Vast federal research programs continue to battle each other for men and funds while all of them together compete with industry and the universities.

Such competition would be more salutary if the supply of scientists and engineers were not already scarce in relation to projects needing their services. By and large, projects involving military space research are now outbidding those oriented toward the commercial sector of the economy or toward the extension of basic knowledge. The National Aeronautics and Space Administration's own research centers and industrial subcontractors alone could have easily absorbed all of the 30,000 new engineers and scientists who became available in 1963. Of the 400,000 American scientists and engineers currently engaged in research and development, 280,000 are employed in government-sponsored projects such as defense and space, while the remaining 120,000 work in industry on civilian objectives. Likewise, over 70 per cent of the $18.5 billion total expended in 1963 for research and development in the United States was spent by the government for military and related projects.[16] The major redeployment of our scientific manpower made possible by these enormous government appropriations has not allowed a proportionate strengthening of other sectors of the scientific front and has given rise to much concern.

During the late 1940's and the 1950's, it was often argued that, far from retarding innovation in the civilian sector of the economy, the shift toward massive military research would not only produce the necessary weapons but also simultaneously generate a flood of peace-time applications far surpassing in quantity what existing industrial laboratories could produce with purely commercial backing. We have now learned that this is not the case. Thus far, investigations with military potential in the 1940's and 1950's in fields such as radar, atomic energy and space exploration have not made as great a contribution to the gross national product, despite the vast resources devoted to their development, as a number of far more modest research programs specifically aimed at the civilian market in such areas as agriculture and polymer chemistry. The fact is that the technical adaptation of scientific principles to such civilian needs as transportation, housing, food, clothing and education is a very complicated process requiring much time and labor, and quite different in nature from the equally complicated development of modern weapons. The arms race plus the current shortage of scientific manpower often preclude the simultaneous pursuit by defense-oriented laboratories of promising civilian applications. Thus, despite the fact that our overall national research expenditures tripled between 1947 and 1960, the rate of economic growth actually dropped during that period from a fair 3.7 per cent per annum to a sluggish 3 per cent. Officials of the Department of Commerce now point to the imbalance in our research effort toward military ends as an important cause for the lackluster economic progress made by the United States in recent years, warning us that such vigorous world competitors as the Netherlands, Germany, Japan and Sweden have all been spending about 1.25 per cent of their gross national product on civilian research to our 0.80 per cent.[17]

Another imbalance in our scientific effort, aggravated by the manpower shortage and by the spiraling cost of research, is that which exists between small and big business. As we noted, of 300,000 manufacturing companies in the United States, approximately 300 perform 80 per cent of industrially sponsored research. These same 300 companies account for 60 per cent of the sales of all manufactured products and for 61 per cent of the total manufacturing employment. While these companies spend an amount equal to 2.75

per cent of their sales on research and development, the remaining small firms can afford an average of only 0.9 per cent, or about one third as much.[18] If small business is to remain vigorous, and if it is desirable to try allocating to all sectors of our economy a more or less comparable share of the nation's scientific resources, new measures must be taken. These will possibly involve increasing cooperative research by several firms or by entire industries, assisted where necessary by government, as has been done with considerable success in Europe since World War I.

To these imbalances between military and civilian research and between scientific research in big and small business must be added the imbalance existing between basic and academic research on one side and applied civilian and military research on the other. Furthermore, disparities arise between the various sciences as a consequence of some gaining public favor while others fall into neglect. Thus the magnitude of the problems facing modern science in using its limited resources wisely becomes apparent.

Until recently, the institutional structure of science was built piecemeal and haphazardly as each government agency or business corporation sought to devise, more or less empirically, that organizational pattern which it felt would best meet its immediate needs. Now, as these originally separate units have grown more interdependent scientifically, while at the same time competing more vigorously for scarce manpower, there has arisen a need on the part of each to make the most of its existing research staff, and on the part of all to coordinate their efforts for maximum overall benefit to each other and to society. Yet progress along both these lines is considerably hampered by a dearth of abundant, accurate data relating to the science of managing science, a discipline still in its infancy but which hopefully, when mature, will help to guide the formulation of scientific policy as economics now guides decision-making in the business world.

It is also highly likely that in the future, research institutions will engage the services of efficiency analysts and science management experts trained in scientific fields, to peer over the shoulders of researchers, to evaluate records and team performance and to act as consultants to scientific task forces during all phases of their research work from inception to final evaluation. They may at first be received with smirks and later with resentment by working scientists, who will declare that discovery is an unscrutable, highly personal and necessarily inefficient act; but at that point, the scientists themselves might do well to recall that the artisan and the factory foreman a half century ago accorded them a very similar reception. As the process of discovery becomes more clearly understood, it seems probable that its management will assume a more uniform pattern, and that this trend will be accelerated by government guidance and regulation as the nation seeks both to enhance and balance its scientific effort.

Indeed, a considerable standardization already exists among big laboratories. Differences between academic, government and industrial research are dwindling as all three types of institution have become active along the whole spectrum of research from basic, through applied, to routine testing, though admittedly each still applies the weight of its effort to different parts of the spectrum. All three types of institution are also in the business of scientific education and extension, both in training their own staffs and in spreading appreciation and knowledge of science among the wider public. The director of the Atomic Energy Commission's Oak Ridge laboratory, Alvin Weinberg, recently advocated converting that institution into a bona fide graduate school in atomic science to help universities train more scientists while at the same time to bring the benefits of a genuine graduate school atmosphere to the Oak Ridge laboratory.[19] He explained that this was not as drastic a step as one might suppose at first, because the laboratory was already deeply involved in scientific education, conducting seminars at and away from Oak Ridge, granting summer research fellowships to graduate students and university professors, cooperating closely with the Massachusetts Institute of Technology in training nuclear engineers and taking part in other related activities. Other government laboratories, such as those of the Department of Agriculture, the National Institute of Health and the Bureau of Standards, have similar programs, as does industry, although to a lesser degree. Scientists from these laboratories often teach specialized graduate courses in nearby universities and frequently take part in academic seminars. Likewise, professors are often in very close touch as consultants with industrial or governmental research.

In fact, as is well known, there has been a marked tendency in recent years to build new research institutions in close proximity to existing ones, especially near large universities. Towns such as Princeton, Berkeley, Ann Arbor, and Cambridge (Massachusetts) have become enormous centers for scientific research. The main advantage in thus concentrating research facilities is to have easy

JOHN J. BEER and W. DAVID LEWIS

access to other experts and to allow the constant trend toward specialization to proceed apace unhampered by loss of contact with parent sciences and with other specialties. If the present trend continues, the majority of our scientists will find themselves working in such communities, in environments so organized as to enable each specialist to serve as many of the local research institutions as his capacity permits. An industrial scientist, for instance, could direct research for his own firm, act as a consultant for a government laboratory and teach at a nearby university. Should government desire to organize some crash program, he and others could be quickly marshaled for this task.

From the very beginning of the second scientific revolution, when academic and, somewhat later, industrial science were first institutionalized, we have noted a trend toward blurring the lines between basic and applied research and between academic and non-academic institutions. The professional scientist of stature, like his counterparts in the professionally older fields of medicine and law, practices, teaches, consults, writes and keeps learning more about his discipline. While on the one hand he has necessarily had to surrender some freedom of action upon becoming an employee of a large institution, he has still retained a considerable amount of self-direction by making the most of society's extraordinary dependence upon his scarce and highly specialized services.

He has, however, not gone so far as Thorstein Veblen urged him to go in the years immediately following World War I. At that time, Veblen sought to organize a seizure of industry and government by engineers and industrial scientists, whom one of his disciples called technocrats.[20] The Technocracy was to come into being by the simple expedient of a paralyzing strike during which these specialists would withhold their indispensable know-how. Nothing came of the movement, for Veblen failed to arouse that class consciousness among the technocrats which he felt sure already existed in latent form. Class solidarity and common political action have never developed among scientists and engineers, since those with administrative ambitions and abilities have found their striving toward the pinnacles of power unprejudiced by their technical background. By climbing up the bureaucratic ladder, rather than by revolution, they have steadily increased their number and influence in the high places of industry and in such government agencies as the National Aeronautics and Space Administration, the Atomic Energy Commission, the National Institute of Health, the National Science

Foundation, the Bureau of Standards and the many research divisions of the Departments of Agriculture and Defense.

It is in some ways surprising that the technocrats have not thus far achieved an even greater control of our society. Businessmen, lawyers and professional politicians continue to predominate in those key positions where the weightiest decisions affecting our national well-being must be made. That this is so may be attributed to the fact that all these professions require the skill of persuasion, and beyond that a keen insight into the ways of men and organizations. Among scientists and engineers such skill and insight often remain underdeveloped. By personal inclination, training, and early job experience they are more likely to focus on scientific and material problems. Yet as the institutional character of science continues to grow, and conversely as the scientific aspects of the work of more and more institutions increase in significance, researchers will wish to sharpen their managerial and cooperative capabilities. As they develop this aspect of their profession, we can look for a still greater influx of scientists into positions of high influence than has occurred to date.

REFERENCES

1. In England, for example, 70 to 75 per cent of a total of 550 graduate chemists were employed in teaching at the beginning of the twentieth century. This percentage steadily decreased, especially after 1918, as graduate scientists who entered industry proved their value to entrepreneurs. In Germany, the shift in favor of industrial scientists occurred earlier; by 1900, 4000 chemists alone were working for business and manufacturing firms there. There is a need for detailed statistical studies to be done for the United States. See D. S. L. Cardwell, *The Organisation of Science in England: A Retrospect* (London: 1957), pp. 135, 155, 160.

2. See especially Arthur D. Little, "The Chemist's Place in Industry," *Journal of Industrial and Engineering Chemistry*, II (February, 1910), 63–66, and Alexis F. du Pont, "The Du Pont Company and Francis G. du Pont, With Special Reference to the Years 1887 to 1900 Inclusive," in Allan J. Henry (ed. and comp.), *Francis Gurney du Pont: A Memoir* (Philadelphia: 1951), I, 14–16.

3. Raymond Stevens, "Little, Arthur Dehon," *Dictionary of American Biography*, XXI, 500–501; N. R. Danelian, *A. T. & T.: The Story of Industrial Conquest* (New York: 1939), pp. 98–100.

4. See William A. Hamor, "Duncan, Robert Kennedy," *Dictionary of American Biography*, V, 511–512; Robert Kennedy Duncan, "Temporary Indus-

trial Fellowships," *North American Review*, CLXXXV (1907), 54–61, and "On Industrial Fellowships," *Journal of Industrial and Engineering Chemistry*, I (1909), 601; Raymond F. Bacon, "The Object and Work of the Mellon Institute," *Journal of Industrial and Engineering Chemistry*, VII (1915), 343–344; Report of R. F. Bacon in *Science*, XLV (1917), 399–403.

5. John J. Beer, "Coal Tar Dye Manufacture and the Origins of the Modern Industrial Research Laboratory," *Isis*, XLIX (1958), 124–125.

6. See "Patents and Profs," *Wall Street Journal*, February 7, 1961, pp. 1, 8.

7. Simon Marcson, "Decision-Making in a University Physics Department," *American Behavioral Scientist* (December, 1962), p. 37.

8. W. Rupert Maclaurin and R. Joyce Harman, *Invention and Innovation in the Radio Industry* (New York: 1949), pp. 172–176.

9. On this and other aspects of the development of the General Electric Laboratory, see Kendall Birr, *Pioneering in Industrial Research: The Story of the General Electric Research Laboratory* (Washington, D.C.: 1957), and Laurence A. Hawkins, *Adventure Into the Unknown: The First Years of the General Electric Research Laboratory* (New York: 1950), *passim*. For a biography of Whitney, see John T. Broderick, *Willis Rodney Whitney: Pioneer of Industrial Research* (Albany: 1945).

10. Simon Marcson, *The Scientist in American Industry: Some Organizational Determinants in Manpower Utilization* (Princeton: 1960), pp. 70–71.

11. Bruce F. Gordon and Ian C. Ross, "Professionals and the Corporation," *Research Management* (November, 1962), pp. 493–505.

12. F. Russell Bichowsky, *Industrial Research* (Brooklyn, N.Y.: 1942), p. 120.

13. Robert K. Merton, *Science and the Social Order* (New York: 1952), p. 234.

14. Earl W. Lindveit, *Scientists in Government* (Washington, D.C.: 1960), pp. 35–54.

15. At the time of Lindveit's publication, about half of industry's research and development expenditures were derived from federal government contracts. *Ibid.*, p. 8.

16. J. Herbert Hollomon, "Science, Technology, and Economic Growth," *Physics Today*, XVI (1963), 42, 44. Unfortunately, Mr. Hollomon does not indicate what proportion, if any, of these scientists and engineers are academically employed.

17. *Ibid.*, p. 38.

18. *Ibid.*, p. 40.

19. Alvin Weinberg, "The Federal Laboratories and Science Education," *Science*, CXXXVI (1962), 27–30.

20. Thorstein Veblen, *The Engineers and the Price System* (New York: 1944), p. 71. This chapter was first printed as "The Captains of Finance and the Engineers" in *Dial*, 66 (June 14, 1919).

SAMUEL P. HUNTINGTON

Power, Expertise and the Military Profession

SINCE 1945 the American military profession has been reeling under the impact of not one but two revolutions. The technological revolution has made the management of violence increasingly skilled, complex and difficult. The strategic revolution—the shift from the pre-World War II strategy of mobilization to the Cold War strategy of deterrence—has required the maintenance of large military forces and a substantial corps of professional officers to command them. It has also required new methods of civilian control over these forces and a new role for the military in the making of national policy. Between them, the technological and strategic revolutions have shaped two important trends in the military profession since World War II: its increasing need for expertise on the one hand, and its declining political power and influence on the other. These two trends, in turn, have given rise to considerable uncertainty, occasional bewilderment and some frustration among the members of the officer corps.

The Struggle for Expertise

Not all officers are professional military officers. The professional military officer is distinguished from other officers by his skill and by his commitment. The skill is, in Harold Lasswell's phrase, the management of violence. Or, as a distinguished British officer recently put it: "The function of the profession of arms is the ordered application of force to the resolution of a social problem."[1] The commitment is to the management of violence as a career. The technological revolution has proliferated the methods of managing violence, but even so only a part of the officer corps consists of professional military officers. Many officers are specialists

131

—albeit relatively primitive ones—in the management of violence, but they have no commitment to officership as a career. Others make a career out of officership but specialize in skills not directly related to the management of violence. Some officers possess neither military skills nor career commitment. Quite obviously all four types of officer are essential to the modern officer corps. The problems of all four types, moreover, are intimately related. This essay, however, is particularly concerned with those officers with both military skills and career commitments.

How large is the American military profession? Military skill and career commitment are matters of degree, and no precise answer is possible. In 1962 approximately 343,000 officers (commissioned and warrant) were on active duty, including 160,000 regulars and 183,000 reservists. If 80 per cent of the regulars and 20 per cent of the reservists qualified in terms of skill and commitment, there would be about 165,000 professional military officers. This would make the military profession just under one half of the officer corps and significantly smaller than either the medical profession (256,000 in 1960) or the legal profession (248,000 in 1960).

The technological and strategic revolutions require of the professional military officer more intelligence, more education and more expertise than he has ever had in the past. These requirements have produced several dilemmas for the military profession. The need for greater professional specialization conflicts with the continuing need for broadly experienced generalists as managers and commanders. The need for officers of ability and education conflicts with the need for career officers willing to devote ten, twenty or thirty years to the military profession.

The increasingly expert character of the military profession is reflected in tendencies toward greater and greater specialization. The Air Force divides its officers among 40 "utilization fields," 198 air officer specialties and 309 specialties and subspecialties.[2] Army officers are assigned to 394 different military occupational specialties. Much of this specialization, of course, takes place in areas not directly related to combat or the management of violence. Hence, as Janowitz and others have pointed out, officers increasingly employ skills which can be used equally well in military life or in civilian life.[3] This, however, is not the whole truth. For the specialties directly related to the management of violence have also proliferated in large numbers. Fifty years ago the methods of applying violence were relatively limited and simple: infantry, artillery and cavalry in the Army; surface ships in the Navy. Now the methods of applying violence are infinitely more numerous and complex. The technological revolution has multiplied weapons for land, sea, air, underwater and space warfare. The strategic revolution has produced an elongated spectrum of violence from subversion and guerrilla warfare at one end to strategic nuclear warfare at the other. Specialists in one type of warfare are increasingly separated not only from civilians but also from specialists in other types of warfare. The same trends which require officers to specialize in skills employed in civilian life also require them to specialize in skills which have no counterpart in civilian life. Specialization produces "civilianization" in some instances, but it also produces more intensive "militarization" in others.

The relation between military and civilian specialties in the technologically most advanced service is symptomatic of these trends. According to the Air Force, approximately 20 per cent of its officer specialties have no closely related civilian specialty listed in the *Dictionary of Occupational Titles*. A rough appraisal of the character of the officer specialties suggests that about 58 per cent are directly involved with military operations and military command and direction, or with weapons development, procurement and maintenance. On the other hand, somewhat over 50 per cent of the officer specialties also appear to involve at least some skills directly transferable to civilian life. The civilian-related skills tend to be heavily concentrated in the technical support (particularly administration, comptroller, supply) and professional support (legal, religious, medical) categories.

The trend toward specialization is found in virtually all professions. Medicine, it is reported, now has fifty-one recognized specialties and subspecialties. Similar developments have taken place in law and engineering. In these professions, specialization has meant the decline of the generalist: there were 112,000 general medical practitioners in the United States in 1931, but only 82,000 in 1959.[4] In the officer corps, however, specialization produces a distinctive problem almost entirely absent from the legal and medical professions. The officer corps is not only a professional body; it is also a bureaucratic hierarchy. In professions like law and medicine, where practice is largely on an individual basis, the practitioner starts with the general professional knowledge learned in law school or medical school and then goes on to become progressively specialized and expert in some distinct branch of law or medicine. No conflict exists

133

between increasing technical specialization and professional advancement; if anything, the latter is becoming more and more dependent upon the former. In the military profession, however, specialization and advancement can and often do conflict. As a bureaucracy, the officer corps needs top leaders who are not narrow specialists. The generals must also be generalists. The requirements of bureaucracy conflict with the requirements of specialization. In the past, when specialists were less numerous and less "special," these conflicting requirements could be reconciled. The technological and strategic revolutions have made this reconciliation much more difficult.

The services have grappled with the problem in two ways. First, they have consciously recognized a distinction between officers who wish to become specialists and those who wish to prepare themselves for top command positions. The former sacrifice the opportunity for high command but develop a specialty which, in many cases, will be transferable to civilian life upon retirement.[5] The latter sacrifice specialization and the possibility of easy transfer to civilian life for the potential opportunity to become generals or flag officers. Air Force policy, for instance, provides that: "The Air Force officer inventory must at all times include both *broadly experienced officers* who are qualified for senior command and managerial positions, and *technically competent specialized officers*." Officers of both types should be "relatively narrowly specialized" early in their careers and then either broaden themselves for high command or intensify their specialization for added competence.[6] In effect, the officer who chooses the "generalist" pattern delays specialization and professional accomplishment to the last stages of his career, when he emerges as a specialist in the most complex forms of military command and management.

The second means of grappling with the specialist-generalist problem has been through increased formal education and training. Today's military profession has an all-consuming passion for education. Education is necessary both to produce technical specialists and to broaden those who are moving on to high command. A prerequisite for advanced education of either type, of course, is a bachelor's degree. In 1953, 44.9 per cent of all male Army officers had graduated from college, and 77.8 per cent of the Regular Army officers and warrant officers were college graduates. In 1960, 57 per cent of all commissioned officers in the armed services had graduated from college, and 85 per cent had attended college.

134

These figures are roughly comparable to those for the legal profession: in 1951, 83 per cent of lawyers had attended college and 49 per cent had graduated from college.[7] Among regular officers, of course, the proportion of college graduates was much higher. Although many obstacles exist, the goal of the armed services is a college degree for every career officer.

Unlike other professions, formal education continues throughout the military officer's career. About 12 per cent of the total officer time in the military services is devoted to education and training.[8] The pressures of specialization and generalization have made graduate work a *sine qua non* for most career officers. In 1958, 45 per cent of all West Point graduates had taken postgraduate courses at civilian institutions. By 1968, it is expected that this figure will be up to 70 per cent.[9] After serving three to six years with the fleet, Naval Academy graduates go to graduate school for a year's work in mathematics, physics, management or international relations. One half of them are expected to remain for a second or third year. Through its Institute of Technology and cooperating civilian universities, the Air Force offers sixty programs for graduate study (including sixteen Ph.D. programs) in engineering, science, management and the social sciences. In addition to these systems of specialized technical education, each service also maintains a system of professional military education: tactical schools for lieutenants and captains; staff college for majors; war college for lieutenant colonels and colonels. Increasingly, the top commanders of the future will be products of both systems.

The technological and strategic revolutions require the military profession to have officers of both high quality and career commitment. These two characteristics, however, can be inversely related. In general, the more intelligent, the more highly educated and the more intensely trained an officer is, the less likely he is to be highly committed to a professional military career. Before World War II the services solved the quality-plus-commitment problem by relying primarily on the graduates of the military academies. The academies still play a crucial role. Their graduates are, by and large, able and well qualified for professional military officership. The average intelligence and ability of the students at the military academies compares very favorably with that of students in good civilian colleges. Maintaining the quality of academy students, however, requires constant efforts on the part of the services. At times the number of applicants for admission to the academies has fallen sharply, and the schools have had less opportunity for choice. A further problem arises from the system of appointment to the academies. In the past, about 61 per cent of the positions at the Naval Academy and about 85 per cent of those at the Military and Air Force Academies were filled through congressional appointment. In 1964 Congress standardized at 75 per cent the congressional proportion of cadets and midshipmen at all the academies. Congressional nominees must qualify for entrance academically, but the system does not ensure appointment of the most able students. Congressional appointees also tend to resign from the service earlier in their careers than those appointed through the competitive processes.[10] The congressional appointment system was a product of the Jacksonian era and is not designed to attract the most able high-school students to the academies. Its defects have long been recognized, but only since World War II have the consequences of those defects been serious for the services. Academy graduates are, nonetheless, highly committed to a professional military career. About 85 per cent continue beyond their initial obligatory tour of duty. At times, however, the retention rate can slip drastically. By 1957, for instance, some 46 per cent of the Naval Academy class of 1946 and 41 per cent of the class of 1947 had resigned their commissions.

In the past academy graduates have been the heart of the officer corps. They set the tone and the standards for the military profession. For most of the first half of the twentieth century they dominated the higher ranks in the officer corps, particularly in the Navy.[11] The outstanding characteristic of the years since World War II, on the other hand, has been the extent to which the academies have *not* been able to meet the needs of the services for regular officers. In the fiscal year 1962, 40,658 new officers were commissioned in the armed forces. Only 1654 were academy graduates. They were just one sixth of the 10,191 officers receiving regular appointments that year and 41 per cent of the new officers entering the forces in regular status. In 1963 academy graduates were 8 per cent of the Regular Air Force officers (4 per cent of all Air Force officers), 22 per cent of Regular Army officers (7 per cent of all Army officers), and 32 per cent of Regular Navy officers (15 per cent of all Navy officers).[12]

At present, therefore, the academies cannot meet the need for officers of quality-plus-commitment. The goal of the services, however, is to procure 50 per cent of their regular officers from academy sources. As the above figures indicate, they are far from this goal. To improve the situation in the Army and Air Force, Congress passed legislation in 1964 increasing the authorized enrollment at the academies of those two services from 2,529 to 4,417 men, thus making their authorized strengths equal to that of the Naval Academy. In due course, this legislation means that the Military and Air Force Academies will each graduate about 930 men every year instead of the current 550 men. These changes will help ease the shortage of qualified and committed professional officers in the Army and Air Force. Academy expansion will not, however, solve this problem for the services.

The alternative is to recruit sufficient officers of quality and commitment from other sources. The two principal sources are the Reserve Officers Training Corps program and the Officer Candidate Schools. Each, however, has disadvantages. Historically, the purpose of the ROTC has been to produce reserve officers who could be called to the colors in an emergency. The Cold War, however, has given the ROTC the new mission of producing regular officers and reserve officers willing to serve on extended duty.[13] By and large, the quality of the ROTC students is high. The problem is to keep the ROTC officers in the services beyond their minimum term of duty. The success of the services in achieving this goal has varied with the type of ROTC program and commission.

Most ROTC officers receive reserve commissions and serve three or four years on active duty. At the end of this obligatory tour, the overwhelming majority of such officers return to civilian life. The Air Force, for example, retains only 15 per cent of its nonrated AFROTC officers and about 45 per cent of its rated AFROTC officers. In recent years the Navy has had a somewhat higher rate with its Holloway plan students. These students are given four-year scholarships at government expense and commissioned in the Regular Navy on graduation. In its first five years of operation, less than 15 per cent of the Holloway graduates remained in the Navy beyond their required tour of duty. In the past four years, however, the retention rate has gone up steadily from 17 per cent of those who graduated in 1955 to 18.6 per cent of the 1956 graduates, 21.5 per cent of the 1957 graduates and 31.9 per cent of the 1958 graduates.[14] In 1963 the Army and the Air Force asked Congress to authorize a somewhat similar program of subsidized education for college juniors and seniors. This program was designed to replace in large part the existing four-year ROTC and was to be geared

SAMUEL P. HUNTINGTON

to the production of career officers rather than reserve officers. The House Armed Services Committee, however, amended the proposal so as also to strengthen the existing ROTC programs, and in December 1963 the House refused to pass the bill in this amended form.

The Army and the Air Force also secure regular officers from the ROTC through the Distinguished Military Graduates program. Under this program regular commissions are offered to ROTC students at the end of their college careers on the basis of their achievements, academic and otherwise, in college. In the fiscal year 1962, 1070 of 11,992 Army ROTC graduates were given regular commissions under the DMG program. Unlike the students who enter the military academies or the Navy Holloway program, these students choose a military career at the end rather than at the start of college. As a result, the retention rate of the DMG officers has been very high. On the other hand, however, the inverse relationship between quality and commitment is not entirely avoided. Students receiving regular commissions through the DMG program are not always the pick of the college crop. In the words of John W. Masland, a leading academic expert on the ROTC:

Although precise data are lacking, it is reasonably clear that the top students in the ROTC programs to whom regular commissions in the Army and Air Force are offered do not include a fair representation of the top students of the entire institution. The acceptance of regular commissions in the Army and Air Force, moreover, is very low among students in the colleges and universities in which the entrance requirements are the highest. It is high at institutions that are not noted for their academic standards, or that do not generally send a relatively high proportion of their graduates into the other professions.[15]

As Professor Masland also points out, a similar problem afflicts the Holloway plan. Those Holloway officers who remain in the service usually come from the lower-ranking academic institutions.

The second principal source of officers is through the Officer Candidate School programs of the various services. OCS is the principal channel through which enlisted men can become officers. In terms of education and general quality, OCS officers do not measure up to those produced from the academies or through the ROTC. The great advantage for the Army and the Air Force, however, is their high degree of career commitment. According to a 1961 sample survey, some 78 per cent of Army and Air Force OCS officers commissioned between 1956 and 1961 had a "high career

138

commitment."[16] In comparison, 62 per cent and 65 per cent of academy graduates in the Army and Air Force and 31 per cent and 37 per cent of ROTC graduates in the two services had such commitments. Only 22 per cent, however, of all the Army and Air Force OCS officers covered in this survey were college graduates. In the fiscal year 1960 the actual retention rate among Army OCS officers, most of whom had not completed college, was about twice that of Army ROTC officers, all of whom had completed college.[17] At least for the Army and the Air Force, in short: Academy graduates have education and commitment but not numbers; ROTC men have numbers and education but not commitment; OCS men have numbers and commitment but not education.

The basic cause of the quality-plus-commitment problem is the lack of prestige and appeal of the military profession. In 1955 a national sample of adults ranked military officership in seventh place after physician, scientist, college professor, lawyer, minister or priest and public-school teacher, and just ahead of farm owner and carpenter. As a whole, the American public does not accord officership the same prestige which it accords the traditional professions. More importantly, those middle class and better-educated groups which traditionally furnish the bulk of recruits for the professions tend to have an even more unfavorable view of the military profession than does the population at large.[18] The services are acutely conscious of the more concrete reasons for their lack of prestige, and they struggle to improve pay, working conditions, housing and opportunity for adequate family life. Improvements in these areas undoubtedly will help in recruiting able and committed officers. But the roots of the problem lie in the traditional American hostility to military values and institutions, the identification of the military with heroism in war and boredom in peace, and the image of the military as something apart from and alien to civilian society. Before World War II the services solved this problem by recruiting a small number of students at an early age to the military academies. Now, however, they must compete actively and intensely with the pyramiding demands of other groups for intelligent and skilled manpower. The problems of the military differ only in degree from those of the government services at large. Careers in business and the private professions have traditionally attracted the largest numbers of able college graduates. The Cold War, however, has increased the need for such people in government work. But as the Herter Committee on foreign affairs personnel observed, the State Department and other foreign affairs agencies "are at some intrinsic disadvantage in this race to employ the best products of the universities." It urged a reorganization of the examination and appointment process to enable the Foreign Service to compete more adequately with private business.[19] The same needs exist for the military. In the long run the quality in numbers which the military profession requires can come only from the graduates of civilian colleges and universities.

The Decline in Power

Immediately after World War II the air was full of alarms about the growing power of the military. These subsided somewhat during the early 1950's. They reappeared at the end of the decade, however, and they were given a major stimulus from President Eisenhower in January, 1961. "In the councils of government," the retiring President warned, "we must guard against the acquisition of unwarranted influence, whether sought or unsought, by the military-industrial complex. The potential for the disastrous rise of misplaced power exists and will persist." The President's words highlighted an increasing concern with the relations between the military and big business, the role of military leaders in shaping foreign policy decisions, their struggles to get more of the taxpayers' dollars, their opposition to disarmament and support for more belligerent foreign policies and their links with Radical Right extremists. In the words of one author: ". . . the sober and shocking and little-realized truth is that today it is less possible than ever before to place any kind of effective check on the Military."[20] If these views were held only by an extremist minority, they would not be worthy of attention. Eisenhower's farewell address, however, endowed them with respectability, and they are now widely held by many reasonable and moderate commentators. In addition, the fears of military power expressed by groups within the United States interact with and help reinforce images of military dominance widely held by intellectual and political groups abroad.

This image of military dominance is false and dangerous. In actual fact, the power of the military profession "in the councils of government" has decreased steadily since World War II. It reached its postwar nadir under the vigorous leadership of President Kennedy and Secretary of Defense McNamara at the very time, paradoxically, that concern about the growth of military power was on the upswing. This concern is rooted in the traditional American tendency to view civilian control in *quantitative* rather than *institutional* terms. Before World War II the United States solved the problem of civilian control by maintaining only minimal military forces. Since World War II, however, substantial military forces have been necessary, and about 10 per cent of the gross national product has been devoted to military purposes. Hence, it seems logical to assume that civilian control is threatened. The strength of civilian control, however, depends not on the size of the armed forces but on the strength of the political institutions and ideology of the country. The Soviet Union devotes about 18 per cent of its GNP to military purposes. Yet civilian control is effective because Communist political institutions and ideology make it effective. Only when the Party was divided against itself in the succession struggle did the military get a foot in the door of power; and when the succession crisis was over, they were quickly ejected. Similarly, in the United States civilian control depends not on how much of the GNP is devoted to military purposes but on the unity, coherence and strength of political institutions and political leadership, and on the attitudes which leaders and public have toward military power.

Between 1939 and 1942, a revolution took place in American civil-military relations. Generals and admirals moved from political isolation into the seats of power. This revolution, however, directly reflected traditional American attitudes that war and peace were two distinct states. In peace, the military should be small in size and divorced from power. In war, however, the goal is victory, and hence military needs should be overriding. As a result, top military leaders played a far more important role in the United States in World War II than they did in any other major belligerent except Japan. The President and the Joint Chiefs of Staff formulated strategy. The Secretaries of State, War and Navy played marginal roles. Unlike the military chiefs, they did not regularly attend the great wartime planning conferences between Roosevelt and Churchill. Congress voluntarily relinquished its control functions. "The War Department, or . . . General Marshall," as one congressman observed, "virtually dictated the budgets."[21] The military were less powerful in economic mobilization than they were in strategy and foreign policy, but even there their power steadily grew during the war. The Joint Chiefs, Admiral Leahy remarked in 1945, were "under no civilian control whatever."[22] Toward the close of the

141

war, the activities and interests of the military extended far beyond military operations. This situation was tolerable, however, because the military exercised their power with the consent and enthusiastic support of the President, the Congress, and the people: they wielded power but they wielded it to achieve the goals desired by the political community as a whole.

World War II thus marked the high point of military influence. Since 1945, the power of the military profession has steadily declined. Military leaders and military institutions were less powerful in the Truman Administration than they were during World War II. They were less powerful under Eisenhower than they were under Truman. They were less powerful under Kennedy than they were under Eisenhower, and there is no sign of any increase in their influence under Johnson. This constant decline in power and influence of the military profession is the single most important trend in American civil-military relations during the past fifteen years. The decline has been marked by a number of changes in the relations between military and civilian groups.

1. *Decline in political influence of the top leaders of the military profession.* In the years immediately after World War II the great military commanders of the war were popular heroes and major political figures in their own right. The Truman Administration was politically weak and needed the help of the great soldier-statesmen of World War II—Marshall, Eisenhower, Bradley—to secure support for its policies in Congress and among the public at large. Marshall served the administration as Secretary of State and Secretary of Defense, Eisenhower and Bradley as presiding officers of the Joint Chiefs, Eisenhower as Supreme Commander in Europe. The single most important foreign policy issue of Truman's second term—the conduct of the Korean War—was essentially a debate between MacArthur on the one hand, and Marshall and Bradley on the other.

The election of Eisenhower created a different, if somewhat paradoxical, situation. A military man was now President, but for this very reason the influence of other military men was limited. Eisenhower, of course, waged a continuing and successful battle to keep down the military budget, which aroused considerable opposition among his Chiefs of Staff. But what could they do? No military man on active duty could compete with the prestige of General Eisenhower, and the prestige of *General* Eisenhower was the principal weapon of *President* Eisenhower in imposing restrictions on military spending. Admiral Radford was the only military officer who played a significant role in policy-making, and he was one officer who also shared the administration's budgetary outlook.

At the close of his term of office President Eisenhower reportedly expressed doubts about the ability of his successor—Kennedy or Nixon—who would lack his military experience and reputation to exercise effective control over the military. President Kennedy, however, demonstrated that the ability to control and to lead can derive as much from political skill as from military knowledge. The top military leaders of the 1960's, moreover, are the products of a peacetime military bureaucracy rather than of wartime military command. This does not mean that they are any less worthy than their predecessors: General Taylor is certainly one of the most brilliant and able leaders the American military profession has produced. But they lack the independent political appeal of their predecessors. In 1948 the Chiefs of Staff were wartime heroes; in 1963 it is doubtful if one American in a hundred could name the five Chiefs of Staff. The military leaders now are the creatures of the politicians, and, as the experience of Admiral Anderson demonstrates, if one of them does stray out of line he can be easily dropped by the administration.

2. *The decreasing role of military men in the civilian agencies of government.* The development of the Cold War immediately after World War II caught the government unprepared with personnel to staff its new foreign affairs activities. The civilians who had joined the government during the war were heading back to their peacetime jobs. Where was the government to find men able, dedicated, willing to serve and at least partially familiar with foreign policy problems? The obvious source was the military. As a result, military officers were appointed to key State Department offices, ambassadorial posts and positions in other foreign affairs agencies. Although the number of military officers occupying civilian positions declined after 1946 and 1947, it remained high throughout the Truman Administration.[23]

Unlike Truman, Eisenhower was able to enlist the services of large numbers of businessmen for his administration. Although he initially appointed several top military officers to civilian positions, the overall participation of military officers in civil office declined significantly during the later years of his administration. Under Kennedy this tendency was intensified. In Kennedy's first two years no professional military officer was appointed to a top civil position in the government. The officers had performed a notable service in stepping into the breach in the early years of the Cold War, when civilians were either unqualified or unwilling to serve. By the 1960's, however, the foreign assistance, overseas information and intelligence agencies had developed their own professional staffs. The State Department, which had suffered under the attacks of McCarthy and the administrative indifference of Dulles, was beginning to refurbish the professional skills and esprit of the Foreign Service. Below the top levels of the foreign affairs and defense agencies, there was an increasing interchange of personnel as military officers were temporarily assigned to the State Department and other civilian agencies, and representatives of these agencies temporarily worked for the Department of Defense. This, however, was an educational device designed to improve understanding and coordination. Unlike the massive movement of military men into civilian posts in the 1940's, it reflected strength rather than weakness in the civilian agencies.

3. *The increasing expertise and influence of civilian groups in the formation of military policy.* Not only have the military retreated from the civilian side of foreign policy, but a variety of civilian groups have moved into the military sphere and have begun to play a major role in the determination of strategy and military policy. Most important among these groups are the so-called "defense intellectuals," the physical scientists and the civil servants of the Department of Defense. The involvement in military policy of the first two groups was a direct result of the changing nature of war and strategy; it was evidence of one way in which the decrease in the differences between military and civilian skills could serve to limit the power of the military. It was also persuasive evidence of the extent to which innovation in strategy and technology was dependent on the actions of groups outside the military hierarchy.

The increasing complexity of war and the decreasing relevance of the traditional distinctions between sea, land and air warfare caused military officers to lag behind in the development of strategic ideas relevant to deterrence. Most of the significant writings on strategy produced after World War II were produced by civilians. Increasing attention was paid to strategy in the universities, in the various centers for the study of foreign and military policy problems such as the Council on Foreign Relations, and in specialized research organizations such as RAND. Experts such as Brodie, Kaufmann, Kissinger, Wohlstetter, Schelling and Kahn took the lead in articulating theories of stabilized deterrence, limited war, tactical nuclear war, arms control and civil defense. Divorced from service interests and trained in the exact or social sciences, they were able to bring a fresh approach to the problems of strategy. During the Eisenhower Administration, their role was largely critical. In the Kennedy Administration, they moved into the White House and the Pentagon. They were able, in a sense, to beat the military at their own game. Traditionally, the professional military officer is supposed to be contemptuous of the ignorance of civilians on military problems and strategy. One striking aspect of the Mc-Namara Pentagon, however, has been the allegation that the civilian "whiz kids" are unduly contemptuous of the military officers for *their* backwardness and ignorance.

The natural scientists are a second civilian group challenging the military on their home ground. Their entrance into military affairs followed inevitably from the atomic bomb. In 1946 they played a major role, on both sides, in the struggle over civilian vs. military control of atomic energy. In the early 1950's, some scientists were leading figures in the development of thermonuclear weapons. Others took the lead in pushing continental defense and low-yield nuclear weapons. Subsequently, sputniks and space again brought the scientists to the center of the scene. A Special Assistant to the President for Science and Technology was appointed, and the office of the Director of Research and Engineering was established in the Department of Defense. The latter official supervises all military research and development. In the debates of the late 1950's and early 1960's concerning technology, space activities, nuclear testing, arms control, disarmament and even weapons development, the role of the scientists was as important or more important than that of the soldiers.

A third civilian group lacks the glamor or public prestige of the defense intellectuals or the physical scientists. In the fifteen years following the unification of 1947, however, the civil servants in the Department of Defense also quietly gained in power and influence. Military officers are normally rotated through top staff positions in tours of three or four years. By the late 1950's, however, some top civil servants had been with the central defense establishment since its creation in 1947. Continuity of service gave them experience, knowledge, contacts and power. The civilian scientists and defense intellectuals primarily play a critical, innovating role in military matters. The civil servants in the office of the Secretary of Defense, on the other hand, primarily play a restricting, controlling role. As a result, the growth of their power is a popular target for criticism by military leaders.[24]

In addition to these three groups of civilians, the top political leadership of the Department of Defense is becoming more knowledgeable in military policy and strategy. These leadership positions are normally occupied by bankers, lawyers, industrialists and educators. Over the course of years, however, each political party has built up a reservoir of talent with experience in military matters. At the end of the Eisenhower Administration, "most civilian leaders in the Pentagon had spent periods of 4 to 8 years in defense work, if not in the same post."[25] The Kennedy Administration, in turn, did not start from scratch but included executives like Gilpatric and Nitze, who had held responsible positions under Truman. The next Republican administration presumably will have its share of Eisenhower appointees. Thus, after fifteen years of Cold War, civilians are playing more and more important roles in shaping military policy. In the late 1940's, few civilians would have dared challenge the wisdom of the Joint Chiefs on strategy. Those who did carried little weight. In the early 1960's, initiative and leadership on strategic matters were shared among a variety of groups, some military, but many civilian.

4. *Centralization of authority over military policy in the executive branch.* Historically, Congress has played an important role in determining the size and weapons of the armed forces and in sharing responsibility through its treaty and war-making powers for their use. After World War II, however, the power to determine the military budget, force levels, weapons and uses of the armed forces became securely lodged in the administration, that is, in top leadership of the executive branch of the government. This decline in the power of Congress also meant a decline in the power of the military professionals. So long as Congress could act independently on force levels, the commanders could appeal executive decisions to Congress with the expectation that they might well be overruled. After World War II military leaders continued to look to Congress to correct unfavorable executive decisions. Frequently Congress heeded these appeals and added additional sums to the military budget. In almost every case, however, the President wielded an effective veto over the congressional action by impounding the appropriated funds or by refusing to authorize larger forces. Congressional groups, of course, can lobby with the administration and

harass it in a variety of ways. But the administration can, if it wishes, always have the last word.[26]

5. *Continued divisions among the military.* The above-mentioned factors have all contributed to a marked rise in civilian authority vis-à-vis the military professionals. Conceivably these developments might have been counterbalanced by other changes on the military side of the equation. By and large, however, they were not. In particular, the single most significant factor abetting the rise of civilian influence was the continued division of the military against itself. Interservice controversy, intraservice divisions, interprogram rivalries all helped to weaken the voice of the military. On few, if any, major issues did the military professionals develop a coherent military viewpoint. Split among themselves, they invited civilian intervention into military affairs. When they were able to compromise their differences and agree on a common program, the result was often so obviously a political compromise that civilian leaders were justified in tearing it apart on grounds of sound military logic. This competition went on not only in the Joint Chiefs of Staff but also in the broader reaches of the "military-industrial complex." Those fearful of the power of the complex assume that it is an entity acting with a singleness of purpose. In actuality, however, it is more of an arena than a unity. It is divided against itself and quite incapable of unified action. The services compete with each other over strategy, weapons and budgets. Corporations compete with each other for defense contracts. Scientific and technical advisory groups offer conflicting advice. Local communities and congressional representatives clash with administration leaders and the chiefs of staff. The lines of conflict and alliance are continually changing. Seldom, if ever, are they drawn on a civilian vs. military basis.

Throughout the Cold War years the determination of military policy has remained firmly in the hands of the civilians. Three major revisions of overall strategy occurred in 1950, 1953 and 1961. In each case, the political leadership of the government took the initiative in changing strategy and supplied the basic ideas and concepts. Most of the other important changes in American policies and programs have been inaugurated by civilians. Civilian Pentagon leaders have not hesitated to overrule military chieftains on the need for particular types of weapons. Inevitably, the pressure from the military is for the proliferation of programs and expenditures. But as the history of the Eisenhower Administration demonstrates, an administration can keep military spending down if it wishes to. Military expenditures (in constant dollars) were less in the last year of the Eisenhower Administration than they were in any earlier year in that administration.[27]

The Military Prospect

Increasing intellectual challenge and decreasing political influence is a recipe for frustration rather than for responsibility. And frustration and discontent have been reflected in the attitudes of at least some military officers. This discontent has had three main foci. First, the requirements of the new strategy of deterrence conflict with many traditional military ideas and goals. The object of military force now is not to win a war but to prevent it. Total victory becomes synonomous with total disaster. Military forces must be constantly ready to fight, but if they do fight they must operate under onerous political restrictions and close top-level political supervision. In the implementation of foreign policy, military means become hopelessly intertwined with political and economic means and goals. These aspects of deterrence caused some military officers in the 1950's to favor a "victory" strategy and what Morris Janowitz has termed "absolutist" military doctrine. By the 1960's, however, this particular source of frustration was losing its sting. The clashes between the advocates of total war and limited war, pragmatic doctrine and absolutist doctrine, were fading. To a remarkable degree, military officers have become reconciled to deterrence and its implications for political control and limited warfare.

A second, more continuing source of frustration lies in the nature of the American policy-making process. As an acute British observer has remarked, "the procedures of democratic politics will often strike the military mind as being inefficient or even immoral."[28] The military officer, typically, wants explicit policies, firm decisions, clear-cut choices. The American policy-making process is designed to produce none of these. Consequently, military officers at times have expressed exasperation at what one general described as the "morass of discussion, argument, delay, and indecision" prevailing along the Potomac.[29] Closely linked to this feeling is the view that military methods and thinking can provide the answers which the politicians seem unable to find. In a 1954 survey, for instance, 32 per cent of high-ranking Pentagon staff officers attributed the differences between civilians and military to the professional virtues

148

of the military and the absence of these virtues among the civilians.[30]

Discontent about indecisiveness was particularly strong during the Eisenhower Administration. The crisp efficiency of McNamara put a stop to this line of criticism. Instead, military officers grumbled at the speed with which the administration went about deciding matters either without the "proper" military advice or in defiance of that advice. The defense intellectuals or "whiz kids" became a standard target. Reacting against the purported role of operations analysis and computers in shaping military policy, the professional officers again stressed the importance of experience and the human factor. The full gamut of military discontent with deterrence, compromise and "computerism" is reflected in the words of General Thomas D. White, retired Air Force Chief of Staff:

> In common with many other military men, active and retired, I am profoundly apprehensive of the pipe-smoking, tree-full-of-owls type of so-called professional defense intellectuals who have been brought into this Nation's Capital. I don't believe a lot of these often over-confident, sometimes arrogant young professors, mathematicians and other theorists have sufficient worldliness or motivation to stand up to the kind of enemy we face. . . .
>
> . . . it seems to me the old strengths still apply. In my opinion the two that count for most in the nuclear space age, regardless of academic cerebrations, are national determination and military forces designed to achieve victory, not tailored to obtain compromise. Professional military training teaches the philosophy of victory, whereas politics is based on compromise.[31]

It is impossible to say precisely how many professional officers share these views. Undoubtedly, they are a minority. Such views embody a negative reaction to the strategic and technological revolutions and the changes which these have precipitated in the expertise and power of the military. Indeed, the tone of General White's remarks resembles nothing so much as the complaints of the old Indian-fighting generals displaced by the bright young officers whom Elihu Root brought into the General Staff in 1903. Such attitudes do, however, raise questions about the general position of the military profession on the American political scene.

In the Cold War the great dividing line in American politics has not been between Left and Right but between the "Establishment" and the "fundamentalists." The Establishment is predominantly East Coast, Ivy League, Wall Street, big business and executive-branch oriented. The fundamentalists are rural, Midwestern and Southern, small business, small town, and Congress oriented. The

Establishment outlook is more international and "sophisticated"; the fundamentalist outlook more nationalistic and "moralistic." In Janowitz's terms, Establishment military doctrine has been pragmatic, fundamentalist doctrine absolutist. In terms of education, experience, functions, skills and organizational position, the military profession is essentially part of the Establishment. At the same time, however, the rapid changes in strategy and technology, the difficult struggle to keep up in the race for expertise and the visible decline in military power give rise to feelings and attitudes more oriented toward the fundamentalist current in American politics. It is not the "unwarranted" power of the military which is cause for concern, but rather the feelings of resentment and frustration which develop when the military believes that it is unaccountably and unjustifiably losing power. At least some elements of the military profession belong, in Daniel Bell's expressive phrase, to "the dispossessed." They share in the "revolt against modernity and the requirements of planned social change" and in "an anti-intellectualism which is a defensive posture against the complexities of modern problems."[32] General White's views certainly parallel attitudes held by other dispossessed groups in the fundamentalist camp. Such attitudes can lead a small minority of extremists to full-fledged participation in Radical Right organizations. A number of officers on active duty eagerly seized the opportunity presented by the Eisenhower Administration in 1958 to alert the country to the dangers of Communism and to organize right-wing seminars and meetings. The primary appeal of the Radical Right, however, has been to the older officers, retired from the military hierarchy and unfamiliar with and hostile to the new expertise.

These activities are an essentially fruitless response to the problems of expertise and power. Of the two, the displacement from power is far less important than the need for expertise. Too much power—too great a role in the making of policy—can indeed lead to partisan and political involvements and thereby undermine military professionalism. Too little professionalism—too little expertise—on the other hand, can also undermine political power. Immediately after World War II the balance of civil-military relations was disrupted by weakness on the civilian side, and as a result the military leaders and institutions were drawn into political roles. This was unhealthy, and a restoration of the balance was clearly in order. If the pendulum is now swinging too far in the other direction, the cause lies in the slowness of the military response to the strategic and technological revolutions.

Older generals may bemoan the new expertise and invoke old truths. The younger and more forward-looking officers, however, are acutely sensitive to the need to catch up in the race for expertise. The obstacles are many. Within the military profession, there are the forces of traditionalism, anti-intellectualism, and the image of the fighting combat commander. Outside the military profession, there is the quasi-acceptance of the military which complicates the problems of recruitment and retention. Far more important to the military profession than political power in government is the full acceptance by society of military officership as a vital, challenging and rewarding professional career. In the absence of a major upheaval, the political dispossession of the military is permanent. With effort, however, the intellectual losses can be recouped. A good start has already been made in the struggle for expertise. Success in this struggle is a precondition to establishing a viable long-term civil-military balance in American policy-making. The future general with his Ph.D. will lack the political halo of a Marshall or an Eisenhower. Both characteristics, however, should help him in making a creative, professional contribution to national security.

REFERENCES

1. Lieutenant General Sir John Winthrop Hackett, *The Profession of Arms* (London: The Times Publishing Co., 1963), p. 3. On why military officership is a profession, see Samuel P. Huntington, *The Soldier and the State* (Cambridge: Belknap-Harvard University Press, 1957), chapter 1.

2. See U. S. Department of the Air Force, *Officer Classification Manual* AFM 36-1, April 15, 1963.

3. See Morris Janowitz, *The Professional Soldier* (Glencoe: The Free Press, 1960), pp. 64-74.

4. Selig Greenberg and David D. Rutstein, in Marion K. Sanders (ed.), *The Crisis in American Medicine* (New York: Harper, 1960), pp. 23, 33.

5. On the mounting problems of military retirement, see Albert D. Biderman, "The Prospective Impact of Large Scale Military Retirement," *Social Problems*, 7 (Summer, 1959), 84-90, and "Sequels to a Military Career: The Retired Military Profession," paper prepared for Inter-University Seminar on Military Organization, Center for Social Organization Studies, University of Chicago, to be published in Morris Janowitz (ed.), *Essays in Military Sociology* (Chicago: University of Chicago Press, 1964).

6. U.S. Department of the Air Force, Officer Career Management, AFR 36-23, September 12, 1960.

7. Lieutenant Colonel Russell O. Fudge, "Informing the Army Officer," *Military Review*, 34 (October, 1954), 33; U.S. Office of the Secretary of Defense, Directorate for Statistical Services, *Selected Manpower Statistics*, February 1, 1963, p. 45; Albert P. Blaustein and Charles O. Porter, *The American Lawyer* (Chicago: University of Chicago Press, 1954), p. 193.

8. The Committee on Foreign Affairs Personnel, *Personnel for the New Diplomacy* (Carnegie Endowment for International Peace, December, 1962), p. 105. Only 5% of the total time of foreign service officers is devoted to education and training.

9. Hanson Baldwin, *New York Times*, June 12, 1958, p. 16.

10. A substantial number of the competitive appointments are reserved for the sons of regular officers and enlisted men. The higher career commitment of the competitive appointees may thus be a function of parentage rather than method of appointment. See Janowitz. *Professional Soldier*, p. 149.

11. For data, see Janowitz, *Professional Soldier*, pp. 58-60.

12. U.S. Department of Defense, *Annual Report for Fiscal Year 1962*, pp. 158-159; S. Rept. 869, 88th Congress, 2d Sess. (Feb. 6, 1964), p. 3.

13. See, in general, Gene M. Lyons and John W. Masland, *Education and Military Leadership* (Princeton: Princeton University Press, 1959).

14. *Department of Defense Appropriations for 1964*, Hearings before Subcommittee of the Committee on Appropriations, House of Representatives, 88th Congress, 1st Sess. (1963), Part 3, pp. 163, 288.

15. John W. Masland, "The Bearing of Military Education upon Civil-Military Relations in the United States," paper prepared for 7th Round Table, International Political Science Association, Opatija, Yugoslavia, September, 1959, pp. 14-15.

16. Mayer N. Zald and William Simon, "Career Opportunities and Commitments Among Military Officers," paper prepared for Inter-University Seminar on Military Organization, University of Chicago, to be published in Janowitz (ed.), *Essays in Military Sociology*.

17. Kurt Lang, "Recruitment and the Military Profession," paper prepared for Inter-University Seminar on Military Organization, University of Chicago, to be published in Janowitz (ed.), *Essays in Military Sociology*.

18. U.S. Department of Defense, News Release, No. 1237-55, December 31, 1955; Janowitz, *Professional Soldier*, p. 227.

19. Committee on Foreign Affairs Personnel, *Personnel for the New Diplomacy*, pp. 67-75.

20. Fred J. Cook, *The Warfare State* (New York: Macmillan, 1962), pp. 29-30.

21. Quoted in Elias Huzar, *The Purse and the Sword* (Ithaca: Cornell University Press, 1950), p. 58.

22. *Department of Armed Forces, Department of Military Security,* Hearings before Committee on Military Affairs, United States Senate, on S. 84, 79th Congress, 1st Sess. (1945), p. 521.

23. Huntington, *The Soldier and the State,* pp. 355-361.

24. Major General John B. Medaris, *Countdown for Decision* (New York: Putnam, 1960), pp. 55, 270-271, 274; Lieutenant General James M. Gavin, *War and Peace in the Space Age* (New York: Harper, 1958), p. 166.

25. Gene M. Lyons, "The New Civil-Military Relations," *American Political Science Review,* 55 (March, 1961), 57. This article is an excellent discussion of the emergence of the new civilian expertise in military affairs.

26. Samuel P. Huntington, *The Common Defense* (New York: Columbia University Press, 1961), pp. 126-146.

27. Huntington, *Common Defense, passim,* and esp. pp. 113-15, 207-234, 277-283.

28. Michael Howard, "Civil-Military Relations in Great Britain and the United States, 1945-1958," *Political Science Quarterly,* 75 (March, 1960), 37.

29. Medaris, *Countdown for Decision,* p. 158.

30. MacAllister Brown, Andrew F. Henry, and John W. Masland, "Some Evidence on the 'Military Mind,'" unpublished paper, Dartmouth College, June, 1958.

31. General Thomas D. White, "Strategy and the Defense Intellectuals," *Saturday Evening Post,* 236 (May 4, 1963), 10-12.

32. Daniel Bell, "The Dispossessed—1962," *Columbia University Forum,* 5 (Fall, 1962), 4-12. This article identifies the changes in the military profession as part of a general shift in American society toward increasing technicality and expertise.

NORMAN E. ZINBERG

Psychiatry: A Professional Dilemma

THERE ARE many different schools of psychiatry—psychoanalytic, behavioral, eclectic, organic or psychopharmacological or even existential. In order to discuss psychiatry as a profession in the United States, it is necessary to specify which school is meant. This article is written from the point of view of psychoanalytic psychiatry.

Furthermore, it is necessary to clarify the peculiar relationships of psychiatry in general to the rest of the medical profession. While psychiatry is part of medicine and, during the last fifteen years, has been given a position of increasing importance in the medical curriculum, it is not usually treated as an ordinary subdivision of medicine. If there is a psychiatric division in a general hospital, it is usually physically separated or clinically differentiated from the medical divisions. In army hospitals, until very recently, psychiatric patients were issued gowns of a different color from those given to other patients. Psychiatric hospitals have traditionally been located far from large population centers, presumably because of public fear and suspicion of mental patients. The proposed federal program of community-based mental hospitals promises to change this, but whether the program will be accepted by Congress and, more importantly, by the communities which will have to feed, house, employ and share social facilities with patients, is questionable.

One cause of the relative isolation of psychiatrists from their colleagues in other specialties is that the training of psychoanalytic psychiatrists differs so greatly from that of the other specialists. The personal analysis, so obviously essential to the psychiatrist, is seen by other medical men as a rite of passage rather than as scientific training. The gulf between psychiatry and the rest of medicine, however, is most strikingly exemplified by the connotations, to both physicians and laymen, of a psychiatric referral or request for a psychiatric consultation. Even a surgical referral, which can be more frightening, does not have the pejorative moral and social connotations that for many people still accompany a psychiatric referral.

This separation between medicine and psychoanalytic psychiatry is partly inherent in the nature of psychoanalysis. "Psychoanalysis" is a method of treatment; a technique by which the processes of the mind are investigated; and a broad psychological theory. In the first and second of these meanings, it is anchored in medicine, but equally and partially overlapping in the second and third it is anchored in the social sciences. The roots of psychoanalytic psychiatry are in psychoanalysis, and psychoanalysis, even though this country insists on an M.D. for its practitioners, has had a foot in both medicine and the social sciences since the establishment of the psychoanalytic movement. This connection with social science was strongly reaffirmed as recently as 1961, when the American Psychoanalytic Association made a controversial decision to reject the establishment of psychoanalysis as a subspecialty of psychiatry similar to child psychiatry.

But the separation of psychiatry from medicine is also maintained by outside forces related to the history of psychoanalysis in this country, and by the conflict between the value systems of much of today's culture, including those of the medical profession, and those of psychoanalytic psychiatry. These factors may make intelligible the current situation of psychiatry as a profession in a dilemma which, if not resolved, could lead to disappointment and waste for all. This professional dilemma preoccupies many leading psychiatrists more often in their discussions with colleagues than in their writing. However, in 1958 in *Young Man Luther*, Erik Erikson, while specifying the book as a study in psychoanalysis and history, summed up the problem in this statement:

Psychoanalysis has tended to subordinate the later stages of life to those of childhood. It has lifted to the rank of a cosmology the undeniable fact that man's adulthood contains a persistent childishness: that vistas of the future always reflect the mirages of a missed past, that apparent progression can harbor partial regressions, and firm accomplishment, hidden childish fulfillment. In exclusively studying what is repetition and regression and perseveration in human life, we have learned more about the infantile in the adult than was ever before known. We have thus prepared an ethical reorientation in human life which centers on the preservation of those early energies which man, in the very service of his higher values, is apt to suppress, exploit, or waste. In each treatment, and in all our applications, this reorientation governs our conscious intentions. To formulate them on an historically valid scale, however, it is necessary to realize that the psychopathologist, called upon to treat in theory and practise the passions, anxieties, and rages of the race, will always have to make some kind of convincing philosophy out of a state of partial knowledge; while neurotic patients and panicky people in general are so starved for beliefs that they will fanatically spread among the unbelievers what are often as yet quite shaky convictions.

Because we do not include this fact in our awareness, we were shocked at being called pansexualists when our interest (that is, the affects of curiosity and confirmation) was selectively aroused by the minutest references to sexual symbolism. We were distressed when we saw ourselves caricatured in patients who, in social life, spread a compulsive attitude of mutual mental denuding under the guise of being alert to the defensive tricks of the ego. And we were dismayed when we saw our purpose of enlightenment perverted into a widespread fatalism, according to which man is nothing but a multiplication of his parents' faults and an accumulation of his own earlier selves. We must grudgingly admit that even as we were trying to devise, with scientific determinism, a therapy for the few, we were led to promote an ethical disease among the many.[1]

It is hardly necessary to document the extent to which psychoanalytic thought has pervaded every aspect of modern American life. When a candidate for President of the United States made a slip of the tongue and called his running mate "my distinguished opponent," many newspapers speculated on their front pages whether the motive for the slip was not Mr. Nixon's dissatisfaction with and political assessment of a recent speech by Mr. Lodge promising a cabinet post to a Negro. This line of thought was so natural that no one felt it necessary to acknowledge the debt to Freud for its initiation. In 1922 our representatives to the Hague disarmament conferences were lawyers and military scientists who specialized in international law and firepower, respectively. In contrast, a statement given out by Mr. Averill Harriman before leaving for Moscow on a similar mission in June, 1963, contained in the first three sentences the word "psychology" and the phrase "emotional climate," to show his understanding of what pertained to international affairs. Again, such thinking was so automatic that no one commented on its origins. This degree of diffusion is almost unbelievable in view of the fact that in 1963 the American Psychoanalytic Association, for the first time in its history, included more than 1000 members.

But the spread of ideas is by no means synonymous with accuracy and clarity. Acceptance of psychoanalysis in the language and thinking of our time has been matched by misuse and misconception. In everyday use, psychoanalytic terms not only often have a pejorative connotation but are divorced from any kind of conceptual precision. In conversation, "compulsive" usually means "finicky" or "repetitious." To say at a party that a girl "acts out a lot" may mean something different from saying that she "sleeps around," but the difference is hard to distinguish.

Sadly, even in the many professions which employ psychoanalytic theories in their own work, even those few concepts that have come to have specific meanings in the semantic jungle of psychoanalytic theory are used generally or in contexts so different from the original ones that the meaning is altered. What is worse is that many of the people in other fields using these ideas have had little opportunity for comprehensive training in psychoanalytic theory, which is always based on clinical evidence and experience. Instead, they have rooted around in the psychoanalytic literature, especially that of Sigmund Freud, and when they wish to "apply" something, they quote isolated passages. These quotations are misleading because of Freud's and others' continuous reformulations, modifications and revisions of their hypotheses in the light of accumulating clinical data. This is not to say that in psychoanalysis there has not been a relatively orderly development of ideas, but that the complex nature of these developments lends itself to diverse formulations and popular misconceptions.

We can now turn to the origins of the acceptance of psychoanalysis in the United States. A leading puzzle to students of the history of ideas has always been the fact that psychoanalysis caught on so quickly and overwhelmingly in the United States, although it did not in Europe. It is impossible to consider psychoanalytic psychiatry as a profession without discussing this question, although no final answers can be offered. Among the factors that encouraged the spread of psychoanalytic ideas, three seem especially important: the acceptance of Freudian thought by key people; the social climate of the culture; and, finally, the intellectual positions in psychology and psychiatry at the time Freud's work was introduced.

A survey of the first of these areas shows that a surprising number of professors of neurology or neurologic psychiatry had expressed a need for a more organized theory of mental illness. This need is indicated by a remark of the famous professor of neurology, Dr. C. L. Dana, in 1904, probably before he had ever heard of

Freud. Dr. Dana said: "Clinical psychiatry is in fact only morbid psychology." It is not surprising that after Freud's visit to the United States, Dr. Dana became one of those enthusiastic supporters of psychoanalytic theory who gave it a foothold in American medicine.[2] C. P. Oberndorf, in *A History of Psychoanalysis in America*, emphasizes the importance of the receptiveness of men such as Dr. Morton Prince of Boston, who in 1906 published in his *Journal of Abnormal Psychology* the first of Freud's papers to be published in this country; James Jackson Putnam, Professor of Neurology at Harvard University; Adolph Meyer, skittish but important; Dr. Frederick Peterson, Professor of Neurology at Columbia University, who persuaded Dr. A. A. Brill to go to Vienna; and a surprising number of others. In the field of medicine this experimentation and interest in the "new" psychology proved not to be a fad. It was carried on by numerous famous practitioners, such as William A. White, Smith Ely Jeliffe, Nolan D. C. Lewis, and, of course, that tireless proselytizer for psychoanalysis, A. A. Brill.[3]

The oft-told event that really represented the introduction of Freud to the United States came not from medicine but from academic psychology, when G. Stanley Hall invited Freud to commemorate the twentieth anniversary of Clark University with five lectures, "On Psychoanalysis." The warmth of his reception delighted Freud, and his admiration of Hall and William James and others who greeted him was great. These men were prominent psychologists, and their recognition of Freud sanctioned the attendance at his lectures of the distinguished audience. However, most of the people who heard the talks, now considered classics, were not favorably impressed. James quickly cooled in his ardor for psychoanalysis, as did Hall. Freud did not like the United States for many reasons, including the fear that psychoanalysis would be "diluted," and later he seemed to think of Hall as a type of enthusiast who liked to "make and unmake kings." So, paradoxically, Freud on his trip won some adherents in medicine, like Putnam, who never deviated from their support for psychoanalysis but for many years were not able to find a place for it in the curriculum of the medical schools; while those in the social sciences, who introduced him, lost interest but lived to see psychoanalytic concepts run wild in their disciplines.

A discussion of the social climate of a culture must always be based to some extent on speculations. Nevertheless, the topic cannot be ignored. Certainly in the United States the psychological novels of a physician as revered as Oliver Wendell Holmes[4] and the popular movement led by Dorothea Dix,[5] both concerned with the mentally ill and their plight, left a residue of interest in this subject that must have helped the acceptance of psychoanalytic concepts. Both these people represented the belief in progress and activity that has always been an important component of any description of the "American character." Americans have always impatiently sought out new treatments and ideas, particularly if they offer the hope of a more effective cure or a more definite answer.

Descriptions of the American character usually also recognize that the pioneer and melting-pot heritages have left for the people what, in modern parlance, would be called an "identity crisis."[6] Americans have always wanted to "find themselves" personally and socially, while until recently the more rigidly stratified class structure of Europe, which attempts to classify every man from birth, resulted in the fact that Europeans too definitely knew their place. Psychoanalysis offered the chance for each person to investigate his emotional origins and to be emancipated by resolving his overwhelming doubts about who he was. The psychoanalytic emphasis on the freedom of the individual appealed strongly to the American democratic tradition.

A case might also be made for psychoanalysis as a philosophy which offered a middle course between Herbert Spencer's Social Darwinism and Karl Marx's economic determinism. These were two of the most important bodies of thought of the first part of the twentieth century. In a broad, oversimplified version, Spencer's philosophy saw human existence in terms of struggle and competition, each man for himself, survival of the fittest without mutual assistance. The Marxist view of society, where each must care for the others and relinquish his individual aspirations for the greater goals of the society, was embodied in the idea that each person diffuses his identity in the state or even in the factory. But the first of these social theories seemed too close to the unbridled primitive aggressions of mankind, while the second, although shiny with idealism about man, seemed too restrictive of personal aspirations. Psychoanalysis, which allowed for conflict between the basic nature of man and his environment but which—although pessimistic as compared to Marx—did not despair of resolution, offered a middle way.

There were other, more concrete, social factors at work. The difference in academic hierarchies in Europe and in the United States seems to have been important. In Europe, the academic tradition was a rigidly structured, static system where a professor was surrounded by disciples who carried on his work. Although much could be accomplished in such well-organized structures, the rate of change and acceptance of new ideas was slow. With the exception of Bleuler, Freud's work won few adherents among the powerful professors of Europe who controlled the universities. In speaking of the academic system, Freud once said bitterly, "I learned that the Old World is ruled by authority as the new is ruled by the dollar."[7] His dissatisfaction with both sides of the Atlantic is evidenced by this remark, but in the United States students were freer to differ with their professors and still obtain jobs at the many new universities and colleges that were being founded. Anyone who thought that psychoanalysis might add a dimension to his work was free to investigate it.

Freud's comment calls attention to the materialism, the consciousness of money and possessions, that he thought characterized America and Americans. This feature of the American personality and the American dream attends any discussion of the success of psychoanalysis in this country. Certainly, knowledge of one's self is a possession, and, as mentioned before, knowledge of the jargon of psychoanalysis can be conspicuously displayed. Also, characteristically, the newly rich believe that wealth can buy happiness and health and so might chance even so odd a procedure as psychoanalysis. The relationship of the materialism of a prospering middle class to psychoanalysis is receiving considerable attention currently because of the extent of interest in psychoanalytic psychiatry developing in western Europe and Japan. Psychoanalysis per se demands a kind of wealth, not always of money but rather of time and psychic energy that cannot be expected of people struggling for survival. This requisite of some form of excess recedes in importance when psychotherapeutic interventions available to the psychiatrist other than psychoanlysis are considered.

Materialism alone as an answer falls short. For one thing, a previous form of psychotherapy propounded by S. Weir Mitchell in this country in the years after the Cival War became very popular both here and in Europe. Mitchell suggested a rest cure because he believed that emotional disturbance was caused by physical exhaustion of one kind or another. The cure consisted of the patient's going to bed for a considerable period of time under the supervision of a nurse with no visitors, no reading, and no writing. In fact, the only activity that Mitchell encouraged was the consumption of large quantities of rich food. In his book *Hints for the Overworked*, Mitchell comments with some concern on how few people could afford this cure, and he mentions the bitterness aroused because this hope of relieving emotional disturbance was open only to those who were wealthy.[8] It seems that any active individualized psychiatric treatment has always been expensive and has led to social concern and a resulting guilt in the psychiatrist, who is faced with a conflict between his social conscience and the form of therapy he practices.

Another social factor is difficult to assess, but it undoubtedly had some bearing on the differing receptions of psychoanalysis in Europe and in the United States. Anti-Semitism in parts of Europe at that time was strong, and it cannot be denied that many of the early followers of psychoanalysis were Jews. It is well known that Freud, in 1910, insisted on Jung's being made president of the International Psychoanalytic Association at least partially because he wished to dispel the idea that it was an all-Jewish organization. This is not to say that there was no anti-Semitism in this country, but it does seem that parochial Americans saw psychoanalysis more as European, which gave it status, than as Jewish.

The third factor under consideration, the intellectual positions in psychiatry and academic psychology in the United States at the time that Freud's work was introduced, has been carefully considered by Donald Fleming. Fleming argues convincingly that although William James' endeavor to vindicate the role of introspection and consciousness in psychology went into realms of religiosity and metaphysics that were not congenial to Freud, James nevertheless prepared the way for psychoanalysis. He further argues that when J. B. Watson and the behaviorists displaced James with a doctrine that confined attention only to the overt behavior of the organism and eschewed introspection as a psychological technique, an intellectual vacuum was created for many workers which was filled by psychoanalysis. Fleming points out that Freudian psychiatry, with the most searching form of introspection ever practiced, took up the slack to precisely the degree that the experimental psychologists and other scientists forswore introspection.[9]

In medicine, overlapping in time with these developments in psychology, was the already mentioned increasing dissatisfaction with neurological psychiatry. During the latter half of the nine-teenth century, Virchowian pathology, which taught that the ana-tomical seat or locus of any disturbance including the functional could and would be discovered by the skilled anatomist, was pre-eminent. This development is traced by Fleming to the experience in warfare—the Civil War in this country and the Franco-Prussian War in Europe—where wounds of the head demonstrated the rela-tionship between nerve fiber connections and thought disturbances. These observations, until the turn of the century, led to a full triumph in psychiatry for the neurologists, best exemplified by a quote from the most famous alienist of his time, Dr. John Gray: "The mind can *not* become diseased, only the body. In all so-called mental derangement there must be an anatomical lesion of the brain. An insane man had either been physically ill or he was not insane." The increasing dissatisfaction with so narrow a view won and kept important adherents for psychoanalysis. But the overpowering nature of this hope for anatomical precision has never lessened for many physicians, and their suspicion of psychiatry, because it is immeasurable in the laboratory, interferes with the standing of the psychiatric profession in medicine. Ironically, Freud from the time of his biological training with Brucke, an originator of the "physi-calist" school, was as zealous an adherent as any, and he never re-ceded in principle from his original position that a neurological substrate for psychiatry could be established.[10]

Given the multiple factors that may have played a part in the acceptance of psychoanalytic psychiatry in this country, it might be assumed that the implicit values of psychoanalysis would be consonant with some of these forces. Surprisingly, this does not seem to be the case. Any investigation of the value system of psy-choanalysis—the way of thinking or the structure of beliefs—reveals little in common with much of American culture. The entire implicit and explicit value system of psychoanalysis has never been thor-oughly delineated, but we will touch on a few values that seem to conflict with the culture and especially with the general value system of the medical profession, of which, after all, psychiatry is a subdivision. These differences in values may explain something about the separation of psychiatry from medicine, and why a psy-chiatric referral has unpleasant moral and social connotations.

Psychoanalytic psychiatry is, if it is nothing else, introspective and devoted to the proposition that insight—greater emotional and intellectual understanding of self—is good. A very fair percentage of the population is otherwise convinced, believing that what you don't know won't hurt you. In medicine especially there is a tradition that the patient should be kept uninformed for his own best interests.

In no area has there been more conflict between the culture and psychiatrists than on the topic of candor about sex. The controversial libido theory, which outlined a broad definition of sexuality, led the earlier psychoanalysts to be seen as libertines and the modern ones as conformists who subscribe to middle-class morality. In general, the rejection by psychoanalysis of morality in favor of a system of thought that considers what "fits," what "makes sense" for a person rather than what is absolutely "right" or "wrong" has led to misunderstanding. The psychoanalytic idea includes the relationship of the person to himself and to his culture. When it includes the culture it imposes limitations on absolute individual freedom, and in that sense it is conformist. But in its emphasis on the person's relationship with himself, it takes individual release and gratification into account, and in that sense it is opposed to absolute morality.

Probably this dependence on morality and conscience accounts more than anything for the unpleasant implications of a psychiatric referral or consultation. Right and wrong may be translated into strong and weak as well as good and bad. Here the ethic embodied in concepts of strength and virtue is misapplied. Awareness of emotional difficulty irrationally becomes synonymous with giving in to and acting on the anxieties and passions of childhood mentioned by Erikson, which are closer to and symbolic of the repressed biological urges.

The psychoanalytic psychiatrist also insists on a primitive instinctual unconscious, where the law of the jungle holds sway, as a biological given in each person. Many segments of the population find such a belief antithetical. They wish to believe that man can become "good" in thought as well as deed. They feel that the psychiatrist, in his insistence on this instinctual life, is looking for what is "bad," and that he overemphasizes that part of human personality.

The rejection of instinctual life has a counterpart in the response of many people to the insistence of psychoanalysis on the reality of conflict. The belief that a mature identity develops through the opposition of intense feelings, that one cannot love without hate and that such conflicts continue in various forms throughout life is abhorrent for many people. This belief carries with it, moreover, an insistence on the necessity of individual choice. A person chooses what he does with some kind of awareness that other possibilities, no matter how painful or shameful, are open. Many people think that it is easier to adjust if doubts and uncertainty are denied. Psychoanalytic psychiatry is well aware that life from the moment of birth changes and narrows the sequence of choices open to each individual, but it insists that some choice remains. This belief that conflict is forever part of life sadly cannot be fitted together with Thoreau's idyll of contentment and tranquility, so treasured by Americans.

One other way of thinking essential to him separates the psychiatrist from other doctors. The other branches of medicine make a diagnosis by exclusion. That is, a doctor will list the most likely and often the most serious diagnostic possibilities, then the next most likely, and so on. He will carry out the tests and procedures necessary to prove or disprove each possibility until his list is exhausted or a diagnosis is made. The psychiatrist thinks oppositely. To make a diagnosis he wishes to know more and more, and each piece must fit with the others. A diagnosis is made by inclusion: what the patient says now must be fitted together with what the patient said before, or a diagnosis is not possible. The psychiatrist's method of diagnosis represents a difference in thinking which can become an important difficulty in his communicating with the other medical specialties, as well as with the general public.[11]

How do these differences in value systems affect the individual psychiatrist? In general, because of both his experiences with patients and his own psychoanalysis, the psychoanalytic psychiatrist accepts the values of psychoanalysis. But this variance of the psychoanalytic values with those of the larger culture, and the stance of psychoanalytic psychiatry in medicine and in the social sciences simultaneously, makes professional life complex for him. As a result, the psychoanalytic psychiatrist is usually a teacher and a proselytizer.* The desire to teach stems from several sources. Spending hour after hour in an intense relationship with individual patients

* A recent paper surveying the psychoanalysts and trainees of the Boston Psychoanalytic Society and Institute, Inc. found that over 90 per cent of its members spent part of their time, and held teaching appointments, in medical schools, schools of social work, hospitals, social agencies, universities, and federal organizations (Levin, Sidney and Joseph J. Michaels, "The Participation of Psycho-analysts in the Medical Institutions of Boston," *The International Journal of Psycho-analysis*, XLII [1961], 271–283).

is a hard and passive occupation. The activity of teaching or hospital work provides a welcome respite. Moreover, the psychoanalytic psychiatrist traditionally believes that he has a special and deep understanding of the human animal that would be of great value to other professions if correctly understood and applied. The psychoanalytic psychiatrist tries not only to demonstrate new facts, but also to teach that well-known ideas and objects can be looked at in a new way, changing the appreciation and perception of them.[12] Such a change requires a change in forms and modes of thinking. Teaching of this kind is extremely subtle and demands a high level of communication which can easily be disrupted by objections raised because of the differences in values.

There is another reason why his teaching is so important to the psychoanalytic psychiatrist: he suffers from a degree of dissatisfaction because he can treat only a few people at a time and at great expense to the patients. The psychoanalytic psychiatrist rationalizes in part by seeing each case treated in depth as a form of research which can never be repeated as no two people are identical. But in reality he moves out of his office and into situations which offer a broader social scope for psychoanalytic concepts. There is precedent for this. It is not that the individual psychiatrist is guilt-stricken because he cannot heal the mentally ill of the world. Freud stated firmly that it was not the actual patients analyzed but the influence of psychoanalysis as a system of thought that would affect the world. The psychiatrist, recognizing the positive contributions he makes to individuals as a therapist, also recognizes the need to broaden the base of his work. This need impels him to take a greater share of the responsibility for solving the communication problem in teaching than do other teachers, and to try to do more teaching than do the practitioners of any other branch of medicine.

The problem of the individual practitioner reflects but is not identical with the problem of the profession. The individual psychiatrist knows that he wants to teach, but he has to struggle to find or to open avenues that will allow teaching. Although no one person can speak for the profession, it is safe to assume that psychoanalytic psychiatry feels that it has much more to contribute to medicine and other disciplines than it has yet been permitted. It also seems fair to say that the problems of communication outlined above have made psychiatrists aware of difficulties that have to be surmounted and of limitations that may have to be accepted. But at the same time that psychiatrists are searching for ways to teach more and better, they have to contend with the extremely serious problem of overpopularization. This fact of having succeeded too well has almost fulfilled Freud's old fear of the vulgarization of psychoanalysis.[13] More important is the possibility of disillusion with psychoanalytic psychiatry resulting from excessive hopes—disillusion that could produce a negative reaction in the very areas where it has not reached its full potential. To maintain appropriate scientific growth and still protect itself as a profession is indeed a dilemma for psychiatry.

The psychoanalytic psychiatrist today is called upon in every organized attempt at the rectification of social difficulties. He is asked to work with children's courts, criminal courts, domestic relations courts, prisons and reformatories, and to consult with social agencies, churches and educational institutions of every level from nursery school to graduate school. He is increasingly asked by industry for help with personnel problems and with the allocation of men to appropriate tasks and work loads. Sometimes his aid is sought on larger issues of national and international import, and he participates today in many federal organizations. This list does not yet touch on his prime function as a physician and part of the medical profession. He shares here the work on medical and surgical wards and the specialty services with adults and children in every outpatient clinic, and especially in institutions devoted to chronic disabling impairments. Not yet mentioned are his important duties as a teacher and administrator in medical schools and general hospitals. And last, but far from least, are the needs for his services in the psychiatric hospitals, in the psychiatric outpatient departments, in the psychoanalytic institutes, in the supervision and training of psychiatric residents, and in the actual clinical practice of psychiatry. Even if it were agreed that psychiatry is capable of attempting all of these duties, certainly the number of well-trained psychiatrists necessary to answer all the calls is impossible to supply.[14]

An excellent example of what is being discussed has occurred in the field of college mental health. Until well after World War II there were few, if any, psychiatrists attached to college health services. About 1950 several colleges added psychiatrists, and limited psychiatric attention became a service covered by the annual college health fee. Then college after college added psychiatrists, and they soon found themselves constantly increasing the services offered as the demand grew. As college psychiatrists surveyed their referrals, they recognized that many of them represented an abdication of responsibility by professors, administrators, tutors and deans. On the other hand, the college authorities found themselves erring on the side of overreferral because they did not wish to make mistakes with serious consequences to the student. But the result was that too often a psychiatric referral became a way out when a student presented a knotty problem.

This is a classic instance of the sort of problem that psychiatry faces everywhere. The psychiatrist was glad to be in the college and felt he had just begun to do an important job. Furthermore, there were innumerable colleges which had not yet recognized the importance of a psychiatrist as part of the college health team. Yet, almost before he had begun, he found it necessary to ask the college to slow down its demands for his services, and found himself faced with the enormous task of teaching the college authorities when best to ask for these services. The college authorities, furthermore, quite appropriately wanted advice and even training in how to handle those cases that remained with them. And the psychiatrist himself was having to learn to apply his techniques to the college student—a relatively new kind of patient for him—a task which requires modification and relearning. This description is not intended to elicit sympathy for the poor, put-upon psychiatrist, but to point out the extent of the problem. The fact is that psychoanalysis and its discoveries are willy-nilly a social force. The professional dilemma of the psychiatrist represents a social dilemma of our culture.

The already mentioned relationship of psychiatry to medicine is part of this problem. When psychoanalytic psychiatry was less well accepted by medicine fifty years ago, it was more concerned, as mentioned earlier, with the biological basis of human behavior as represented by an unconscious dominated by inborn desires or instincts. Freud's physicalist belief lent a certain support to the idea that a true "cure" for mental illness could be effected. Psychoanalysis continues to be a theory that centers on motivation in human behavior with drives rooted in the biology of the organism. However, without minimizing biological underpinnings, psychoanalytic theory has concerned itself more and more with the relationships and impact of the social structure on the developing organism. This shift in emphasis to concerns that seems more social-psychological and sociological has been disillusioning to many physicians. Certainly, when dealing with forces of such magnitude, the possibility of a cure for emotional disturbance seems remote. There are enough remnants of Virchowian pathology extant to cause much of the medical profession to look to someone other than the psychoanalytic psychiatrist. Let it be clear that these psychiatrists recognize psycho-pharmacological, endocrinological and neurophysiological research as essential. Several psychoanalytic psychiatrists are in the fore-front in such research. Nevertheless, attention should be called to the possibilities in medicine for irrational disillusion and desertion of what psychoanalytic psychiatry can offer in order to chase a false promise. In the social sciences the trend has, as could be expected, gone in the opposite direction. Here the biological base of psycho-analytic psychiatry represents the lack of hope for a cure, and social scientists tend to be infatuated with the environmentalists or so-called neo-Freudians.

This dichotomy between biological drives and social strivings seems an unnecessary one. Current psychoanalytic theory says that the variations on the great themes are infinite and specific to a time, place and person. The same basic underlying conflict or motive can be expressed in different ways, the way determined exclusively by the society and culture.

It is the awareness of the uniqueness of the individual that is the essence of psychotherapy. Too little has been said about therapy, but, whatever his aspirations, it is as a therapist that the psychiatrist is a physician. Considering the difficulties, good therapists appear to have a fair measure of success. But there is a great deal of bad psychiatric training and bad therapy. As the tenets of good training are so hard to define, inadequate or insufficient training is accepted as it is nowhere else in medicine. In this fact lies another possibility for the proliferation of disappointment and disillusion.

An interest in psychoanalytic psychiatry is awakening in Japan and in parts of Europe. The increased flexibility of psychoanalytic theory and the falseness of the culture-biology dichotomy outlined above indicate that differences in the forms in which problems appear are not differences in underlying motive, as Bronislaw Mali-nowski would have assumed. But the therapist and the theorist must be trained to understand that the person's feelings are most bound up with those very differences in presentation of the prob-lem that are culturally determined. With this understanding there should be no barriers to psychoanalytic psychiatry's becoming a truly international institution. To avoid a repetition on a grand scale of the problems attendant on growth exemplified by what has happened in American colleges, careful thought should be given to the dilemma of the psychoanalytic psychiatrist in this country and to the reactions to psychoanalytic concepts as a social force. Psychoanalytic theory does aspire to become a total psychological system including cognitive and adaptive considerations as well as motivational ones. Disappointment can discredit these aspirations before they are realized. Psychiatry is in need of a professional definition that will permit it needed scope but will allow for its limitations.

REFERENCES

1. Erikson, Erik H. *Young Man Luther.* New York: W. W. Norton, 1958.

2. Oberndorf, Clarence P. *A History of Psychoanalysis in America.* New York: Grune and Stratton, 1953.

3. White, William A. "Forty Years of Psychiatry," Nervous and Mental Disease Monograph Series, New York, 1933.

4. Oberndorf, C. P. *The Psychiatric Novels of Oliver Wendell Holmes.* New York: Columbia University Press, 1945.

5. Oberndorf, *A History of Psychoanalysis in America.*

6. Erikson, Erik H. *Identity and the Life Cycle.* Psychological Issues, No. 1. New York: International Universities Press, 1956.

7. Freud, Sigmund. *The Origins of Psychoanalysis.* Edited by Marie Bonaparte, Anna Freud and Ernest Kris. London: Imago Publishing Co., 1950.

8. Rein, David N. S. *Weir Mitchell as a Psychiatric Novelist.* New York: International Universities Press, 1952.

9. Fleming, Donald. "Freud in America." Presented at conference of the Psychiatric Service, Beth Israel Hospital, Boston, Mass., 1962.

10. Freud, Sigmund. *History of the Psychoanalytic Movement.* London: Imago Publishing Co., 1946.

11. Bibring, Grete L. "Medicine and Psychiatry." Discussion at conference of the Psychiatric Service, Beth Israel Hospital, Boston, Mass., 1959.

12. Kris, Ernest. *Psychoanalytic Exploration in Art.* New York: International Universities Press, 1952.

13. Freud, *History of the Psychoanalytic Movement.*

14. Kubie, Lawrence S. "Need for a New Subdiscipline in the Medical Profession," *Archives of Neurology and Psychiatry,* 78 (September, 1957), 283–293.

WILLIAM ALONSO

Cities and City Planners

THE CITY planning profession, like most adolescents, is self-conscious. It worries about its appearance, it strikes poses, it adopts and discards heroes, it revolts against its parents while depending on them. It tries, in short, to establish its own identity. This identity is the product of its intellectual ancestry and of its early development, of its current situation and, perhaps to a greater extent than other professions, of the appearances and realities of the object of its concern, which is the city. It is a profession in rapid change, full of contradictions and given to excesses. Such a subject cannot be portrayed at rest and separately from its object, and so we will consider some of the forces that have made it what it is, but principally we will consider some of the issues that confront it and how it is coping with them, for it is in action that the importance and the weaknesses of the profession can be seen.

City planning in the United States stems from several roots, of which the earliest is architectural. The 1893 Columbian Exposition in Chicago dazzled Americans with the classic magnificence of the fairgrounds, and many visitors returned to their communities eager to ennoble their appearance in a movement called City Beautiful. The common manifestation of this movement was a superficial playing with boulevards, waterfronts and neoclassical architecture, but some of the writings of the period show a sensitive awareness of the society and the economy to be housed in this splendid container. The City Beautiful faded gradually out of American planning. Aesthetic concern for three-dimensional design returned with vigor only after World War II, and then largely as a result of European influences such as the Congrès International de l'Architecture Moderne (CIAM), of which Le Corbusier was the principal figure. However, those who now practice in this vein owe their first allegiance to architecture rather than to city planning, and they often call themselves urban designers.

Other seminal influences are harder to differentiate from one another. The muckrakers and other early reformers focused interest on the housing of workers, considering finances, family life and social organization as well as design. The development of urban sociology, mostly in Chicago in the 1920's and 1930's, served to document the conditions of urban living and shifted attention from the aesthetic of urban form to an analytic geography concerned with the social and economic landscape of the city. The New Deal provided funds and a national program for reform, emphasizing slum clearance and public housing. The naive social darwinism popularized by Herbert Spencer had held that poverty and slum conditions were the just deserts of the inferior and necessary conditions for social progress. It now became an article of faith that slums and bad housing were the cause of ill health, criminality, illegitimacy and other social evils. Consequently there was as much effort directed to tearing down slums as to providing new housing for those displaced. Today this seems a gallant charge against windmills. We have learned, for instance, that the slum is often a tightly knit social fabric that provides security and gradual acculturation to urban life, and that moving its inhabitants to antiseptic piles of brick can be cruel. We have learned that slums are often manifestions of racial as well as of class inequality, but we have not learned much about solving this thornier problem. This does not mean that nothing need be done about slums, but that the brave solutions that had seemed so evident have proved inadequate, and that learning advances slowly and painfully.

Advocates of city planning, as most urban reformers, were deeply suspicious of corrupt municipal governments, and they advocated the use of appointed commissions that could keep their hands clean of the filth of politics. From the 1920's to World War II untold planning commissions were organized, and each would hire a planner to produce a Master Plan. This consisted of proposals for parkways, a waterfront improvement, a new city hall and other items, and, always, a zoning ordinance. Public works, for obvious reasons, could often be sold by the commission to the city government. The zoning ordinance, stating what land could be used for what purposes, was often adopted, but it tended to degenerate. Seldom prepared with sufficient understanding of structural relationships, its administration consisted of a joyful or reluctant granting of variances and

171

exceptions, so that it soon became riddled with holes. The planning commission in a social sense, and the zoning ordinance in a real estate sense, represented middle and upper class values and were too often holding operations against the forces of change. Since zoning combined conservatism with the planning advocated by the progressives, it often enjoyed considerable support together with indifferent success.

Faith that technical analysis is superior to the political process as a means of arriving at decisions has been another fountainhead of planning, at least since Hoover's 1920's. Techniques have improved by leaps and bounds in recent years in such areas as the estimation of the demand for housing, offices and highways and the calculation of the impact of particular measures. Many questions have thus been validly removed from the politician to the analyst, and this has given strength to the apolitical view of planning.

But there is a strong counter-current, and in many cases planning is moving closer to politics with the realization that what is needed is not so much a plan as a planning process. That is to say, the Master Plan, reflecting its architectural ancestry, presented a picture of an ideal final stage, much as the plans for a building represent the completed building, and the only question was how to carry it out. Today it is clear that in the nature of things every plan is tentative, both because information is imperfect and because there is no final stage: there is always a future beyond the stage projected. What is needed is continuing planning, which produces every year a plan for the next few years, and every few years a plan for the next two or three decades, so that the next steps and the distant goals are known at all times. With this concept, plans have become the companions of policy and the planner has moved inside government into a position similar to that of a general staff in an army. When plans are statements of policies the emphasis shifts from the solution of particular problems through particular projects to a view of the city as a complicated system to be guided as well as corrected.

These are the architectural, the reformist and the technocratic roots of planning. Other influences might be mentioned, such as the utopian movements with their long and colorful history, or the paradoxical importance of the romantic anti-urban attitudes in England and America, of which Lewis Mumford is a representative. There is also the British version of city planning, which is called town planning, and the continental versions, which are often called urbanism.

Suffice it to say that they are closer to physical design and further from the social sciences than is American city planning.

Training for the profession is offered in the United States and Canada at some three dozen accredited schools of planning, almost all offering postgraduate programs only, two to three years long and leading to the degree of Master of City Planning. People are attracted into the profession from many fields. Students from an architectural background are now only a modest plurality. Most of the others come from liberal arts and the social sciences, some from law and the natural sciences. Their motives for entering planning are mixed. Because of the great shortage of planners, good wages and rapid promotion are certain to attract people. But altruistic motives are also important: a desire to improve our environment, to help make the good life possible in cities. Some people, although very few now, are dedicated to particular ideologies, from New Deal liberalism to several forms of socialism. The majority are apparently not interested in political ideas. Rather they feel good will toward their fellow man and, in a general way, they wish to improve his lot.

In recent years doctoral programs have gained in importance. These are offered by half a dozen universities, and they direct their training to research and teaching rather than to professional practice. Their development has raised again the question of whether the field has a valid body of knowledge or of expertness. No clear answer emerges. Certain topics interest planners principally, and others fall within traditional academic disciplines. Perhaps the answer is that the planner brings a point of view, an area of concern or a set of questions that he must answer as best he can because of the urgent problems of cities. The approach is eclectic in that it takes much from others, but the pressure of responsibility for action rather than of knowledge for its own sake forces a shifting synthesis which, whatever its intelectual inadequacies, goes to the issues and does not trouble itself with the territorial rights that tradition has established between, let us say, economics and geography. Had city planning the self-confidence, it might paraphrase the well-known definition that mathematics is what mathematicians do.

The situation of planners in this respect is very similar to that of medicine some time ago. Medicine is also a goal-oriented activity that makes use of other academic fields such as chemistry and biology. It uses their tools and findings and raises questions which may be explored by people in the field itself or in related fields. In the same way, in recent years, planning has produced a great deal

173

of research activity under a variety of labels, including that of planning. There has resulted an explosion of knowledge and, unfortunately, a greater flood of literature with which no one person can hope to keep up, leading to the paradox of specialization in a profession that a decade ago prided itself in producing generalists in an age of specialists.

The naming of the planning association, which was founded in 1917, stimulated a revealing debate in choosing between American Institute of Planners or American Institute of Planning. The issue at stake was whether the organization should represent the activity of planning, in which anyone can participate by thinking intelligently about the future, or whether it should represent a particular body of men who labeled themselves city planners. The second alternative was chosen, and today the American Institute of Planners follows a policy of professional closure. It has persuaded agencies to write into their job specifications educational and experience requirements, and it has been discussing the establishment of registration examinations. The British Town Planning Institute, unconcerned with the semantics of its name, has had such examinations for years.

This is the profession that is trying to meet the challenge of urban change. By and large, it is right and sensible to train people to deal with urban problems and to permit them to advise the public and the authorities on these matters. It is true that our knowledge of urban phenomena is rudimentary, comparable perhaps to the knowledge of the human body at the time of Harvey's discovery of the circulation of blood. That is to say, we know a great deal, not nearly enough and much of it wrong. Still, the problems are there and decisions must be made. The advice of a good planner is probably the best available, but it is likely that in ten or fifteen years our understanding will have advanced through research and experience to where the advice of the average planner will be better than that of the best today, just as today's planners are better than those of one or two decades ago.

Knowledge is inadequate and solutions shallow, and to improve this situation it is right to be impatient with the profession. It has attracted as yet relatively few first-rate minds, and these must be prodded to produce their best. The apostolic zeal of the aesthetic and reformist heritages and many years of frustration still manifest themselves in a crusading attitude of yea-saying and a distrust of criticism. City planners are more influential than ever before, and there is a danger that power may corrupt, that mistakes will be repeated and justified rather than teach how things may be better done. Success can too easily be measured by activity and expenditure.

Perhaps these dangers to the profession can best be made clear by considering the urban situation today and by showing the inadequacy of the more popular solutions. A modern city is the most complex social and economic system that has ever existed, and, to keep from getting lost, we will focus on the interplay between size and structure of cities as the background for current planning practice.

When things change in size, they tend to change in structure. A grown man is not, at least physically, merely a very large baby. Science fiction to the contrary, being a fly implies being neither bigger nor smaller than the usual size of flies. A mutant the size of a freight car is impossible: it could not fly, its legs would buckle if it tried to walk, and, anyway, it would die of asphyxiation, since its breathing mechanism can serve only bodies a fraction of an inch in diameter. Size and structure depend upon each other. The critical relation between size and structure applies as well to social organisms such as nations and cities. But while the relation is easily accepted by most people in the biological realm, for some reason we seem to have difficulty in understanding it in the social realm, and this often leads to trouble. The fact is that, with economic development, cities and countries tend to grow, and as their size increases, their structure changes.

Looking at it from the other side, a change in structure tends to demand a change in size. Economic development is a continuing change in the structure of a society. With economic development the size of cities has changed. In the eighteenth century, a city of a few tens of thousands was a large and important city, and a few hundred thousands made a very large city in the nineteenth. In the twentieth century we have seen the city of a few millions emerge as the dominant form. Of course, this many people simply do not fit into the municipal boundaries which had been established for the earlier, smaller cities. The population has spilled over, and the urban mass covers a number of municipal units, in many cases in the United States straddling two and even three states. This urban mass, which we call by the awkward names of metropolitan area or metropolis, is the true city of today. We still refer to parts of the metropolis as "cities" or "towns," and these parts maintain their existence as municipal corporations, but they are no longer true cities in the sense of a geographic community of work and home. The facts have changed, but our thinking—much less our system of government—has not kept up with them.

But the metropolis is no mere large-scale model of the older city any more than the *Queen Mary* is a large-scale model of the *Santa María*. It is well known that economic development has brought specialization to the work of men. It has also brought about the specialization of space for men's activities. Work, home, shopping and recreation are more separated than they have ever been. Vast areas of homes specialize by race, income, family, size, age and tastes of residents. Shops cluster and separate according to price, style, variety and type of goods offered, and according to whether they are reached on foot, by car or by mass transit. Factories and offices gather and separate in complicated rhythms of their own. The great variety of indoor and outdoor amusements distribute themselves in this space according to the markets they serve.

Those who disparage the monotony of our metropolitan areas see only half the picture. There are in fact more things under the sun than there used to be, but these things are usually grouped together rather than mixed. There is therefore little variety in any one place, although there is more variety to the whole. Curiously, those who complain of monotony often also complain of the chaos of our urban areas. This apparent contradiction disappears if we think of these critics as on foot in the first instance and in a car in the second. If one is walking, the immediate area seems large and unchanging. But if one is in a car, one travels much faster and sees more things in a short time, and then the great variety of the city may become bewildering.

Bewildering, yes; but is it chaos? Chaos is only the absence of order, and order is nothing but the understanding of structure. There can be no question that our metropolitan areas have a structure, and that serious students of cities understand it fairly well, know how it got to be that way, and how it is likely to develop. The chaos of which the critics complain, then, refers not to the lack of structure but to the difficulty of perceiving it; and the problem is not one of restructuring but one of making understanding easier. A person moving through a city must be given visual clues and explanations of where he is and where he is going, of what these places are and of how they are related to each other. Many suburban residential areas should be given a more intense focus and clearer edges. Adjacent areas, such as the financial and the commercial in most downtowns, should be differentiated and articulated. People must be given a clearer image of the structure of urban areas while preserving variety and surprise within the elements of that structure. This is a very recent way of looking at urban design, but it should have considerable impact, taking the aesthetics of city planning beyond the architectural consideration of groups of buildings to the treatment of urban form as such.

The bigger pieces making up the mosaic of the metropolitan structure have also been criticized on grounds other than aesthetic. That side of sociology that used to be called social philosophy has attacked the social monotony of the suburbs, and most planners have concurred. The organization man, the member of the lonely crowd, seeks status in the endless urban sprawl by living in a house with a picture window which is usually cracked. These critics deplore the anonymity, the dullness, the conformism and the shallowness of suburban living, and they point out how short the suburbs fall of that pastoral ideal which they question in the first instance. Children brought up in this synthetic environment know nothing of the real world outside, meet only children of families exactly like their own, and grow up to be intolerant, uninteresting, ignorant conformists. The meeting place for men is the town dump, which is lacking in dignity. The women lead lives of intolerable loneliness and boredom or of frantic activity as charwomen, chairwomen, nursemaids, or hostesses, according to whom one reads.

These portraits or caricatures have proliferated recently. Some of the strokes in these portraits may be questioned, such as the relative ranges of experience of central city and suburban children, but the distaste of the authors for this suburban way of life is what is important. These critics are not just reporting on a way of life: they are judging it. By the skillful use of language they are criticizing and trying to change the tastes of their readers to have them see the suburban way of life in a new and most unflattering light. The fact, the evidence shows, is that this way of life is what most Americans want, that they are getting it and that they feel, and are supported by any reasonable comparison, that they never had it so good. Whether these people are instances of ensnared *Boobus americanus* or latter-day Candides happily tending their gardens depends on one's viewpoint. In my opinion, they are achieving their ideal, however imperfectly. Various city planners have proposed alternative modes of considerable merit and ingenuity, but their schemes have had only local and partial success. If there is to be any fundamental change, it will have to be by an extraordinary innovation in the field of taste, offering an alternative type of housing and manner of living which is as deeply rooted in the traditions and feelings of our society as is the present suburban house. What this alternative may be, if there is one, we will not know until it succeeds.

The changes in size, and therefore in structure, of cities have affected their centers as well as their edges. While the suburbs have continued to grow very fast, virtually every central city has lost population in the last decade. This has brought about a strange alliance between the intellectual—usually liberal—critics of the suburbs and those businessmen—usually conservative—with an interest in central city real estate. Their combined argument runs: the city (the central city is meant) is dying; the city is the focus of our economy and the center of our culture; therefore, unless something is done, our economy is endangered and our culture is weakened. This, of course, is nonesense. The city today is the metropolitan area, and it is growing lustily. As it grows it is developing and changing in structure, redistributing people and activities. What is in fact happening is that, as a result of this redistribution, businesses and people are shifting out from the center. This hurts some downtown businesses, though it benefits business at other locations, where new centers are forming. Like all transitions, it has its costs and dangers, but to argue that it imperils the economy as a whole would be like arguing that the development of the automobile hurt the horseshoe and buggywhip industries, and that therefore it imperiled the economy. On the cultural side as well, the argument is weak. People can move about very rapidly (this is what has made the suburbs possible), and can attend lectures, concerts, museums or the theater regardless of where they live. It may be that the suburbanite prefers to watch television, but that is a fundamental problem of our culture's tastes and attitudes, not of geographic location. If he were somehow dragged back, kicking and screaming, to the central city, once he quieted down a bit he would presumably turn on his television set.

In the past few years there has been a great deal of effort to put new life into the central cities, spearheaded by the federal Urban Renewal Program and generally endorsed by city planners. This program has much good in it, but the obsolete fractioning of our metropolitan areas into many different tax units has perverted local motives and has resulted in many futile and very expensive projects.

Suppose, for instance, that a central city has a slum area. It is a well-documented fact that slum areas cost a city, in terms of police and fire protection, welfare payments, schools and other expenses, much more than they pay in taxes. On the other hand, an area of wealthy residents in apartments pays into the city much more than it takes out in municipal services. A city is, in legal terms, a municipal corporation, and like any other corporation it will be anxious to exchange a losing line for a profitable one. In other words, any municipality will gladly trade its poor for some other municipality's rich.

Under the Urban Renewal Program, a city may do just that. It may acquire a slum area under eminent domain, clear it of its buildings and sell it to a developer. No one today can afford to build for the poor without subsidy. On expensive central land it is nearly impossible to build at all except for the rich, and even that must be done at high density by means of apartment towers. On central land, the city can be quite certain that it is exchanging the poor slum-dwellers for wealthy apartment-dwellers. The cost of this operation to the city is one third of the difference between what it paid for the area to its previous owners and what the developer pays the city for it. The federal government pays the other two thirds. The profits to the city will be the increased tax revenue resulting from newer and more expensive property plus the savings in city services. This is likely to prove profitable to the municipal corporation. For instance, one large recent project cleared an area where the average income of families was $234 per month and built there apartments with an average rent of $200 per month. Only families with a monthly income of $1000 or more would normally pay such rents.

But if this type of renewal eliminates slums in an area and improves municipal finances, what is wrong with it? The answer is simple. One must look not at areas but at people; not at the finances of one tax unit but at the finances of the metropolitan area. The poor who lived in the slum have simply moved elsewhere, and the municipality hopes that they have moved to some nearby municipality, which will then be obliged to contend with their money-losing presence. Usually, the poor not only receive no direct benefit, but the clearing of the slum may reduce the housing supply for their income group, making higher rents and more crowding likely in the low-rent housing market. The high-income groups could have had housing, new or old, elsewhere, probably in the suburbs. What has happened is that the various tax units

WILLIAM ALONSO

in the metropolitan area are playing an expensive game of musical chairs with the poor and the rich for tax dollars. The poor that one city has got rid of go to another city; the expensive housing that one city has gained has been gained at the expense of another city, and there is no net gain for the metropolitan area.

The federal government is playing an equivocal role with respect to metropolitan structure. With its right hand, the Urban Renewal Program, it is trying to breathe new life into the centers of metropolitan areas, counter to the ongoing structural trends. With its left, however, it is reinforcing these trends and weakening the center. It does this with its F.H.A. mortgage insurance policies and its income tax policies, which permit the homeowner to deduct the interest on his mortgage and the property tax on his home, while the renter can deduct no part of his rent. This makes owning much more attractive financially than renting and provides a powerful extra push to the suburbs. Suburbanization is the basic trend of large cities, deeply rooted in taste and the economics of land. It would take government intervention and controls of a different order of magnitude than the current Urban Renewal Program to reverse these trends, even without contradictory policies.

Meanwhile, preserving the fiction that the metropolis is composed of independent parts makes the process of growth more painful for the suburbs as well as for the center. While central cities worry because they are losing the middle and upper classes and are left only with the poor, who tend to be minorities such as Negroes, Puerto Ricans, or Mexicans, the suburbs pretend that these poor are not *their* poor, and that the suburban population is not made up of stockbrokers, professionals and insurance men but rather of homesteaders and Jeffersonian farmers conducting their affairs in a small, self-contained community not affected by the problems in the central cities. But the suburbs have their problems too, both social and financial. Because they are composed of families with children, one third to one half of their population is in the public schools; because they are absorbing most of the population growth of the nation, they need new streets, sewers and other facilities; and much of their energy is spent in anxious battle to keep out people with incomes lower than their own as well as others who would not "fit." Every part of the metropolis is encouraged to beggar its neighbor, and the egoism and short-sightedness of fictional independence serve only to create new problems.

Business and industry as well as population are also being redis-

180

tributed, and Urban Renewal is also trying to preserve these activities in the central city. But again, the geographic fragmentation of an obsolete governmental structure tends to distort and pervert the renewal decisions. A recent federal publication, trying to show that the renewal of commercial and industrial areas makes economic sense, presented approvingly the case of a central city in which renewal had resulted in $180,000,000 of new construction and an increase of $200,000 in yearly property taxes to the city. This makes no economic sense to me: the increased tax revenue is only about one tenth of 1 per cent of the total investment, not big enough to be a justifying factor. Furthermore, from the point of view of the private investor, taxes are an expense, not a profit. When we look at the public share of the investment we can understand what has happened. The federal government contributed $8,000,000 and the city, $4,000,000. The new taxes represent 5 per cent on the city's investment. This is a reasonable return on the city's investment of $4,000,000; but to base the economic sense of an investment forty-five times as big on a reasonable return to the city is akin to basing the decision to have a major operation on the attractiveness of his fees to the surgeon. Such things happen, but they are not often considered desirable. They are, in fact, unethical and immoral.

The important questions are whether the total private and public investments are an efficient use of capital, profitable by ordinary business standards; and whether the total public investment to have the development take place in the central city is productive when compared with the efficiency of development elsewhere or of no development at all. This is a difficult question, but it is seldom asked by city planners, let alone answered. It may be that such an investment is wise, but we do not know that it is.

The ordinary investment criteria are not the only ones that apply in such cases. There are important qualitative changes which do not appear in any balance sheet, but which nonetheless may benefit every inhabitant of the metropolis. Without positive action the urban center may wither, and the metropolis may become a vast, amorphous, headless amoeba. A strong center is needed socially, economically and psychologically, for it is here that urban life is lived in full, and virtually all activities in the metropolitan area focus towards it. Here is the center of power, where a new enterprise may be conceived over lunch; here a woman may shop at a department store, look at expensive merchandise in exclusive shops, have dinner in a fine restaurant, and then go to the theater; here one may find a shop that specializes in stringed instruments or clothing for six-foot women, a man who can repair jade or ivory, someone who is an expert in importing from Hong Kong, an agency that can supply the names and addresses of a few thousand street railway enthusiasts or likely opponents of the death penalty. But this variety and richness is possible only because there are enough things and enough people downtown to attract more things and more people. Let the size of the downtown area drop below the necessary critical mass, and dissolution will follow. There will not be enough six-foot girls coming downtown for there to be a shop especially for them. There will not be enough lunch-time demand to keep a fine restaurant going, and if there are no restaurants, the theaters will suffer. Unless downtown is big enough, there will be no downtown. Some activities will move to the suburbs, but many will die or will never come into existence. Life will become much duller and more homogenized.

But why, if metropolitan areas are getting bigger, should the downtown area be in any danger? Once again, it is a matter of critical size. The suburbs have grown enough, and are far enough away from the old center, for there to be enough local demand to justify local department stores, lawyers and architects, fashion and furniture stores, and other services. Of course, these do not have the variety and size of their downtown equivalents, but they have grown largely at the expense of the downtown area. Industry has been shifting from railroads to trucks, and increasingly it prefers one-story buildings with ample parking, leading, of course, to suburban locations; and industry pulls related activities along with it. Even some large offices have tried moving to the suburbs, but with indifferent success.

These changes in metropolitan structure have indeed placed the downtown area in danger, for each move reduces its size and its attractiveness. But is this a short-run danger or a long-run destiny? Consider the trends that favor downtown. The employment composition of every country, as it develops, shifts increasingly to white collar jobs, and these are typically downtown jobs. Automation and rapid communication not only increase the proportion of "head" over "hand" workers; they permit their spatial separation. As physical production is automated and depersonalized, and as communications improve, managers and supervisors can send impersonal orders to a more distant production line and still be downtown for the advantages of personal contact with other decision-makers.

Therefore, although the physical production part of industry may continue to become suburban, the management of that production may become more centralized. And as our population becomes richer and better educated, it seeks the luxurious, the sophisticated and the specialized, which are the major attractions of downtown. In short, then, there are very powerful forces which in the long run will mean a resurgence of the downtown area. It will be a different downtown in that it will be a more purely distilled essence of what we have today; but it will be all the better for that.

Is Urban Renewal in the downtown area a holding operation to counteract the short-run forces which are endangering the urban center until these long-run trends establish themselves? The answer is yes and no. Urban Renewal is for the preservation of the downtown area, but it uses short-run arguments and short-run thinking. It uses subsidies to create new and glamorous buildings without asking how these buildings will be used in thirty years. For instance, most of our important metropolitan areas were founded next to water, and downtown was based on proximity to the port on the edge of the urban area. But, as the port decreases in relative importance (which it almost universally has), and the urban area increases in size, downtown tends to seek the center of the urban mass. It creeps away from the water, at a rate of perhaps one-half mile every twenty years. Are not many of today's projects in the older parts of downtown trying to recreate a center on land that is fated to be an edge? Are they not trying to bring an old center back to life, rather than being midwives to the birth of a new and more viable center?

It makes excellent sense to subsidize the center if the danger to its critical size is a temporary one and a return to health is likely in the long run. But it is less than wise to pour money into glamorous architectural groupings looking with admiration and civic pride only to the size of the capital investment, the increased tax base and the added floor space. If the urban centers are shrinking, their immediate problem is overcapacity, and adding floor space will not solve it; if rents at the center are too high, so that suburban locations are more attractive by comparison, expensive buildings, strongly assessed and paying high taxes, are unlikely to be the solution. It cannot be denied that new and well-designed buildings have a glamor that attracts businesses and customers, and that they may give the downtown area a feeling of effervescence and restore confidence. But new buildings get old very quickly.

To save the downtown area, what is needed is a downtown that works well. Many of the new downtown projects are composed mostly of free-standing buildings, handsomely set about in open space, designed as sculpture on a grandiose scale. The emphasis is put on the project as such, not on the downtown area as a part of the urban system. Not enough attention is paid to the way one element relates to another. For instance, most downtowns have evolved with buildings standing side by side, filling up the blocks, with the streets as channels between them. According to their economic strength and ability to pay rent, activities take locations on the main street, on the side streets, or on the back streets, all close to each other and dependent on each other. Most of the new developments place their buildings standing free *within* the block, and little or no provision is made for those businesses that would go on side and back streets because they cannot pay prime rents. Yet many of these smaller businesses are the lubrication and the ball bearings needed for the smooth operation of the larger businesses, and many of them, such as restaurants, bars and book and specialty stores, make downtown interesting and human. The downtown area is the brain tissue of the metropolis, a complex, evolving, and little understood organ. If it is sick, it may require surgery, but this surgery should be done with sensitive fingers, with the finest surgical instruments, and with the closest attention to what is in fact being done.

In the past half-century our cities have outgrown our concepts and our tools, and I have tried to show how the lagging understanding of the changes in kind that go with changes in size has led us to try remedies which are unsuited to the ills of our urban areas. In this sense, I have been writing mostly about the past and present. What about the future? For the past few years there has been growing professional and popular interest in the step beyond the metropolis, even though we have yet to digest the present reality. The words *megapolis* and *megalopolis* are being heard with increasing frequency, usually applied to an almost continuous string of cities running from Washington, D.C. to Boston. And once this idea is launched, similar patterns are seen emerging on the West and Gulf Coasts, in Argentina and Venezuela, in Indonesia and in Europe.

The pattern does not consist of a string of metropolitan areas standing shoulder to shoulder, fighting for space like a crowd in a subway, but of metropolitan areas in a functioning group, interacting with each other. In the same manner that economic development has made the size of the typical nation inadequate and has called for super-nations, it seems that soon—at least in historical time—urban units will go beyond the scale of the metropolis to the scale of the megapolis. And just as the metropolitan area is not made up of an accumulation of little cities complete in themselves but on a system of specialized and therefore dissimilar areas, the various metropolitan units of megapolis will specialize and become more different from each other than they are today. No one knows with any certainty what the fields of economic specialization will be, or how the social specialization which occurs in metropolitan areas will reappear at the megapolitan scale, though comparisons between Washington, New York, Boston, and other cities are quite suggestive. It does seem likely that history may continue to outpace our ability to grasp and deal with our urban problems, and that, like generals, city planners may be fated always to fight the day's battles with the outworn ideas of their last war.

But even today, at the level of metropolitan development, perhaps the ultimate question is who is to be the planner's client. Is it the commission, the mayor, the council or the voters? Is it only the residents of the city, or future residents, or those who work there but live elsewhere? Should consideration be given to the interests of the region and the nation when they run counter to the city's? When we say a plan is good and desirable, who will benefit and who wants it? I have emphasized the effects of the municipal fragmentation of urban areas. Most city planners are in favor of metropolitan government but work for a particular municipality. What is their responsibility and who is their public? Questions of goals and clients are particularly difficult for city planners, but ultimately it is these questions of ethics and responsibility that distinguish a profession from other occupations.

JOHN CONWAY

Politics as a Profession in the United States

AT A TIME when public affairs are paramount in the United States
and when the popular attitude toward politics has a new seriousness
and government itself enjoys an unprecedented prestige, there is
no certain method of channeling the energy and idealism of the
politically gifted into the political process. There is no certain way
of relating policy decisions to the representative organs of the
political machine. The outlets for political concern are, in the nature
of things, imprecise; and the ambition and decision for a political
career must involve a leap in the dark, full of uncertainty and
characterized by discontinuity, for the political institutions of the
United States in the twentieth century assume that it is still the
eighteenth century. The young man who wishes to serve his country
in a public capacity may, to the extent that his time and resources
permit him, begin in local politics, but almost invariably he will aim
at the executive or the group that advises the executive, for only
here can he be convinced that his personal sacrifices are worth the
effort. If he has already achieved a position of distinction he will in
a similar fashion direct his endeavors toward Washington if his party
is in power. If it is not he will wait on the sidelines until the opportunity is ripe. If he comes from a different class background from
that of the majority of those in executive positions, he will aim at
the executive of his labor union rather than at the executive in his
city, state capitol or Washington. If he has special training and special gifts he will concentrate on their development and wait to be
consulted or try to get into a position where it is likely that he will
be consulted.

What this young man will not do is reinforce with his gifts the
legislative elements. Because this is so, what Walter Bagehot calls

186

"a polity of discussion" is in this country weakened. At his wildest and most perverse the late Senator McCarthy did not allege that Congress was infiltrated with Communists. It was the Administration that was supposed to be populated with Marxists, for it was there, not in Congress that the country could be changed, there, not in Congress, that decisions were made. Put in that setting the myth could be convincing, and it convinced a very substantial number of well-meaning citizens. On the other hand, Rose, the Canadian Communist accused of treasonable dealings with the Soviet Union, was in fact a member of the House of Commons in Ottawa. It was to that body, as in Great Britain, that the prime minister had to explain and defend his policies and it was there that his role as leader of the country would be endorsed or brought to an end.

The lack of any organic relationship between the executive and the legislative is the crux of the problem of politics in the United States today. The problem of the expert is something new in our time. A great deal more experience will be necessary before we can assess his proper role in government. What is more serious and at the same time more comprehensible and manageable is the inevitable erosion in the part played by the representatives of the people in decision making and policy planning, that is, in the most vital national problems.

How has this difference between the prestige of a political career and its difficulties and limitations come about? Politics has emerged as a respected profession only relatively recently in the United States. In theory it was not supposed to be a profession but an avocation, the activity of the citizen when he was called upon to serve in public office but not his chief activity. Calvin Coolidge's remark that "the business of this country is business" is usually quoted ironically, but this is a mistake. By the time Coolidge became President his statement was a misreading of what had taken place since the beginning of the twentieth century. It was, however, an understandable misreading, for, leaving the Civil War aside, it was a reasonably accurate explanation of the American experience in the period between the War for Independence and the Great Depression. The congressman was a delegate of his constituents sent to Washington to express their views. This was not of course entirely the case; but the electorate and the representative both believed it to be true. The Constitution, a distinctively eighteenth-century document, expresses the faith that government can be a self-operating mechanism which, through the balance of powers, can leave the citizen free for his proper concerns, "life, liberty and the pursuit of happiness." Until our own time a positive view of government has been alien to the American historical experience; it still is, in some respects, alien to the fundamental American political philosophy. It would not have occurred to the eighteenth- or nineteenth-century American to say with Edmund Burke that the restraints upon men's liberties are to be counted among their rights. Burke's argument requires an acceptance of a view of human nature and human possibilities that did not seem reasonable during the first century and a half of the history of the Republic. Alexis de Tocqueville remarked that "aristocratic nations are naturally too liable to narrow the scope of human perfectibility; democratic nations to expand it beyond reason."[1] The profession of politics is closely related to beliefs about human perfectibility.

Tocqueville wrote elsewhere, "On my arrival in the United States I was surprised to find so much distinguished talent among the subjects, and so little among the heads of government. It is a constant fact, that, at the present day, the ablest men in the United States are rarely placed at the head of affairs; and it must be acknowledged that such has been the result, in proportion as democracy has outstepped all its former limits. The race of American statesmen has evidently dwindled most remarkably in the course of the last fifty years."[2] Tocqueville was right in one sense and wrong in another. It was true that the heads of government, as he observed them, were not very impressive. But the race of statesmen had not dwindled. They were devoting themselves to other pursuits, for politics is, among other things, a means for arriving at a position of power and creativity. The problem of government having seemingly been solved by the Founding Fathers, those who wished power and who had creative impulses looked to areas of American life other than the political arena in order to fulfill themselves. Imagination, drive and energy did not seem to be necessary in the government of the country. But there were other problems that very clearly had not been solved. The country had not been opened up. Its resources were hardly known, let alone utilized. It was economic development, then, rather than political life that commanded the best talents, the highest ambitions and the greatest energies of Americans almost until the dawn of this century.

For the great majority of people there was the constant move west as new lands were opened up. For the gifted, for the born leaders, there was the complex and demanding challenge of industrialization. The obvious and urgent task was the construction of railroads, the introduction into New England of the textile factories of old England, the problem of organizing industry and finally the whole corporate structure of American business and finance. The rewards were great for those who had the necessary ability. The task required those qualities of statesmanship, farsightedness and complete commitment which in other countries at the same time, notably in Great Britain, were being devoted to government in its several aspects. Lord Curzon governed the Indian Empire. Andrew Carnegie organized and governed a hardly less vast and equally important empire.

The situation that Henry Adams deplored toward the end of the century was not due, as he believed, to something innately wrong with the American experiment. It was due rather to the fact that the qualities he expected to find in Washington were absent, not because they were nonexistent in his fellow countrymen, but because they were being devoted to other and at the time perhaps more important objectives. Washington did not need qualities of statesmanship and imagination; it provided little outlet for them. The major problem was maintaining the Union and preserving a delicate *status quo*. Both before and after the Civil War what was wanted in Washington was the ability to compromise and to bargain. Naturally, men whose gifts lay in that direction were attracted there. These are often able, but rarely commanding men. It is significant that when the compromise broke down an Abraham Lincoln appeared; but he appeared only then. It is not until the Union was re-established on a new basis, the economy had matured and the United States began to emerge as a world power that men of Theodore Roosevelt's distinction were attracted to national politics.

Because political life lacked the distinction and the strong personalities that accompany creativity, it was particularly open to corruption. The enabling powers required for the development of the national economy lay almost exclusively with the states. Able men, however, with their eyes on other objectives, had neither the time nor the interest to enter politics so as to control the exercise of these powers. Instead, they bought politicians to do it for them; hence the almost legendary corruption of state governments during the century. This corruption was enhanced by the problems which arose when the flood of immigrants began to arrive from Europe. Still alien in their new home, inevitably exploited in the period of laissez-faire capitalism, they had to band together to protect

189

themselves. The natural leaders among them seized what came to hand in order to protect and elevate their people. Almost invariably, on the city and state levels, political corruption was the result. A negative view of government in the first place, the preoccupation with opening up the country's resources and organizing of the national economy, and, finally, the arrival of millions of uneducated immigrants, concentrated in the cities, combined to give the term "professional politician" a measure of opprobrium which is accurately reflected in the political cartoons in the thirty years before the turn of the century. It was a profession which few gentlemen would choose to enter.

Today it is very different. A political career or some other form of public service is increasingly the goal of large numbers of able college graduates. Apprenticeship to a congressman or a senator is eagerly sought after as summer employment. The family house in Maine is cheerfully given up for the acute discomforts of a Washington July and August if only there is the opportunity to observe and to some small extent take part in a politician's life. What has happened to make Adams' indictment of little more than antiquarian interest? For one thing, the pleasures of power, the exercise of creativity no longer find their expression exclusively in the world of business and industry. The great industries have been created once and for all. The mines have been discovered and organized. The great railway systems which built the Harriman and Vanderbilt fortunes have been completed and now tend to be irritating problems rather than challenging opportunities. There is little room left for the solitary, adventurous entrepreneur who shaped the nineteenth century. For the beneficiaries of the great fortunes, there are few alternatives if they are able and ambitious. The role of *rentier* does not go well with the restless American temperament. Nor can they participate in a lingering feudal and ritualistic past as their English counterparts still can do to a degree. To be a duke is, however anachronistic, self-justifying. To be an American of great inherited wealth is not, as the monumental and now largely empty mansions of Newport amply testify. Industry and business do not need to the degree and in the numbers they did a century ago men of outstanding creative ability, restless, ambitious, very strongly motivated by a passion for power. They want and need able, experienced and level-headed administrators. This is illustrated very well in Mr. Roger Blough's famous confrontation with President Kennedy and its disastrous consequences. Mr. Blough, with a naïveté about politics peculiar to his generation of businessmen, blithely assumed that the age of the elder Morgan was still in full flower. He had not realized that today a man of Morgan's temperament and abilities would be in the White House or close to it, his eye fixed not on organizing the American steel industry—that has been done—but on a position that would challenge his extraordinary abilities and satisfy his extreme ambition.

In fact, although many of the historic attitudes toward politics and the politician persist in the general public, in the minds of most educated people the words conjure up an image very different from that held sixty years ago. The reasons for this change are not hard to find and I think they are chiefly three—the Great Depression, the introduction of the intellectual into government, and the disappearance finally of isolationism as a basis for this country's foreign policy. The experience of the depression added a seriousness to the notion of government that it had not had before. It was made clear except to the most obdurate that the American world was not economically self-operating, that national authority was entrusted with a task of the utmost gravity. In the starkness of the early 1930's, Americans turned to the federal government to save them. It had never occurred to them that, except in case of war, this would be necessary. Business had proved, or so it seemed to the average citizen, inadequate even in its own area of activity. State government was helpless in the face of a national economic disaster.

There always has been in the American temperament a crusading zeal, an awareness of something better than what exists. The desire for reform is one of the few characteristics all Americans share in common beginning with the first settlers in New England, however differently various groups may have interpreted the word. In the years between the Civil War and the depression, politics was usually considered to be the object of reform rather than its agent. Franklin D. Roosevelt and his advisers, quite apart from the validity or success of their policies, mark the end of this era and the beginning of a new and probably permanent view of politics. Roosevelt's success in investing politics with idealism is certainly one of his greatest achievements. There is now the belief, largely new, among educated people that government is the channel for necessary change, not its obstacle. It has taken three decades for this to sink into the American consciousness. It becomes increasingly clear in successive generations of undergraduates I have observed that a political life of some sort or other ranks on a level equal with, if not

191

higher than, business and the traditional professions. This reinterpretation of government as positive and good rather than as a necessary evil is the fundamental change that has affected the profession of politics today. It is the reason why thousands of young men who fifty years ago would never have approached their adult lives in this way engage in politics not only in Washington but in state and civic affairs as well. Patriotism and idealism for the young man of action can find their fullest expression in the political arena.

The appearance of the intellectual in every role on the political stage came with the New Deal. It was immediately apparent to Roosevelt, as it was to a great many other people, that the problems confronting the United States in 1932 could not be left to the operation of laissez-faire principles, nor could they be solved by amateurs. The economic philosophy upon which nineteenth-century developments had been based was clearly indequate if not positively detrimental in the setting of the 1930's. With notable exceptions practicing politicians did not have systematic ideas about what should be done to bring the country out of its crisis. They rarely had a real grasp of the causes of the crisis. His pragmatism, his freedom, as a rich and privileged man of long lineage, from the beliefs and shibboleths of conventional business thinking, together with the seriousness of the situation allowed Roosevelt to call for the professional assistance of people who knew—or thought they knew—the causes and cures of the ailments that were afflicting the United States. The President turned to economists, lawyers and social scientists for the expertise which was essential if the nation's economic balance was to be restored.

The past thirty years have only intensified the intellectualization of government, and it seems unlikely that this trend will be lessened. It certainly will not be reversed in the foreseeable future. Trial and error and ordinary common sense are not adequate to cope with the internal problems of this or any other country, let alone the complexities of foreign policy. Many of these problems only the expert can understand. The layman, even though he may be a senator or representative, has no natural and rarely any acquired competence in many areas that call for policy decision. The result has been a steadily increasing galaxy of intellectuals clustered in and around Washington. If one of Franklin Roosevelt's great achievements was investing the whole sphere of national politics with idealism, another and equally important achievement during his regime and since then has been the investing of politics with intellect. This now enduring marriage of government with academia and with the intellectual life of the country, of which Wilson and the Progressives were the fleeting precursors, has great significance in several directions. It has made Washington and life there very different from what they once were. Washington is moving to a position where it can lay claim to being in some sense an intellectual as well as the political capital of the country. Far more importantly, however, it has modified the position of senator and representative in ways which I will discuss later.

The disappearance of the possibility of isolationism as the basis of American foreign policy is the third change that has affected the profession of politics, for it has introduced problems unknown or largely ignored in the country at large before the coming of World War II, problems of a magnitude sufficient to challenge the ablest and the most ambitious, to command the devotion of the most committed. The direction of American foreign policy since 1939 can be compared to the opening of the continent and the organization of American business and industry during the last century. The stakes are as high—much higher in fact. Demands for intelligence are of as high an order. The demand for courage, imagination and initiative is even greater, for what is being attempted is a reversal of attitudes first expressed in Washington's Farewell Address and ever since then reverently maintained. The founding of the United Nations, of NATO, the negotiation of the atomic test ban agreement and the problem of arms limitation, the situation in Cuba have required and received the attention of some of the best talents in the country. The business of the country is no longer business.

The chief business of the United States is the world situation, its problems and their resolution. American foreign policy is and must be creative. It must involve itself actively in the affairs of other nations, in direct contrast to its previous aloofness from foreign political entanglements. It is a matter of the most immediate concern to this country what regime is in power in any part of the world and how that regime must be approached and handled. The task is difficult and it has been complicated by the change in attitude to the United States of so many foreign countries. The United States was able for a long time to rest comfortably on the conviction that however foreign despots might fear and despise the democracy across the seas, their oppressed subjects saw it as the promised land and hastened to go there as soon as the opportunity arose. This is not true any longer. Just at the time when this country has been

forced to concern itself with the world, the world, now free entirely
from despots in the old monarchial sense, shows a surprisingly large
amount of anti-Americanism. The downfall of the Hapsburgs, the
Hohenzollerns, the Romanovs and the other lesser dynasties did
not bring about an automatic adoption of the American system
or some variant of it. In many instances it brought about a new
ideology based upon a different political philosophy and apparently
capable of gaining the allegiance of millions of people. Moreover,
the Marxist world is not the only problem to be dealt with. The
new Europe, the emerging African and Southeast Asian states and
Latin America cannot, for better or worse, be told what to do. They
must be negotiated with, carefully and skillfully.

In these circumstances the political arena is not that of Chester
Arthur. It is that of Chatham and Pitt. For the first time in American
history public life offers to the aspirant of talent the greatest of all
satisfactions. Patriotism, power, the responsibility for ruling men,
problems worldwide in their scope, the task of remaking the world
and keeping the peace under the threat of a formidable antagonist
have combined to raise public life and the profession of politics to a
level of prestige, to give them a challenge and color they never knew
before. Averell Harriman inherited his father's railroads and is a
very competent railroadman himself. The fact that he has devoted
himself single-mindedly and with selfless commitment to public
affairs is significant of the change I have been describing. The
phenomenon of the Kennedy family is without precedent. Nelson
Rockefeller, Adlai Stevenson, Paul Nitze, Douglas Dillon, Dean
Acheson have no parallel as a group in that happy period before the
Great Depression and the war brought home to Americans the fact
that the government was not a self-operating mechanism. How
could they have a parallel? There was no task of sufficient dimensions in the political world to attract their attention, challenge their
abilities or command their devotion. The real world was elsewhere.

The arrival of the profession of politics at its current level of
prestige raises some difficult and interesting problems in a political
society based upon the assumption that such a profession does not
exist. What is the profession of politics in the United States today
and how is it entered? The rubrics for the professions of law and of
medicine are clear. The young man who wishes to rise in the world
of business knows exactly what he must do. The man who desires

a career in politics is in a different position. There is no straight road to the top. Here there is a striking contrast with political life in Great Britain, where the route is through the House of Commons. A young man who wishes to enter public life tries to get elected as a member of Parliament. If he is successful his problem is simple—to stay in the House and to rise in eminence both as a member of the House and as a member of his party. With luck and with the necessary ability he will in due course be a member of the cabinet. He might even be prime minister. At any rate he can set his eye on those objectives since the prime minister and his cabinet must be members of Parliament. In the United States it is very different. The road to power is tortuous and unpredictable. If a young man wishes to be President or to hold a cabinet post there is no certain way of planning his future, although it is easier to aim at the Presidency than at any other office, as President Kennedy demonstrated. The road to cabinet office is not through the political process but through the achievement of distinction in some business or profession. The aspirant for high office must aim at being a partner in one of the large and influential eastern law firms or the head of a great industry. One thinks of Dean Acheson and John Foster Dulles, of the present Secretary of Defense and Secretary of Treasury.

The basic determining fact is that the road to office is not through the elective bodies—the Senate or the House of Representatives—excepting insofar as the Senate might possibly be a springboard to the Presidency and the House of Representatives a springboard to the Senate. Almost by definition, the House of Representatives can rarely if ever be the ambition of absolutely first-class talents. The two-year term of office is in itself a limiting factor, for it gives the representative barely time to get to know his job before he has to return to electioneering once again. But, much more importantly, the seniority system prevents youthful talent from expressing itself. The congressman cannot hope to hold high office. He can, however, hope to head in due course one of the important committees—but only in due course and that may be a very long time indeed. If he wishes to achieve such a post his fundamental preoccupation must be with his electorate at home. If he is not successful at the next election, even though he should be re-elected at some later time, his seniority is lost and he must begin again. His only hope is to pay such careful attention to his electorate that his return is as certain as possible—and wait. This is not a form of political activity, although it has its own virtues, that is likely to attract the brilliant, the ambitious and the impatient.

At Westminster the brilliant, the ambitious and the impatient, if they have political sagacity, do not have to wait very long. This is why in the United States there is so much political talent on the sidelines, in law, in business, in the universities, in journalism. That President Kennedy drew so heavily for his close advisers on the universities should have surprised no one. In the British cabinet system most of these men would not have been members of a university faculty in the first place. They would long since have been in the House of Commons and in many cases would have already had their first taste of cabinet office. There are no counterparts in Great Britain to Walter Lippmann or to Joseph Alsop and the other political commentators at their level. The reason for this is that their counterparts are in the House of Commons. If the young Walter Lippmann or Joseph Alsop or McGeorge Bundy were in the British system, with their gifts and their intense political concern they would surely run for Parliament. If the late Hugh Gaitskill had been in the American system, he would have been a member of a university faculty or the author of a bi-weekly syndicated column on public affairs. If the party this educator or journalist supports wins the election there is a chance—by no means a certainty—that he will be drawn into the administration. If not, he remains outside the government permanently, since there is no forum within the political machinery in which his voice would be as influential as in his newspaper column or on his lecture platform. As educator or journalist he can hope to form public opinion to his way of thinking.

In the House of Representatives, supposing that this educator or journalist found himself resident of a district where there was a chance of his being elected, he would have few if any peers, little influence and at most a dubious future. The Senate is a different matter, even if the difference is somewhat illusory. It is recognized to be a body of higher status than the House. It is much smaller. By reason of the fact that one third of its members is chosen every two years it has a continuity which the House lacks and thus a rather clublike cohesiveness. Because the senatorial term is for six years the Senate can approach its responsibilities in a more leisurely, less harassed manner. Its members come generally from a higher social position than do the members of the House. Appointive until the Seventeenth Amendment, it is less of a tribune of the people, more of an independent body. This fact, together with its powers to advise and consent and its particular concern with foreign affairs, gives to it a certain, unmistakable patrician flavor. To be a representative might mean anything. To be a United States senator has always implied a particular distinction. The representative must bring distinction with him if he has it. This the Senate confers on its members, and it takes the exertions of a Joseph McCarthy to lose it. However, distinction is not power. The Senate, prestigious though it may be, does not rule. The fundamental importance of both Senate and House and their range of activities are limited in Section 6 of the first article of the Constitution: "No person holding any office under the United States shall be a member of either house during his continuance in office."

The separation of the legislative from the executive has been almost too successful. The powers of the Senate and the House are great, but they are negative powers, for it was not assumed in the Constitution that there would be many policies to make at a national level. However, able and ambitious men concerned with the public welfare do not wish only to approve or disapprove of policy. They want to make it, for that is the creative area of public life. The range and complexity of policy making and of executive decision today, placed in the context of the separation of powers, has changed the nature of American politics and therefore of the profession of politics. It has introduced a new class of public men who can properly be called politicians. To call them anything else is to cloud the issue, for they have to do with and in fact control the most important areas of American policy. What is significant is that, although they are vested with great powers, they are not part of the legislative body nor are they, even in the remotest sense, representatives of the people. They are appointed by the President and removable at his will. In the crises that face the world the destinies of this country are in their hands. They are its governors. Men concerned about public affairs and with a desire for power are attracted to this new area of public life. Given the American Constitution and the world today this is bound to happen, but it will not enhance the power and prestige of the legislative bodies nor strengthen their intellectual qualities.

The two Cuban crises are cases in point. Each of these could have brought the country to war. Both decisions moved the country into positions which committed it to certain course of action. These decisions emanated in no sense from elected representatives. Certain of the representatives may have been called in and informed of the direction in which one of the crises was moving, but its control was not their affair, nor could it have been. The position of the two houses has been not unlike the Dominions in the British Empire and Commonwealth at Imperial Conferences before the Balfour Report of 1926. Their representatives are summoned and informed by the group that is making or has made the decisions. They are confronted with a *fait accompli*. In such a situation they can only consent, for to do otherwise is to put their theoretical rights above the safety of the country.

This situation arises from the political philosophy on which the Constitution is based. It makes the federal legislature static and incapable of growth. Only the executive can grow and develop and add new devices necessary to meet unprecedented situations. For it to be otherwise would require a rethinking of fundamental American political principles and a new constitutional convention. This seems highly unlikely. Until this happens, however, the CIA, the National Security Council, the Atomic Energy Commission, the experts and the special presidential assistants, all of them wholly unrepresentative in the traditional sense, all of them inconceivable seventy-five years ago, will govern the country in the most important matters. The exigencies of government today have outgrown the constitutional machinery, which was until recently assumed to be able to take care of every situation that could arise. It is just as well to face this situation and reflect about it, even though very little can be done about it at the present time.

But there is still another factor that should be considered. This is the role of the expert, and it affects government not only here but in every civilized country and in all those countries that hope to become civilized. It raises a difficult question. For a long time in the western political tradition—since the seventeenth century, if not before—political progress has been measured in terms of increased representation by the masses of the people in the political process, for it was assumed—Rousseau gave the idea its classical expression—that the people *en masse* were capable of solving the problems of society. This is so deep in our political consciousness that we are hardly aware of it and we scarcely ever examine it, so deep that even modern totalitarian dictatorships rest their legitimacy upon it or upon some variant of it. Neither Hitler nor Mussolini nor Stalin based their assumption of power on a mandate from heaven. They claimed that they represented the will of the people. The appearance of the term "peoples' democracy" is a comment on the profound degree to which this belief has affected political thinking in the modern world.

This belief is hard to hold with anything like the passion and conviction that brought about its acceptance in the past two centuries. For it is clearly apparent that the generality of people and their representatives cannot understand many of the most urgent contemporary issues and that the constitutional machinery was not devised for dealing with them. The Rousseauistic idea is consistent with the age of laissez-faire and the early phases of the Industrial Revolution, that is, the sovereign people can decide all issues so long as there are no important issues to decide. It is not consistent, in its totality, with the age of nuclear fission, highly developed technology and underdeveloped countries.

Internal problems are no more susceptible of an amateur approach than are external ones. Gladstone, with a classical education and a good business mind, could bring down his celebrated budgets. The organization of the United States' finances and its economic policy are beyond the capacity of any except the most highly trained specialists in these fields. Even the right of the legislative bodies to agree or disagree with their recommendations in theory is not as unassailable as it once was, for it is difficult for the ordinary man to act as judge in issues which he does not understand. Farm policy, foreign trade, city planning, urban renewal and public health are vital issues not only on which expert advice is essential, but also on which specialists must do the planning. Furthermore, specialists are in many instances the only really qualified judges of policies advanced. This is not to overlook the real and continuing importance of the legislative bodies. Since they reflect public opinion—particularly the House of Representatives—it is largely through them that public opinion can be modified and changed. Certain areas of American life cannot be changed by executive action nor very much influenced or affected by the views of experts. Civil rights and the future of the American Negro in the end rest upon the attitudes of the electorate and how those attitudes can be modified. So does the way in which the country views the rest of the world, its relationship and responsibilities to it. As the link between the electorate and the executive, the House and the Senate interpret the one to the other and influence both. In this sense Congress is the custodian of the American conscience. This is a profoundly important function, but it is not the creation of policy. It is not ruling.

If expertise is essential to the right ordering of the country's internal affairs, it is even more important in the planning and execution of American foreign and defense policies. The secrecy that is necessary in these areas of government today in itself acts to limit the power of the representative to participate in their formation. The decision to oppose Russian shipments of material and personnel to Cuba could not be made publicly, nor could the public through their delegates take part in making the decision. It was made, and had to be made, by the President and his advisers, by the National Security Council, all of them acting on information provided by the CIA and the scientific experts. It was likewise the case with the atomic test ban agreement. This latter depended first of all upon scientific knowledge. The practicability of such an agreement had to be established before any agreement could be negotiated or signed. In this instance the President's chief scientific adviser, Jerome Wiesner, had a position of power to which no senator could aspire. Nor is this situation peculiar to the United States. Sir Solly Zuckerman in Great Britain has a similar role, is not a member of Parliament and is called upon to provide the information and give the advice which the prime minister must have if he is to decide and to act. Only the foolhardy in Washington or at Westminster would act upon the assumption that their common sense or intuition were superior to Jerome Wiesner's or Sir Solly Zuckerman's considered judgment. In such situations Congress is, and probably must be, by-passed.

In this situation the profession of politics must be redefined and its scope widened. Some kind of organic relationship between the legislative and the executive would have several happy results. It would raise the intellectual level of the legislative bodies because able men, in this age of political concern, would wish very much to belong to such bodies once they were an effective force in the actual government of the country. It would expose the brilliant to the salutary criticism of the matter-of-fact. It would help to harness the abilities of numerous potential politicians who now stand on the sidelines. Finally it would strengthen free government. The basis of free government is discussion. But it must be a *polity* of discussion, that is, the discussion must be politically effective. It has the power to influence governments, ideally to bring them down. The French in the seventeenth century and the Austrians under the Hapsburgs talked endlessly and brilliantly, but that did not mean that their governments were polities of discussion.

Finally it would do something to relieve the almost intolerable burdens on the President if only by diffusing responsibility so that he is not always in the end psychologically isolated when the great decision has to be made. It is commonplace that the developments I have been describing have operated to increase presidential power and therefore responsibility enormously. Under the Constitution there is no way of dealing with unprecedented situations except by handing them over to the executive, and this when the President is not only the executive but the symbol of all that his country stands for. He is not a private citizen as is the prime minister in Great Britain or Canada. He is monarch as well. Louis XIV could be both in an age of simple problems and leisurely government. It is too much to ask of one man in the middle of the twentieth century.

The American political system has continued, essentially unchanged, since the foundation of the Republic. It is carried on today by the momentum of faith in ideas which appear to have been brilliantly successful. It is not the ideas or the democratic belief that one questions. It is rather the political machinery by which those ideas and beliefs are implemented. One endorses the American political faith with few reservations; but it is difficult to avoid the conclusion that the political machinery by which that faith was to be protected was designed on the assumption that the world of the twentieth century would never exist. At least one of the Founding Fathers anticipated this and he was one of the greatest of that distinguished group. Thomas Jefferson wrote:

> Some men look at constitutions with sanctimonious reverence, and deem them like the ark of the covenant, too sacred to be touched. They ascribe to the preceding age a wisdom more than human, and suppose what they did to be beyond amendment. . . . I am certainly not an advocate for frequent and untried changes in laws and institutions . . . but I know . . . that laws and institutions must go hand in hand with the progress of the human mind. As that becomes more developed, more enlightened, as new discoveries are made, new truths disclosed and manners and opinions change with the change of circumstances, institutions must advance also, and keep pace with the times. We might as well require a man still to wear the coat which fitted him when a boy, as civilised society to remain forever under the regime of their barbarous ancestors.[3]

What Jefferson feared has indeed come to pass. The Declaration of Independence and the Constitution are guarded and revered with no less awe than the ark of the covenant. The problem of

201

politics and the profession of politics in the United States has been complicated by this confusion of the relative with the absolute. It is time that some clarification was attempted.

REFERENCES

1. Alexis de Tocqueville, *Democracy in America* (Cambridge: Sever and Francis, 1864), II, 39.

2. *Ibid.* I, 253.

3. *Basic Writings of Thomas Jefferson*, ed. Philip S. Foner (New York: Willey Book Company, 1944), p. 750.

C. RICHARD SODERBERG

The American Engineer

I. Introduction

THE ENGINEER deals with the material needs of man: food, shelter, transportation, communications, energy, materials, structures, and machines. From primitive beginnings these activities gradually became systematized into technology. Later they evolved into a process of intimate interaction between science and technology. The principal domain of the engineer is technology in the service of economic and industrial objectives, but he has played an equally important role in the technology of war. In this relationship to technology of peace and war, the engineer represents one of the professional groups whose work directly influences our material well-being and national strength and also provides one of the major foundations of foreign policy. He is a member of a team which also includes the scientist, the businessman, the industrial organizer and manager (a position he frequently holds), the economist, the banker, and representatives of many other groups.

The outstanding fact of the modern world is its commitment to technology as a way of life. When technology enhanced its potentialities through the systematic application of science, this commitment became a fateful one. Man can now satisfy almost any material need, provided that he is prepared to make the necessary social choices. This new power over the environment, so earnestly hoped for by our forebears, has come about suddenly, out of a period of wars and social upheavals. Confronted with the problem of survival in wartime, we have been content to accept levels of public activities and taxation which would have been unthinkable without this incentive. The intimate relationship between modern war and technology thus enabled us to take many important steps without really facing up to the social choices involved.

The period has also taught us that collective man's rationality is only a thin veneer. Underneath there are frightening propensities for cruelty and irrationalism. The technological process is neutral to many of the most important things in life: compassion, tolerance, ethics, morals, and religion. In the long run it can probably be made to flourish under any of the existing economic and social systems; it may even be in the process of creating its own social and international environment. It can lend strength to evil as well as to good causes. It lends itself with equal impartiality to the service of trivia and tripe as to genuine needs of utility and beauty.

The engineer, besides being an agent in this transformation, is also a citizen with a stake in the outcome. His special knowledge and experience do not confer upon him automatic wisdom, nor is he always able to speak with true independence. As a member of a profession, however, he can add his voice to others in advancing dispassionate, enlightened views on important issues. The engineer's position among the professions in modern society is an ambiguous one, in stark contrast to his key role in technology. The reasons for this are complex and not yet fully understood. The recent years of unparalleled technological developments have brought about needs for new talents, particularly in science, which have put the traditional qualifications of engineers in the shade. Engineering itself has failed to make distinctions between professional activity and technicianship. To the average citizen the word "engineer" carries no distinction between the professional practitioner and the technician, in spite of the Webster definition of "engineer" and "engineering." In this situation the public seems to have found a clearer resolution by extending the definition of the term "scientist." It can be argued, of course, that the distinction between scientist and engineer is merely a semantic one; that the now popular usage of "scientist" for both activities is an improvement on the old-fashioned nomenclature. Semantic usage often has a deeper significance than mere caprice on the part of the public, however. The present lack of distinction between engineer and scientist is symbolic of the fact that our entire social outlook, including that of many scientists, is becoming increasingly subservient to technology. In this environment the scientist and the engineer appear to the public as twin professionals in the service of technology.

It is true that in modern technology engineers and scientists often do play identical roles. Many scientists function essentially as engineers; many engineers devote themselves to scholarly scientific pursuits. In spite of this, and in spite of the inevitability of semantic usage, I believe that this ambiguity of professional definition is unfortunate, not the least for science. The technological process requires much more than applications of science. Science itself must have purposes other than that of being a mere servant of technology. We may earnestly hope that science for its own sake, with restraint on the itch to control the environment, will continue in its cultural mission. The informed voice of science is needed, particularly when the process of technology threatens irreplaceable values in our environment. Here science can function as a cultural force of restraint on technology. But popular usage of words is not easily influenced by deliberate efforts of reform, even those based on sound logic. In the long run the only significant results will come through the impact upon the popular image of the activity and personality of individual engineers. This requires, first of all, a deeper awareness on the part of engineers themselves of the historical background and the cultural role of their profession.

The engineer filled some of society's material needs by rational activities long before modern science was born. As society emerged from primitive beginnings it created niches of material needs, the fulfillment of which required certain traits of intelligence and character such as imagination, inventive ability, and the power of observation and generalization, which led to the accumulation of specialized craftsmanship and knowledge. It is difficult to decide at which point in this evolution a craft develops into a profession. The use of science as a technical tool is one criterion, but equally important is the maturing of the social and philosophical outlook. The mere desire to exploit specialized knowledge is certainly not enough; there must also be a desire for unique personal accomplishments and service, the desire for contributions of a scholarly nature, the interest to learn by experience, the desire to share the experiences with fellow workers and with society. In particular, there must be the desire and ability to achieve a position of independence to voice the dispassionate professional point of view on important issues. A sense of participation in contemporary culture as a whole is no less important. Whitehead's observations, already quoted in the introduction to this volume, apply with special force to the engineer.[1] His is perhaps one of the most culpable of the professional groups in this respect.

The engineer is still in the midst of the transition from the attitudes and traditions of the craftsman and skilled artisan into concepts of greater intellectual depth and broader social awareness. He still has a long way to travel before this process is complete. The inevitable slowness of this process must be kept in mind. The engineer and the scientist are newcomers among the professions. The older professions of theology, law, and medicine found a place in the medieval university, thereby acquiring a head start in time of centuries which is still to be made up by the newer professions. It can be argued, therefore, that the true professional role of these newer categories is yet to be fully developed. Modern society is truly built around their contributions, however, and it may be that the term "professional" is in the process of acquiring yet another meaning.

II. Historical Background

Human material needs, even relatively sophisticated ones, were attended to by various nonprofessional members of society long before man was conscious of specialization into engineering. This was particularly so in agriculture. Relatively advanced forms of technology, such as those related to fibers and cloth, soap-making, and dyeing, were expertly run by women in their homes, particularly in Western society. This intimate association between human needs and their satisfaction by empirical procedure is as old as man.

The first organized activity arose in connection with architecture, roads, waterways, bridges, fortifications, heating, and sanitation. Supporting these activities was a growing need for metals, hence the importance of mining with its associated activities of pumping, hoisting, ventilation, and purification and smelting of ores. In this role we find engineering performed in the antique world, particularly in Egypt. At the height of Roman civilization there had developed the image of the professional engineer, perhaps best illustrated by Vitruvius, who not only functioned as an engineer but also wrote about engineering.[2] The antique world, because of its dependence upon slavery, lacked the incentive to exploit natural resources of energy. As witnessed by the nomenclature which has come down to us, wind and water mills played a role in it, although mainly as toys for the diversion of the mighty or for mysteries exploited by priests.

The slow transition from Roman to Western society was not wholly a "dark age." There was a steady advance in technology even during these years.[3] The climate of northwestern Europe and its natural resources, the classical heritage and Christianity, and the gradual elimination of slavery played their roles in forging the character of Western man. Out of this transition came impulses which by the fourteenth century had inaugurated the development of Western technology. Lewis Mumford has suggested that technology evolved through three overlapping epochs: the "eo-technic phase" to about 1750, the "paleo-technic phase" to the period after World War I, and the present "neo-technic phase."[4] These periods signify more than mere divisions in time; each phase had its peculiar technological and social character.

The eo-technic phase represents modern man's first thrust towards control over his environment, and it is here that we find the beginnings of engineering as a recognized profession, often coupled with military activity. Among the early engineers there appears the towering genius of Leonardo da Vinci (1452–1519), whose fascinating notebooks did not become known until long after his death.[5] There were also professional engineers such as Simon Stevin (1548–1620), who generalized his experiences with machinery into the early beginnings of modern science.[6] There is Galileo (1564–1642), the founder of modern science, whose observations also dealt with engineering structures.[7] The zest of the age is transmitted to us through observers such as Agricola[8] and engineers such as Polhem,[9] through whose writings we can enter the spirit of a primitive, yet relatively advanced, technology in which the great majority of the mechanical inventions had already been made. The origins of the English designation of engineer go back to this epoch. As early as the time of Edward III, in the fourteenth century, the officer who was responsible for firearms was referred to as "Artilator" or "Ingeniator." The men who ran the ballista, sometimes called gins, were referred to as "Engyners." The modern name engineer undoubtedly has this origin.[10]*

Science owes a debt, not always acknowledged, to some of these forerunners in engineering. We have become accustomed to think

* The terms "engineering" and "technology" have both come into our language without clear distinction between them. In popular usage "engineer" now means anybody operating, inventing, or designing engines or engineering systems. "Technology," referring to the systematic treatment of any art (or science), came into use in the last century, apparently due to Jacob Bigelow. It has found wide application in recent years. The American ECPD accreditation system has introduced "engineering technology" as related to technicianship in engineering or industry. The uncertainty of nomenclature is regrettable. In the following pages I propose to use "technology" for the systematic treat-

of engineering as "the application of science to the fulfillment of human needs." This is, of course, true for most of the activities of contemporary engineers, but the early engineers played a more fundamental role. By their sober attitude and their quantitative approach to nature, they gradually became accustomed to the inherent limitations in the exploitation of natural resources of energy. These engineers were among the first men of intelligence to become aware of some of nature's exclusion principles. Some engaged in aimless search for "perpetual motion," the "universal solvent," or other fantasies, but the majority did not. Most of them remained anonymous.

Galileo's influence upon science was the most far-reaching, but it is worth remembering that he was anticipated, in certain important ideas, by Simon Stevin, the Dutch engineer. Stevin postulated "the exclusion of perpetual motion" as the foundation of the physical world. His device, with the motto "Wonder en is gheen wonder" (a miracle is no miracle),[11] throws a remarkable light on the transition from intuition to knowledge. It contained the germ of the ideas which led to the principles of virtual work and conservation of energy. Ernst Mach has characterized this as "one of the rarest of the fossil indicators that we possess in the primitive history of mechanics . . ."[12] The first faltering steps towards modern science were thus made by the early engineers and guided by their practical sense.

Even though many inventions of decisive importance, such as the Newcomen steam engine, belong to the eo-technic phase, the engineering profession as we know it was born out of the paleo-technic phase, with its greater dependence upon the steam engine, the patent system, the factory system, manufacturing methods and machine tools, industrial organization, banking, and credit. Many of the key developments took place in England. The partnership of James Watt and Mathew Bolton with their factory at Soho[13] may be said to have been one of the first modern enterprises in mechanical engineering. The spirit of the epoch is well illustrated by Armytage as "the age of mechanical engineering." It is in early Victorian England that we see the modern engineer-enterpriser, embodied in personalities such as George Stephenson (1781–1848), William Fairbairn (1789–1874), Henry Maudsley (1771–1831),

ment of the entirety of industrial operations, "engineer" for the professional practitioner, "technician" for the skilled craftsman, "engineering" for the theoretical and practical activity of the engineer and the technician.

Marc Isambard Brunel (1769–1849), Thomas Telford (1757–1834), and many other fascinating characters.

Our technological civilization was initiated in this epoch, and many of the characteristics of engineers may be traced to the influence of these pioneers. The pride of newly won power over the material world; the enthusiasm for the new rationalism, as expressed by the Benthams and James Mill; the belief in freedom and democracy; the potential competence of the early engineers to solve problems of public health; and the general indifference of business and political leaders to the appalling social conditions are all part of the scene. Through the initiative of leaders such as Edwin Chadwick, these social conditions were systematically investigated and reported on through Royal Commissions. The effects in England of these reports came slowly, but they were diligently studied by two émigrés, Karl Marx and Friedrich Engels, the one living in Soho and the other in Manchester. The conclusions of these men on the cause of these social conditions were to have the most far-reaching consequences, leading in our own time to the establishment of the modern communist states.[14]

The later Victorian Age saw developments in chemical engineering in Germany, and electrical engineering in both England and Germany. Finally, during and after the close of the American Civil War, American participation became important. Industry on a scale scarcely imagined before, such as the steel industry, the railroads, and marine transportation, now appeared here. The latter part of the nineteenth century saw the emergence of new prime movers: the internal combustion engine, with its impact upon the automobile and the airplane; the steam turbine and the diesel engine, with their great impact upon electric power and mass transportation.

Professional organizations and journals of publications developed together with education in engineering and science. As the engineering societies were formed they took over some of the characteristics and idealistic motivations of the Royal Society and similar academies in Italy and France. In England the Society of Civil Engineers, later called the Smeatonian Society, was organized in 1771. This eventually led, in 1818, to the Institution of Civil Engineers, organized by H. R. Palmer. Under the presidency of Thomas Telford this organization began to assume the role which has since been followed by so many other engineering societies. Palmer conceived the role of the engineer as "a mediator between the philosopher and the working mechanic." Under Telford civil engineering was formally defined as "the art of directing the great sources of power in Nature for the use and convenience of man," a phrase which has found its way into Webster's definition of "engineering."

Engineering education began to take form in the early part of the last century, when schools of vocational character gradually became converted into universities. The great prototype was the École Polytechnique in France after its reorganization under Napoleon. Under Gaspard Monge, the mathematician and organizer who had already become famous during the Egyptian campaign, this institution inaugurated many of the features which are characteristic of engineering schools today. Instruction in the underlying sciences preceded the professional training, and the students were later encouraged to undertake more comprehensive tasks. Great emphasis was placed on spacial visualization and drawing. Monge's hand in descriptive geometry can be traced to this day in many programs.[15] The École Polytechnique became a training ground for France's great men, even in fields outside of science and technology. Gradually the military and civilian emphasis began to be more clearly differentiated, the term "civil engineering" being originally a counterpart to "military engineering."*

With variations due to national character the "technical university" on the French plan spread to all of the nations of Western Europe. Darmstadt (1822), Karlsruhe (1825), and many other German institutions are examples which were soon followed by others in France, England, and the rest of Europe. It is worth emphasizing that these institutes of technology or technical universities represented the response of European society to the challenges of the modern world. The structure has been extended to many other modern professions. The old universities only reluctantly added to their programs; even the inclusion of science under natural philosophy came slowly. Concern with other human needs was considered part of the outside, vulgar world.

The developments in America followed the English pattern, but there were also other influences, notably from France. Public works and transportation represented the first needs, and political leaders such as George Washington actively sought out European civil engineers. One of the best known, and perhaps the most versatile, was the English engineer-architect Benjamin Henry Latrobe

* In the Scandinavian countries "civil engineer" still designates a university-educated engineer, regardless of specialty.

(1764–1820), who emigrated to the United States in 1796 and exerted a powerful influence on many engineering projects. The economic depressions in the late thirties and early forties seem to have created severe difficulties in the form of retrenchments and political investigations.[16]

Generally, early America seems to have teemed with enthusiastic inventors, amateur engineers, and enterprisers both before and after the Revolution. The real advance into technology was triggered off by the Civil War, however. Prior to this America had depended chiefly upon the United States Military Academy for formal education in engineering. This was established in 1802 at West Point, when Congress also authorized the Corps of Engineers. This action was strongly influenced by Benjamin Thompson, Count Rumford (1752–1814), the inventor, physicist, Tory spy, and otherwise fascinating personality.[17] Through his posthumous award to Harvard, that institution created the Rumford Chair in "science applied to useful arts," first held by Jacob Bigelow (1786–1879), whose *Elements of Technology,* published in 1829, was one of the early American treatises on engineering.[18]

The structure and spirit of the USMA was shaped by Colonel Sylvanus Thayer (1785–1872), who served as superintendent from 1817 to 1833. Because of the close relationship to the Corps of Engineers, and due to Thayer's influence, West Point became the first engineering school in the United States, patterned to a degree on the École Polytechnique in France. West Point and the activities of Jacob Bigelow at Harvard thus represented the start of American engineering education. Other institutions such as Rensselaer Polytechnic Institute in 1824 followed; but the real advance into education for useful purposes did not get under way until the end of the Civil War. M.I.T. is a typical example. The voluminous correspondence which preceded the organization of the Massachusetts Institute of Technology is of interest. The attitudes to useful education and their evolution during the years of the Civil War throw much light on a process which was repeated in many similar places at that time.[19] Later the institution of land-grant colleges, as a result of the Morrill Act of 1862, came to play an important role. It encouraged many of the states to establish colleges of agriculture and mechanical arts. By 1870 there were a large number of such institutions.

The period from the Civil War to World War I was truly the epoch of the American engineer. His contribution to the creation of the new nation was a fundamental one. Like most of his fellow citizens, he was not yet bothered by any doubts as to the ultimate blessings of technology. The educational system in engineering grew to maturity during this epoch, and it appears to have been well adapted to its role of providing great leaders as well as efficient servants of the growing industrial complex.

World War I and its aftermath, besides revealing the real complexity of the modern world, also exposed weaknesses in the American educational system. It had failed to anticipate the growing need for more advanced education in science; it also failed to realize that the engineer had a role beyond technical proficiency and material success. Certain fields, such as chemical engineering, showed considerable foresight in more advanced education; but on the whole, the American system of engineering education was inferior to those in Europe. In many scientific fields education in Europe was considered essential for American engineers and engineering teachers. American industry in those years was aided not only by the influx of immigrant labor but also by technical intellectuals who by their superior training served industry and education. Many of these worked in modest positions as draftsmen and technicians. Some of these men, who later became well known, were surprised to find little appreciation of their services. Stephen S. Timoshenko, who arrived in the United States in 1922 as an emigré from Russia at the age of forty-four, and who was already well known in Europe, spent month after month in vain seeking a teaching position in any school of engineering. He finally got a start in industry and later played an important role in advancing engineering education in America. Many men of similar background had the same experience. An industrial and educational complex which desperately needed the services of such men had not yet awakened to the importance of better education and research in science and engineering. These circumstances were to alter dramatically in succeeding decades. It was out of these impulses that the American engineering profession began the phase of self-searching and critical examination which is now bearing fruit.

III. Characteristics of the Engineering Profession in America

THE MAKE-UP OF THE PROFESSION

In 1963 there were in the United States about 935,000 individuals, mostly men, who classified themselves as engineers.[20] By comparison there were about 500,000 scientists and about 1,000,000 technicians. A decade earlier the number of engineers was about 633,000; at that time it was estimated that about 57 per cent of this number had college degrees.[21] This percentage is certainly greater now. At the same time, 93 per cent of all the people who had received degrees in engineering were still living, although not all were active within the classification indicated by their degrees. In 1953, 3,800 of these engineers, a little more than 0.5 per cent, had Ph.D. degrees or their equivalent. In 1963, this number had risen to about 10,000, or over 1 per cent of the total.

No exact distribution with respect to details of employment is available for 1963, but for 1960, when there were 840,000 engineers, 77 per cent were employed in industry and about 7 per cent in government.[22] Of the remainder, about 135,000 engineers, the majority were employed in occupations not listed under "industry," a considerable number were self-employed, the rest were teachers. In 1958, there were about 11,500 teachers of engineering, of whom 8,200 constituted the core faculty. The remaining 3,300 were part-time teachers or instructors seeking advanced degrees at the institution of employment.[23] The number of teachers seems small, but there were, in addition, many teachers in engineering schools not listed as engineers.

PROFESSIONAL ORGANIZATIONS

The engineering profession in the United States has been in perpetual transition for many years, but most of the important changes can be traced to the period after the 1920's. Many of the new developments in engineering education took place in industry, particularly in industrial complexes such as General Electric, Westinghouse, du Pont, American Telephone, and others. There was a beginning of appreciation for the role of research in these relatively mature industries as well as a conscious search for men of high intellect.

The American Society for the Promotion of Engineering Education, later changed to the American Society for Engineering Education, had been formed in 1893. In a series of studies and reports this Society had exerted a strong influence on the destiny of the profession.[24] Perhaps the most important is the Wickenden Report,[25] issued in 1929 after several years of study. This presented an unusually mature assessment of the problems and their background. Its role in engineering is not unlike that of the Flexner Report for medicine. It has been followed over the years by many similar assessments, such as the Grinter Report on Evaluation of Engineering Education. The present phase of the movement is led by the "Goals Committee" under E. A. Walker.

The message of the Wickenden Report led to several measures on the part of the profession to improve education, to certify minimum standards, to coordinate certification with the expanding system of state registration, and to give the young engineer a better understanding of his professional role and duties. These objectives were attained by the creation of several new organizations, of which two are relevant to the present discussion. These developments were part of the movement of accreditation for undergraduate curricula in many fields. This had much earlier origins, but the actions during the 1930's were particularly significant.[26]

The Engineers Joint Council (EJC) was formed in 1946, succeeding the earlier American Engineering Council as a federation of engineering societies in which the respective officials meet to consider problems of public policy. It now speaks for twenty-six engineering societies. On the direct initiative created by the Wickenden report, there was formed in 1932 the Engineers' Council for Professional Development (ECPD), which has since become the main agency for united activities on professional problems.[27] This is also an affiliation of engineering societies, the present list being: American Institute of Aeronautics and Astronautics, Inc.; American Institute of Chemical Engineers; American Institute of Mining, Metallurgical and Petroleum Engineers; American Society of Civil Engineers; American Society for Engineering Education; The American Society of Mechanical Engineers; The Engineering Institute of Canada; The Institute of Electrical and Electronics Engineers, Inc.; and National Council of State Boards of Engineering Examiners. The inclusion of The Engineering Institute of Canada indicates a link with the Canadian institutions, but the ECPD does not accredit curricula in Canadian engineering schools.

By the inclusion of the National Council of State Boards of Engineering Examiners, the structure has been coupled with the state licensing system of engineers in the United States. Through these activities the corresponding state laws have had a degree of coordination, even though they are not identical.

The system of accreditation under the ECPD has exerted a powerful influence upon the development of curricula in engineering, particularly in upgrading the weaker ones. The accreditation procedure applies only to curricula in engineering and does not apply to the institutions themselves. An account of its activities is presented each year in the annual report of the ECPD, which also contains the current list of accredited curricula and the corresponding institutions. The annual report for the year 1963 contains a listing of 163 engineering schools with 866 accredited curricula. The accreditation also includes the programs for technicians, for which the term "engineering technology" has been adopted.[28]

The existing system of professional organizations[29] at first sight appears confusing, with many overlapping roles. Like other professions, engineering also grew by the accretion of specialties. Each new field—civil, mechanical, chemical, electrical engineering—was established as a more or less independent profession with its individual systems of professional standards, journals of publication, and so on. These organizations frequently were adopted by the respective industries as vehicles of commercial promotion. The fact that the supporting sciences and the elements of basic training were common to all of them did not at first seem important. The process of the formation of new organizations and the merging of older ones presents an interesting development which deserves closer study. New specialties such as nuclear engineering were started in several organizations, later to emerge as independent societies. Similar developments have taken place in specialty fields such as applied mechanics, which has had an active development in the American Society of Mechanical Engineers, or experimental stress analysis, which has become the basis for another separate society. Many of these subprofessions have acquired a degree of stability and permanence which makes it unlikely that the system will change rapidly. The mere question of size makes major consolidations difficult. It thus seems that this type of fragmentation is an inevitable aspect of the profession, at least in the United States. The creation of the EJC to handle problems external to the profession and the ECPD for problems within the profession were important steps. However, they have not wholly resolved this problem.

Most of the professional societies came into existence in response to a complex set of impulses: genuine industrial needs, opportunities for promoters and publicity seekers, opportunities for commercial exploitation, and many others. In the modern scene there are genuine professional and social needs for a better recognition of the larger entities, such as transportation, communications, energy, and materials, which remain as tasks in our society regardless of the fluctuating roles of individual business enterprises or inventions. However, these larger entities lack the appeal of publicity or promotion which is inherent in the lesser specialties. Their recognition can come only from a deeper awareness of the role which technology plays in our society.

RECRUITMENT—SHORTAGE

During the decade 1950–1959 there were awarded in the United States about 350,000 B.S., 56,200 M.S., and 7,000 Sc.D. degrees in engineering.[30] During the same decade, particularly since Sputnik, the problems of our national resources in intellectual manpower have become an important issue. Many people and organizations have taken the stand that the enlargement of the profession by education has been entirely inadequate. With this has come a feeling that "engineering" has ceased to attract the unusual student, and that in the minds of prospective students it has lost out in comparison with "science." It is difficult to make a clear, unbiased judgment of this issue. Some of the confusion stems from the selection of the year 1950 as a standard of reference. The entire period from 1940 to 1950 was strongly influenced by World War II and the Korean War. Not only were the groups of college age unusual by their small size, but the role of women was also unusual. The soldiers in the service delayed their education; the returning veterans later greatly augmented the graduating classes.

A recent study by Brode has put this issue into a much clearer perspective.[31] By making proper allowance for these abnormal factors, it now seems clear that the decisions which determine the enrollment of engineers and scientists are much more stable than we have surmised, the numbers depending chiefly on the size of the age group which seeks a college education. The principal conclusions are:

a. The percentage for each age group which selected engineering has varied between a low of about 8 per cent in 1954 and a high of about 10 per cent in 1959. Since then it has declined to around 8 per cent.
b. The percentage which has taken physical and biological sciences has also remained steady. The physical sciences reached 4.1 per cent in 1955 but has since declined slightly.
c. The cause of this decline in engineering and the physical sciences appears to be a sudden upsurge in mathematics, which started in 1958.
d. The age group reaching 22 declined during this period, reaching a low in 1955. It is now increasing and is due to expand explosively during the latter part of this decade.

There is, nevertheless, a shift in interest on the part of young people away from engineering of the old tradition. This is due to a variety of complex causes. The shift of emphasis in rapidly changing engineering schools, the increased awareness in our society of the role of science, the role of sponsored research, improved education and guidance in high schools, and perhaps a hidden degree of wisdom on the part of our youth are all aspects of this problem.[32]

The engineer and the scientist represent the most highly selective group in our society in terms of intelligence. This means that it is inevitably limited to those who can qualify. The distribution of this type of intelligence in any population is a fairly stable phenomenon and cannot be easily changed. Under the present circumstances, therefore, the percentage of college graduates who take engineering will probably continue to be stationary or decline slowly, even though the total numbers will increase. Brode suggests that we are approaching a ceiling in this type of manpower. Reserves have to come from women, who do not yet play a significant role in American engineering, and from social strata which are now underrepresented among those holding college degrees.

The shortage will continue to be felt in those activities in engineering (defense and space) which can benefit by exceptional gifts of intellect and deep commitment to science. Industry has also learned that the exceptionally endowed man is a precious asset in all kinds of operations. This was understood by a few industries even during the depth of the depression. But the understanding has now become a permanent part of industries' attitude, and exceptional men will be in perpetual demand.

Even with this better appreciation of excellence, the possibility of serious unemployment among certain categories of engineers should not be excluded. Lack of attention to this problem has caused much harm in the past, and it may be earnestly hoped that these mistakes can be avoided in the future. This segment of our intellectual manpower resources is much too precious to be wasted or discouraged by needless despair.

RECENT TRENDS IN EDUCATION

The engineering profession has kept its educational system under scrutiny for a long time, but at no time have the forces of change been stronger and more persistent than now. The reasons are complex, but a few of the major issues can be enumerated. Strongest perhaps is the feeling on the part of many that the older system of

217

professional education at the undergraduate level is inadequate for full professional stature. The attempt to freeze the system at this level resulted in excessive attention to technicianship and too little attention to broader issues. Even though engineering education has broadened its aim and extended the programs into the humanities and the social sciences, this feeling persists.

The proliferation of technology into ever wider fields, contrasted with the static nature of many programs of engineering schools, has been another source of concern. The fact that professional education must primarily focus on fitness to cope with the unexpected is becoming accepted, but the educational system is not fully adapted to this principle. Coupled with this is the emergence into national consciousness of "the scientist" as the man of the hour. The fact that the general public, even the enlightened part of it, fails to make a distinction between engineers and scientists is little comfort to the engineering profession; it would like to see the engineer appreciated on his own. This has led to subconscious and irrational opposition by engineering teachers to needed improvements such as strengthening the education in science and the development of graduate education.

In the meantime graduate education in engineering has increased sharply. This is, in fact, one of the most significant phenomena of recent years and represents the response of youth to the situation. It has been immeasurably strengthened and encouraged by research sponsored by national agencies of defense and space. Even though this has created new problems, it is significant that these agencies were persuaded to put a substantial part of this activity in the service of education. The National Science Foundation has put much of this support on a more satisfactory basis. Many of the private foundations have encouraged experiments in education which otherwise could not have been undertaken.

These issues are part of the problem of transition from craft into profession. The craft tradition carries with it the implication that there is a fixed and relatively stable body of knowledge, which the engineer "must have" as part of his professional equipment. This premise had validity for engineering education not so long ago, but the circumstances are now changing. The most important quality sought now is the ability to cope with wholly unknown situations, to deal with fields which perhaps did not even exist when the engineer went to school.[33] This places a great strain on the educational system in engineering, which has been proud of its systematic and occasionally pedestrian character. On the whole, however, one may

218

conclude that these lessons have been learned and that progress is only a matter of time.[34]

As some of the engineering institutions have grown in stature, they have begun to break away from the older craft divisions. The interaction with the life sciences, the social sciences, and the humanities has been of great importance. The introduction of research centers of greater scope foreshadows a new point of view in which essential human needs such as transportation, communications, and materials are looked at in perspective. These changes are taking place throughout the system, even though they may be more ambitious and dramatic in some of the larger schools.[35]

Perhaps the most potent effect of these changes is the growing conviction that the modern engineer must continue to study throughout life. This has become recognized by special programs in many institutions and by the creation of "centers for advanced study" in engineering in some.[36] These will have a far-reaching effect in the maturing of the engineering profession.

IV. The Engineer's Role

IN SOCIETY

The free culture of the United States represents the first consistent application of technology to human needs. We have yet to develop real understanding of this remarkable phenomenon, which will continue to occupy historians into the distant future. There are, of course, many obvious causes: the ideals of freedom which led to the political system of the United States, its remarkable degree of stability, a steady influx of productive individuals through immigration, the availability of the resources of an entire continent for the exercise of unusual, practical, and pragmatic talents of its people, and the effectiveness of the free enterprise system in launching it are examples. When we look at our present problems, however, and at the working of technology in wholly different social systems, we must conclude that these are only part of the explanation and that some of the real causes have so far eluded us. W. W. Rostow has listed the main qualities needed for a nation to get started on the road to economic growth,* [37] but there is a question whether even these economic factors tell the whole story.

Most of the perplexing problems which beset us nationally and

* "the propensities to develop fundamental science, to apply it to economic ends, to seek material advance, to accept innovation, to consume, to have children"

internationally stem from the impact of technology. It is the success, rather than the failure, of the process of technology which now creates the main issues. We may also ask ourselves to what extent these problems represent inevitable consequences of technology, or whether they are open to conscious choice. Must technology be completely enveloped in unrestrained commercialism? Are we prepared to face the social choices necessary to let the workings of technology reduce poverty and misery? Are the extremes of the affluent society indispensable consequences of technology? Can we imagine a social-political system, agreeable to our own mores, in which technology is the servant rather than the master?

The victories in science and technology have completely altered the international situation. The overwhelming fact that unrestrained use of the new power leads to mutual annihilation has begun to shape international relations. The events of the recent past indicate that true understanding of this fact can lead to constructive improvements in the relations between powerful nations. Internally the process of technology will force us to keep in permanent question the boundary between public and private enterprise. The explosive developments of recent years came from public expenditures necessary to ensure national survival. In the process we perfected the interaction between science and technology into the forced development process, whereby the last restraints on the ambition to control the environment seem to have been removed. Nuclear power, air transport, radar and short wave communications, as well as ever deeper penetration into the secrets of nature, are monuments along the way.

These advances in the process of technology cannot be halted or reversed; they are with us permanently. The true implications of this added power in almost any of the major categories of human needs are yet to dawn upon man. Many ventures which we have been accustomed to label visionary, impractical, or impossible have now become real possibilities; some of these, such as climatic control, may have awesome implications. When such ventures were clearly impossible, they could be dismissed as foolish dreams. Anything which is possible in human affairs is likely to be tried. This will require much more in the way of wisdom and restraint than any previous situation in the history of man. Many examples can be cited, but the supersonic transport is a pertinent example at the moment. Putting aside the question of whether supersonic civilian air transport is socially desirable or not, we now appear to be in a position where we dare not let the venture go by default. Yet the cost is likely to run into many billions of dollars, of which private enterprise is willing or even able to pay only a small fraction. In the course of time most of our major industries will be confronted with super projects of this scale.

Modern technology is already beginning to intercede in our social and political systems. We may be reluctant to call it socialism, and we may hope to bypass the distasteful choices involved, but in the end technology will demand resources beyond the capabilities of the free enterprise system. The courage to face these choices rationally can be sustained only by better education in all aspects of the process of technology. In this situation we need desperately the voice of dispassionate reason. Professionals in technology must play an important role, and they must consciously prepare themselves for this task. It must be constantly reiterated that neither scientists nor engineers have any monopoly on the wisdom required. A world wholly dominated by them would surely turn into a nightmare. The guidelines for this role may be found in the traditions of the older professions.

The older professions came to play a dual role in society; they were the custodians of learning and practice in their own domain, but they also exerted a powerful influence on their contemporary world in other ways. The minister not only attended to the religious needs, but he also played an important role as one of the few men of learning and culture in rural society. This was particularly so in those countries where the ministers were the product of first-class university education. The lawyer and the doctor also influenced society outside of their professional domains. These influences are no longer quite as strong as formerly; perhaps they have never played the same role in America as they did in the older agrarian type of European society.

Whitehead, in a celebrated chapter on "aspects of freedom,"[38] has identified the important guardians of liberty in society. He arrives at the conclusion that the professions, by means of self-governing institutions, which can "claim liberty and exercise control" play a most important role. The combination of character, intelligence, and wisdom with independence of expression thus becomes the important criterion of the professional leader. The important voices in our society most frequently come from men who have achieved success, power, and wealth. Many of them are wise and impassionate, but it is only through exceptional qualities of character and integrity that they have acquired a position of prestige and independence. Even so it may be argued whether true independence can be reconciled with great power. The politician seeking election, the businessman furthering the interest of his enterprises, the advertising man trying to influence the consumer, the labor leader seeking to maintain his following among labor, the engineer managing an industrial complex, or working as an employee in it, may all be men of integrity; but in these roles they cannot always speak with true independence on social issues, particularly those which have become "sensitive." Their own success is, in a measure, proof of their ability to view things from the point of view of their own self-interest.

This need not involve direct questions of freedom of expression or democracy. Lack of freedom does not stem from tyrants or tyrannical political systems alone. It can also be caused by a social and intellectual environment which encourages the use of slogans and platitudes through which the true issues are obscured and which eventually imprison their users. Political and cultural leaders with wisdom must play their principal role here, but informed and independent voices of reason are equally important. The professional man has a great responsibility in this respect, and his education must anticipate this role.

This influence must come from the vantage point of prestige, created by unusual qualities of character, education and culture, high professional accomplishment, and dedication to this independence. It is difficult to achieve in any profession, but particularly so in engineering. The fundamental motivation of the engineer stems from the desire to create useful material things at a profit and to make them work—a combination of artistic, scientific, and economic motives. He usually does not enter the profession with inherited wealth; most often he is out to succeed on his own towards power, wealth, and prestige. Most engineers are content to reach recognition within their own field, and only a few are privileged to view in perspective the entire process of technology and its role in society.

It is primarily in teaching that our society has been able to confer such a position of independence on professionals. This is true in engineering as well as in the other professions, but here the relationship between teaching and practice is a much more complicated one. Something more than the present scheme of professional education is needed. The position of the teacher in the professions and in society must be better recognized. There are, nevertheless, signs of improvement. Some of the great universities have found it possible to create distinguished professorships in teaching and research related to engineering, which in the long run will attract outstanding and potentially great men. It is worth remembering also that in spite of these difficulties there have always been a few teachers of engineering who have played this role. But generally science has done better. Achievements in science are more readily assessed, and the great men of science have perhaps been more aware of this role.

The developments in engineering education of recent years have brought along new problems, which in turn threaten to obscure the position of the teacher in engineering. They stem from the doctrine, adopted by all professions, that professional teaching must have its roots in the contemporary world. Government-sponsored research programs and consulting service to industry and government are part of this picture, but so is the practice of operating business enterprises from the secure vantage point of a professorship in a university. These activities have rescued engineering education from the doldrums of fifty years ago, but they have also brought the problems of the market place into the university. There are many perplexing questions which have as yet to be faced squarely. What should be the attitude of the university to rights of inventions and discoveries which may have great financial value? What about the faculty members' loyalty—is it to the university which provides him with a center for his career, or to his own business interests? Can the university under these altered circumstances properly discharge its obligations to the students and to society in general? What about questions of conflicts of interest when faculty members render advice to the government? Equally important are the subtle changes of ideals which imperceptibly tend to favor the skillful promoter and the operator in comparison with the unselfish creative worker. Most important, perhaps, is the potential loss of independence of professionals. We are learning that even the soundest of doctrines must be applied with wisdom. The devotion to true independence may have to become one of the important qualifications for a high university position. The problem is now receiving much attention.[39]

In most European countries bureaucratic positions play an important role in the same connection, a role comparable to teaching. Until recently the position of engineers in civil service has not carried high prestige in the United States, but the situation is now changing rapidly due to the role of the federal government in science and technology. The American civil service has grown rapidly in maturity and professional strength. It is worth noting that about

60 per cent of all the federal professional civil service personnel are scientists, engineers, and health professionals. In the highest grades the percentage is even greater. As in industry, there is an unfortunate tendency to relate success to bureaucratic or management functions rather than to creative and professional activities.

Lastly, the engineering profession itself must improve its means of public identification of outstanding men. Apart from the EJC, the principal means for this has been within the engineering societies themselves. Recently there have been encouraging instances of high national recognition. The National Academy of Sciences (NAS) has come to play an important part. This is an example of a private agency under government charter, which through the prestige of its membership has been able to speak with understanding and wisdom on important public issues. This agency also includes engineering. The National Research Council, organized by the NAS in 1916, besides its role in World War I has participated in a substantial research and development program and advisory service financed by private industry as well as by government agencies. Through this agency the NAS has had an indirect influence on a large number of important problems in engineering as well as in science. However, the size of the engineering section (about 50), which is limited by the total membership of the Academy (about 675) and its election procedure, is too small to effectively represent the entire engineering profession in the United States.

A National Academy of Engineering, as a parallel to the National Academy of Sciences, is now in the process of formation. Initiated by the leaders of the EJC, it envisages an institution of the same type as the NAS, with the same congressional authorization and with a similar charter, election procedure, and size. The exact relationship to the NAS has not yet been developed, but the proposal appears to have responsible support. Like the NAS it must grow into its role by gradual development of professional ideals, policies, and election procedures. This will take a long time. It can become an important milestone in the evolution of the engineering profession, but its role lies in the future.

IN TECHNOLOGY

Engineering, like other professions, is faced with a perpetual controversy about the relative significance of the generalist, the specialist, and the administrator. This has become particularly acute in recent years, because of the obviously important roles in modern technology of the scientist and the engineering specialist. Many responsible leaders claim to see in this an inevitable decline in the role of the engineer-generalist. According to this view, all that the process of technology needs is a group of highly trained scientists and engineering specialists under competent management.

In the nineteenth century the inception of new fields usually took place by intuitive invention. The leaders, even outstanding ones such as Thomas A. Edison, Henry Ford, and others, were empiricists. Gradually the demands for deeper scientific knowledge grew more insistent, but the full recognition of science, research, and specialization did not come until World War II. By this time there had developed an array of engineering specialties based on superior scientific background. Subjects such as vibrations, acoustics, stress analysis, heat transfer, lubrication, and metallurgy provided a rewarding scope of activity for a new type of engineer, the engineering specialist. These specialties have had a strong influence upon education as well as on the system of professional organizations. During the war years this process came to its true fulfillment, when many new fields, notably nuclear energy, communications, and computer technology, were taken up by highly trained physicists, mathematicians, and other scientists, and to which they brought a mature scientific background not previously put into full use in engineering tasks.

The engineering specialist and some scientists live in an uncluttered world of deceptive simplicity. The background can be gained by academic studies, the narrow specialization is relieved by varied industrial applications, the information can be put to good commercial use on a private basis, it may be combined with teaching and research, and it may even be claimed that the activity has reached full professional dimensions. All of these circumstances have transformed engineering education into education for specialists; first-class education towards broader objectives has all but disappeared from our engineering schools.

This is not to say that the trend towards education for engineering specialists is wrong in itself, or that it is not necessary. It is perhaps the only method whereby engineering education can be kept alive in the present epoch. It has, indeed, given new life to the academic aspects of the process of technology. It can be taken for granted that the influence of scientists and engineering specialists will continue to increase rather than diminish. The error arises when this activity, so congenial to the academic environment, is automatically equated with the whole of technology, or when the excluded segments are dismissed as "technicianship." It should be obvious from the previous review of the tasks which confront our technological system that we are more than ever dependent upon the ability of at least a few to view the process of technology in perspective. At the moment our universities have brushed off the task of training and inspiring such men as a task uncongenial to the university atmosphere. This may be called the great dilemma of engineering.

The very mode of success of individual engineers must be considered part of this issue. Success of engineers is sometimes due to creative acts of invention and discovery, sometimes to bureaucratic activity as part of a team; sometimes the success is managerial, sometimes it is purely financial. All of these mainsprings of individual action are important, and no profession can afford to adopt a set of ideals which is not calculated to lead to success of one kind or another. But the kind of wisdom needed for the development of these ideals comes hard. Professional education deals with time constants of the order of at least one lifetime, and during this period there will be inevitable changes of emphasis. Periods of innovation (such as we have experienced recently) will be followed by periods of consolidation. Hence, when value judgments are applied to different forms of talent, they must be value judgments seasoned by wider perspectives and greater wisdom.

Engineering education has not yet faced up to this issue, and perhaps new forms of professional education are needed. It may be that the "centers of advanced study" already mentioned will in the end help to resolve the issue. Admittedly the task is a difficult one. The kind of professional background sought can be achieved by only a few. Along with a mature scientific background in many specialties there must be the interest and ability to view the process of technology in perspective. It may even require modification of our preparatory education, in which the process of technology becomes a major object of study. Our children can be counted upon to fill in many of the complex technical details. What is needed most urgently is exposure to the social and economic context in which technical inventions are used.

Whatever role history will assign to the many professional groups interacting in the process of technology, we can take for granted that the American engineer has been, and will continue to be, one of the important members. It is in engineering that the American genius has found particular expression, and many of our youth are still blessed with these same qualities. The wise use of these gifts will continue to be one of our most important tasks.

V. *Conclusions*

The American engineer is the product of a long process of development which is far from finished. The ideals which have motivated him have undergone subtle changes—from the early zest for invention and a deep belief in the blessings of the new age through the more directly materialistic objectives of the latter part of the nineteenth century to the present phase, in which some of the emphasis is on deeper penetration into science and a broader cultural awareness.

The scientific and humanistic training of engineers will continue to improve, particularly for those who go on to graduate education. This will improve the engineer's competence as a teacher, particularly in relation to engineering science. It can confidently be expected that the adherence to undergraduate education as a base for engineering will become less rigid, so that at least in some first-class institutions engineering will be a graduate discipline, preceded by a "pre-engineering" type of undergraduate education. This process has already started on a modest basis. Technology must have a place in such undergraduate programs, and one hopes that it can be introduced within the social, economic, and cultural context as one of the important objects of study in our society, with less emphasis on isolated technical facts. It can also be expected that the ECPD accreditation system will find a way to recognize these programs without undue control over graduate education.

Not the least important in this connection is a more serious effort in our society to understand the workings of technology. Some day this will become a conscious part of elementary education, no less important than the affairs of rulers and political parties. Society needs this understanding in order to face the future world of technology. Engineering education would mature in such an environment of understanding.

One of the important characteristics of the American system of engineering education is its great diversity. It is hoped that even with a steady advance in quality, this diversity will continue to exist. The highest achievements on the academic side can be reached by relatively few, even though the recognition of the importance of education at the doctoral level is a most important step. It is equally

227

important to remember, however, that the process of technology needs professionals with a very wide spectrum of emphasis, and it is not possible to apply relative value judgment on any part of it. The important objective is to develop to the fullest the great variety of intellectual and personal gifts with which our youth are endowed.

Engineering will continue to depend on scientists and engineering specialists in scientific as well as in more practical aspects of the process of technology. Along with this specialization there will, hopefully, come an appreciation of the few outstanding minds who can grasp the scientific complexities and also see the main aspects of the process. The doctrine that a professional career must involve lifelong studies is gradually becoming accepted for engineering. The response to this, the advanced institutions in engineering, will hopefully bring mature technology into the American university.

These manifold tendencies will help to strengthen the public image of the engineer. However, this remains one of the important problems for which no obvious and simple solution exists. It will not be accomplished by calculated publicity. Only the engineering profession itself can create it—first by better recognition within the profession and next by increased awareness of its role in society. Society will continue to depend on engineering for its material welfare. Let us hope that in the fullness of time it will also accord this activity its deserved social recognition.

REFERENCES

1. Alfred N. Whitehead, *Science and the Modern World* (Cambridge, 1925).

2. W. H. G. Armytage, *A Social History in Engineering* (New York, 1961). This is a recent and welcome addition to the history of engineering.

3. Armytage, *A Social History of Engineering;* Charles Singer, et al., *A History of Technology* (Oxford, 1956), Vol. II.

4. Lewis Mumford, *Technics and Civilization* (New York, 1934).

5. Leonardo da Vinci, *Notebooks,* arranged by Edward McCurdy (New York, 1938).

6. *The Principal Works of Simon Stevin,* Vol. I edited by E. J. Dyksterhuis; Vols. IIA and IIB edited by D. J. Struik (Amsterdam, 1955 and 1958).

7. Galileo, *Two New Sciences,* translated by Henry Crew and Alfonso de Salvo (New York, 1933).

8. *Agricola: De Re Metallica,* translated in 1912 from the 1556 Latin edition by Ex-President and Mrs. Herbert Hoover (Dover, 1950).

9. *Christopher Polhem (1661–1751), the Father of Swedish Technology,* translated from the original Swedish version of 1911 by William A. Johnson, Trinity College (Hartford, Connecticut, 1963). Sweden emerged from the Middle Ages later than the rest of Europe. Polhem's observations on contemporary eo-technic engineering are noteworthy. He urged formal education in engineering and created a museum, which was to serve as "a technological alphabet" in engineering education.

10. Armytage, *A Social History in Engineering,* p. 50; H. W. Dickenson, *James Watt, Craftsman and Engineer* (Cambridge, 1936), p. 13.

11. *The Principal Works of Simon Stevin,* Vol. I.

12. Ernst Mach, *The Science of Mechanics* (London, 1942; original German edition, Leipzig, 1883), p. 35.

13. Dickenson, *James Watt, Craftsman and Engineer.*

14. Armytage, *A Social History in Engineering.*

15. Stephen S. Timoshenko, *History of Strength of Materials* (McGraw-Hill, 1953).

16. Daniel H. Calhoun, *The American Civil Engineer, Origins and Conflict* (Cambridge, Mass., 1960). The history of the engineering profession has not yet attracted many historians or sociologists. This volume represents a promising beginning of systematic study of the emergence of the American engineering profession.

17. Sanford G. Brown, "Count Rumford, Physicist Extraordinary," *Science Study Series* (Anchor, New York, 1962).

18. Jacob Bigelow, *Elements of Technology* (Boston, 1831).

19. William Barton Rogers, *Life and Letters,* edited by his wife (Boston, 1896), Vol. I, Appendix C; Vol. II, page 60.

20. Annual Report of the National Science Foundation, Division of Scientific Personnel, 1963.

21. Dael Wolfle, *America's Resources of Specialized Talent* (New York, 1954).

22. Annual Report of the National Science Foundation, Division of Scientific Personnel.

23. Forest L. Trautman, Thomas E. Cooney, and Carl W. Borgmann, "The Ford Foundation Engineering Faculty Study," August, 1961.

24. "Goals of Engineering Education," Information Document 2, *American Society for Engineering Education* (1962).

25. W. E. Wickenden, "Report of the Investigation of Engineering Education, 1923–1929," *Journal of the Society for Promotion of Engineering Education,* Vol. I (1930); Vol. II (1934).

26. "Accreditation in Higher Education," *U. S. Department of Health, Education and Welfare*, U. S. Government Printing Office (Washington, D.C., 1959); William K. Selden, *Accreditation: A Struggle Over Standards of Higher Education* (New York, 1960).

27. H. L. Hazen, "The ECPD Accreditation Program," *Journal of Engineering Education*, Vol. 45, No. 2 (October, 1954), p. 101; C. E. Davies, "The Builders of the ECPD," *25th ECPD Annual Report* (1957); Thorndyke Saville, "Achievements in Engineering Education," *Transactions, American Society of Civil Engineers* (1953), CT, 147.

28. The *31st ECPD Annual Report* (1963).

29. C. E. Davies, "Organization of Engineers in the USA," *Proceedings of the International Technical Congress* (Paris, September, 1946).

30. W. E. Tolliver and H. H. Armsby, "Engineering Enrollment and Degrees, 1960," *U. S. Department of Health, Education and Welfare*, Office of Education Circular 638, U. S. Government Printing Office (Washington, D.C., 1961); "Doctorate Production in United States Universities, 1920–1962," *National Academy of Sciences*, Publication 1142 (1963).

31. Wallace R. Brode, "Approaching Ceilings in the Supply of Scientific Manpower," *Science*, Vol. 142, No. 3604 (January 24, 1964), p. 313.

32. John R. Dixon, "The Lost Mission in Engineering," *Journal of Engineering Education*, Vol. 53, No. 7 (March, 1963), p. 434. This is an example of how the situation is viewed by some of the engineering teachers; C. Richard Soderberg, "The Trends in Engineering Education: Do They Concern the Power Industry?" *Proceedings of the American Power Conference*, XXIV (1960), 135.

33. C. Richard Soderberg, Report of the Dean of the School of Engineering for the academic year ending June 30, 1959, Massachusetts Institute of Technology, "A Philosophy of Engineering Education."

34. Gordon S. Brown, "New Horizons in Engineering Education," *Dædalus*, Spring, 1962, p. 341; Julius A. Stratton, Report of the President, Massachusetts Institute of Technology for the year ending June 30, 1963.

35. Stratton, Report of the President, M.I.T.; Gordon S. Brown, Report of the Dean of the School of Engineering, Massachusetts Institute of Technology for the academic year ending June 30, 1963.

36. Brown, Report of the Dean of the School of Engineering, M.I.T.

37. W. W. Rostow, *The Process of Economic Growth* (Boston, 1952).

38. Alfred North Whitehead, *Adventures of Ideas* (New York, 1933).

39. Stratton, Report of the President, M.I.T.

JAMES MARSTON FITCH

The Profession of Architecture

UNLIKE MANY OTHER FIELDS of professional activity, architecture
must serve a complete spectrum of social process, stretching from
the largely ceremonial, such as the F.D.R. Memorial, to the wholly
utilitarian, such as the surgical operating theater. Because its jurisdiction thus extends from the poetic to the practical, it is simultaneously subject to two quite different value systems—one derived
from art, the other from science and technology. This confronts the
architect with professional problems which are peculiar, if not indeed unique, to him.

Subjectively, the architect occupies a position closer to the artist
than to the scientist in that in his work he aspires to the creation of
formal order. That is, he hopes like all artists to resolve the contradictions between form and content in such a fashion as to produce
a work of high esthetic value. Here, however, all parallels end, for
the architect hopes to extract from this resolution a building which
will have an artistic validity *above and beyond the basic need which
called it into being*. This dual ambition makes his task, if not of a
higher order than that of his fellow artists, then certainly one of
greater complexity. For though his building may, like a piece of
sculpture, be susceptible of manipulation for purely formal ends,
its content is social process and living human beings, each with in-
eluctably nonesthetic requirements. The relationship between a
painter or poet and his audience is a dialogue, uni-dimensional, limited in scope and easily terminated by either party. But the relationship between the architect's building and its occupants is much
more fundamental. It is a relationship which in the modern world
is terminable only by death. Thus whatever formal characteristics
a work of architecture may share with other categories of art, there
is this fundamental difference: *it has no spectators, only participants.*
This distinction, so obvious and so profound, is too often overlooked

by everyone, including architects themselves. All too often, as a result, any conflict between the formal requirements of the container and the functional requirements of the contained is resolved in favor of the former. The occupant is simply forced to fit.

As though this were not enough to differentiate architecture from all other art forms and artifacts, there is another paradox concealed within the "contained" itself. Usually the environmental requirements of the occupant differ fundamentally from the various processes which he attends, takes part in or supervises. In the preindustrial world this inner contradiction was not usually severe. But in modern life these two sets of environmental requirements are not always congruent. In most of modern industry, they are divergent; in such fields as printing, pharmaceuticals and metallurgy, environmental criteria for worker and process will differ radically. Often— as in chemicals or nuclear power—they will be mortally irreconcilable. Thus, in many of the 270 distinct building types which modern American life requires,[1] contradictions must be solved at two levels: first between the "containees" themselves and then between them and their container. Respect for these two conditions is mandatory if the building is to be successful. But respect for these two conditions will often leave very little room within which the architect can safely exercise his prerogative to manipulate the container for purely formal ends.

Most contemporary failures in architecture and urbanism stem either from a failure to understand this problem or else from the refusal to come to terms with it. Of course, neither buildings nor cities can grow like living organisms, employing cellular division and genetic memory. They require the intervention of human agencies. In this sense they must always be consciously designed by men with preconceived ideas of what forms they should assume. An "unplanned" edifice or city is ultimately inconceivable: no matter how badly designed or executed, it is the result of someone's (or some group's) creative ambitions. Nevertheless, building and city alike must satisfy a whole range of human need—private and social, psychic and somatic—and these needs lie mostly below the reach of simple plastic or pictorial manipulation. Viability is the end result of meeting many interlocking requirements, most of which are simply not the proper media for artistic invention or subjective expression. Though we cannot expect either buildings or cities to grow spontaneously, neither can we expect them to survive a formal manipulation for purely artistic ends.

232

These problems, of course, have always been present in architecture, but they have been acutely complicated by the flowering of science and technology on the one hand, and the unparalleled proliferation of social, economic and industrial processes on the other. It must be remembered that at any time prior to the closing years of the eighteenth century, the architect would have worked within a clear and comprehensible reference frame of needs and means, the exact dimensions of which were established by two sets of complementary but opposing forces. One set of these forces pressed outward, so to say, representing the client's minimal requirements. These minima would vary with class and culture. They would extend from the peasant's irreducible requirements for survival—roof against sun and rain, wall and fire against winter cold, enclosure for crop and beast—to satisfaction of the sensual appetites and ceremonial apparatus of the nobility. But a set of external forces acted to limit survival and satiety alike. These pressed relentlessly inward, establishing limits of span and height, complexity and technical sophistication which sharply restricted the ambitions of pharaoh, emperor and archbishop alike. These forces were six in number: (1) the impact of the climate; (2) a limited palette of locally available materials; (3) the lack of mechanical prime-movers; (4) the limited means of transport and communication; (5) a slow rate of cultural change and technical invention; (6) a well-informed but conservative clientele. Under such restrictive circumstances the margin of error was sharply curtailed; personal idiosyncrasy was strictly contained; the possible solutions to any given problem were limited in number. Under such circumstances, an architect like Thomas Jefferson could easily encompass the poetic and the practical aspirations of his day, designing the curriculum and the campus of his beloved university and then supervising the making of bricks and nails to construct it.

Today this balance of forces is radically altered. Industrialization is making human habitation possible anywhere, including the ocean bottom and outer space. The materials of the entire world are readily available to the architects of all developed countries. The average American has all the necessary mechanical horsepower at his disposal. Communication at the speed of light and travel faster than sound have raised the rate of cultural change to unprecedented levels. Today's clientele is no longer conservative, but it is illiterate in its judgments and insatiable in its appetites. Little wonder, then, that the American architectural profession is today in crisis.

This profession consists of from 27,000 to 30,000 registered architects. In addition to the one national association, the American Institute of Architects, with 29 state chapters, there are 18 state societies, all of whose members are registered architects but not all of whom are members of the AIA. In fact, although the AIA is the unchallenged spokesman for the whole profession, its membership stood at only 16,207 in April, 1964.[2] In addition, there are perhaps 3,500 graduate apprentices—young men and women who have won their first professional degree but who have not yet completed the three-year stint of supervised work in licensed offices.[3] This apprenticeship, the equivalent of the medical internship, is the precondition to standing for the state board examinations.

The profession supports a total of 77 schools or departments, all of them organized into the Association of Collegiate Schools of Architecture.[4] The academic standards and performance of these schools is, in turn, policed by another professional organ, the National Architectural Accrediting Board: it had fully accredited 53 of the above schools as of April, 1964.[5] The ACSA reported a total enrollment of 18,922 students for the academic year 1963–1964.[6] Of these the overwhelming majority would be working for their first professional degree, the Bachelor of Architecture, although many would have already taken their Bachelor of Arts before entering architecture. While only 661 students were working for advanced degrees in 1950 (date of the last AIA survey), both the number and percentage of men and women working for the M. Sc.Arch. and the Ph.D. are today undoubtedly considerably higher.

Admission to the profession is won, as in medicine or law, by passing the licensing examinations held by the authorized agencies, the Boards of Architectural Registration in the various states. Operating under state laws deriving from the public health and safety clauses of the United States Constitution, the first of which were passed by the Illinois legislature in 1897, these quasi-official bodies exercise effective control of the entire profession. The profession has its own national organ, the *Journal* of the AIA, and numerous local publications; it supports five commercial magazines of national or regional significance. Although the AIA publishes all the standard documents and contracts of the profession, the publication of all texts is in the hands of commercial publishers.

Structurally, in other words, the architectural profession closely resembles those of law and medicine. There are several significant differences, however. First, the architect is in nowhere near such complete control of his field as are his peers in law or medicine. For example the civil engineer is also qualified, by the terms of his education and licensing, to design structures involving public health and safety. Most bridge and highway construction, as well as that of airports, dams and seaport facilities will ordinarily be entrusted to the engineer; the architect is involved (if at all) only in the monumental aspects of the work. In addition, whole sectors of specialized industrial and military enterprise are considered the exclusive domain of the engineer. Many aspects of urban planning are now entrusted to professionals with nonarchitectural backgrounds.

Other sections of the building industry lie outside the architect's normal jurisdiction. For example there is the twilight zone of the "stock plan" in which he designs a prototype building—chain store, filling station, single-family house—for serial reproduction. Here the client will be a national chain or a big speculative builder, and the architect will be paid on a royalty basis, having personally little to do with the actual siting or construction of the individual unit. Most of the huge single-family housing market, amounting to a million units a year, is handled in this fashion. Finally, there is the fact that in most rural areas of the nation, any individual can design his own house or barn without recourse to either architect or engineer. This lack of control of his putative field of operations unquestionably makes the architect less influential than the medical doctor, whose monopoly of power often seems absolute even in such peripheral fields as pharmaceuticals, hospitals and health insurance. Perhaps because of such facts alone, the ratio of architects to engineers or lawyers is much lower (26.5 per 100,000 as against 449.8 and 203.8, respectively), and the median annual income is also lower ($5,509 for architects as opposed to $8,302 for doctors and $6,284 for lawyers).[7]

But the architectural profession is developing other peculiarities as well. The traditional first-hand relationship between individual practitioner and client is being increasingly modified as both tend to become corporate entities. Even in 1950, 24 per cent of all registered architects found themselves the salaried employees either of big private firms or governmental agencies.[8] This trend is even more marked today; ever fewer architects stand any real chance of being successful independent practitioners. Abstractly this may not of itself be a bad development, but it has two important implications for the future. First, it means that the man in the big office will tend to become increasingly specialized, seeing less and less of

235

the entire field of practice and of the clients. Second, more and more of the architect's clients are themselves corporate entities—big business, big institutions, big government and the military. And this carries the most disturbing implications of all.

For in modern America the architect's *real* client is less and less his *legal* client. The white collar man in the big skyscraper, the worker in the big plant, the housewife in the big housing project, the child in the big consolidated school—these are the people for whom the architect works and to whom he is ultimately responsible. They are the "contained" for whom the building containers should be accurately and sensitively designed. Yet these are the people whom the architect no longer sees. He deals instead with their agents—those corporate or institutional entities who commission the projects. Instead of first-hand observation of real people and their needs and aspirations, the architect is given statistical data with which to work—peak loads, median incomes, average family size, minimum floor areas, etc. These data, of course, may be essential for the establishment of the broad lines of policy; but they are no more a substitute for first-hand detailed knowledge of the actual "consumers" of the building than statistics on the incidence of cancer are to a physician with an actual patient.

Nor can it be assumed that these corporate or institutional clients, acting though they may be as agents for the consuming public, are always to be relied upon to represent its best interests or requirements. In a profit-motivated society, criteria for actual architectural projects are all too apt to drop to the minima permitted by building codes or by the law of supply and demand. Of course this tendency will vary from field to field. The speculative builders of tract housing are notorious for the venality of their design and construction policies. On the other hand a life insurance company planning a big housing project for long-term investment purposes may—out of sheer self-interest—follow quite enlightened policies. The demand for maximum economy in public projects can often prove quite as limiting a factor as the demand for maximum profit in a private one. Naturally many public buildings with specialized requirements, such as hospitals or schools, must meet factual standards determined by the uses themselves. American public housing, on the other hand, has been permitted to slip to the lowest levels of mediocrity of any country in the West.

Thus, if any generalization is possible, it would be that the general level of American building, whether viewed from a functional

236

or from an esthetic point of view, falls grotesquely short of national capacities. This is in large part due to the inability of the building consumer to understand or implement his demands, requirements, expectations. And the result of the architect's isolation from his real client is the increasing prevalence of the abstract, the formal and the platitudinous in architectural and urban design. This changed relationship is not only expressed in his personal life, whose fortunate position in Galbraith's economy of abundance has served to insulate him against the squalor and discomfort of Harrington's culture of poverty. It is also expressed in subtle but definite changes in his cultural orientation. It is true, of course, that from the very nature of his work the architect has always stood closer to the upper classes than to the common man. For ordinary people his services were always much more rare and much less imperatively required than those of lawyer or doctor. Nevertheless the tradition of the socially conscious, intellectually committed architect has a long history in the United States. One might say indeed that the leading spokesman of the profession in each generation were of this persuasion: Jefferson, Latrobe, Greenough; Sullivan, Wright, Gropius, Neutra. This tradition reached its apex during the days of the Great Depression and the New Deal, when unemployment in normal channels forced approximately three-quarters of the architectural and engineering professions into government-sponsored projects of one sort or another. This switch from the private to the social client gave the architect an exhilarating sense of identification with society. It served to shift his attention, if not his allegiance, toward social architecture.

To a certain extent the afterglow of this Rooseveltian liberalism still suffuses the profession, giving a more liberal aspect to its posture, perhaps, than to those of the American Medical Association or the American Bar Association. But increasingly since the 1950's the profession has returned to "normal." Architects have been reabsorbed into the world of private enterprise. Some of them have themselves become men of big business: in 1964 there were 25 firms *each of which* had over $60,000,000 worth of work on their boards.[9] Ironically, this general prosperity has led to the impoverishment of intellectual speculation and invention. The Utopian element in architectural thinking has largely disappeared; theory itself is in disrepute. The men whose polemics (whether in print or in stone) once galvanized the Western world are either aging or gone. Though Mies van der Rohe, LeCorbusier and Gropius are still active and vocal, few younger men aspire to their prophetic role. The dominant attitude is one of complacent *laissez-faire* whose esthetic expression is a genial eclecticism. The result is a body of work as antipopular and aristocratic in its general impact as anything ordered by Frederick the Great or Louis XV.

This aristocratic esthetic is very evident in all the most prestigious buildings of the day. It is dismayingly apparent in the urban redevelopment schemes which are currently convulsing the centers of many American cities. Aimed at radically altering the social character of the central city, these projects almost without exception end by evicting the poorer worker, the racial minority, the small merchant and tradesman, and replacing them with what is euphemistically called "upper middle income" groups. The result is some of the most outrageous class planning since Baron Hausmann remade central Paris to correspond to the imperial pretensions of Napoleon III. Designed in the self-styled avant-garde manner, these projects are often handsome from a purely formal point of view. But this should not blind us to the fact that this particular mode of expression has been largely emptied of its original functional-democratic connotations. Its main components were formulated decades ago, under conditions quite different from those which obtain today. The spacious and humane iconography of Roosevelt is today being put to quite other uses. It will not be the first time, of course, that the same style has been the vehicle of different points of view. Jefferson and Napoleon alike turned to the Romans for a language of figurative expression; and two such antithetic figures as Emerson and Calhoun could both feel comfortable with the Greek Revival. Whatever one's personal estimate of this aristocratic esthetic, it remains the outward evidence of an internal involution: the abdication by the profession of its claim to be the architect of the whole people, to become instead the agent and spokesman for an elite.

How the profession will extricate itself from this cul-de-sac is a knotty problem. Because of its default, it probably faces that sort of "socialization" the fear of which has convulsed the medical profession, and for many of the same reasons: for just as millions of Americans lack good medical care, so are the same millions deprived of good housing, good schools, good hospitals. The satisfaction of this need undoubtedly implies the increased intervention of governmental agencies; and this probably implies an increase in the bureaucratic architecture so abhorred by the profession. But—

aside from the fact that big private firms are quite as bureaucratic as any counterpart in local or national agencies of government—this "socialization" of architecture will not, of itself, guarantee qualitatively superior architecture and town planning. Only a greatly improved system of education and training, together with a new kind of functional rapport with the building consumer, can accomplish this goal.

The historical origins of architectural education lie much closer to engineering or dentistry than to those of medicine or law. This was due to the fact that competence in the former *could* be acquired through apprenticeship exclusively, whereas theoretical training was of critical importance to the latter. Thus, until the opening of the present century, the vast majority of building was in the hands of men whose origins were closer to the craftsmanship of millwright and mason than to academic scholarship. Professional education at the university level has been a commonplace requirement in medicine and law for centuries. But the first professional school of architecture in the United States was established only in 1868, at the Massachusetts Institute of Technology. The American Institute of Architects itself had been formed only eleven years before in an effort to establish professional standards of training and competence. And it was to be decades before the various state governments, acting under the public health and welfare clause of the Constitution, could be persuaded to pass legislation establishing a system of examination and licensing procedures (Illinois was the first in 1897, Vermont the last in 1951).[10] Only in the last few decades, then, has the training of architects been put upon an equal footing with the older professions.

But preindustrial architecture had one anomaly which it shared with no other profession—the presence in its midst of the amateur and the connoisseur. (Both terms, in those days, had the very favorable connotation of a disinterested love of the field.) From the Renaissance onward, the architect's patron often crossed the line to become, in actuality, an architect himself. But whether these amateurs remained passionate and tireless patrons, like Horace Walpole or the Earl of Burlington, or became the actual designers of buildings, like Jefferson at Charlottesville, they established the other polarity of preindustrial architecture. As opposed to the direct economic incentive of the craftsman, they entered the arena from many other lines of approach: from an enthusiasm for literature, especially the classics; from antiquarianism; from political commitments (Jefferson saw the Roman basilica as the only fit container for his new Republic); even from religious conviction (the Gothic Revival was above all the vehicle for nineteenth-century religiosity).

Formed thus of components from widely divergent cultural milieux and propelled by the most disparate motivations, it must be reckoned as extraordinary the extent to which these early architects managed to resolve the contradictions between craftsmanship and scholarship, poesy and practicality—in short, the contradictions between the formal and the functional. Nevertheless, the fundamental tensions remained; in fact, they grew steadily sharper with the rise of industrialism, and they are accurately reflected in the curricula of our schools today. The effort of the schools to resolve this contradiction has been, generally speaking, to move toward increased emphasis on the academic, always at the expense of the craft elements of the field. From one point of view this has been both inevitable and desirable. Modern architectural problems can no more be solved by carpentry than can space craft be built by village blacksmiths. However, the shift in training away from craftsmanship has been more toward mere technology than toward a truly scientific investigation of architecture as a whole. On the other hand, the "liberal arts" aspect of the curriculum has generally shown a healthy tendency away from simple antiquarianism toward modern historiography, theory and critical literature.

But there can be no denying that the price paid for this new professionalism has been high. It has played an important role in the complete extinction of the conventional wisdom of the entire preindustrial field. Few contemporary architects have any first-hand knowledge of actual construction methods and techniques. Simultaneously, by the same process, the craftsmen themselves are being robbed of their historic competence and wisdom. What with the factory production of building components and the mechanization of the construction industry itself, there is less and less need for the intelligent, well-trained craftsman. Indeed, the modern working drawings from the architect's office objectively tend to *discourage* good workmanship. More and more, as they reduce building to a process of mere assembly, they imply the "headless hand" of the assembly line. The result is the further lowering of the taste and literacy of the workmen, a situation which the old apprenticeship system made impossible. And this disastrous process of impoverishment is then reinforced by the disappearance of the individual patron of architecture and his replacement by the faceless consumer who has no real voice in or control over the buildings in which he is born, lives and dies.

It is not a happy picture to contemplate.

If the crisis is indeed of the kind and dimensions suggested above, then comprehensive changes in several areas of the profession suggest themselves. First of all, the formal education of the architect should be infused with a truly scientific (as opposed to a merely technical) approach to the problems of environmental design. Such an enriched curriculum should be supplemented by required summer field work in three distinct areas: (1) construction work on building projects (masonry, steelwork, mechanical equipment, etc.); (2) staff work in functioning institutions (housing projects, schools, hospitals, etc.); (3) drafting-room experience in architectural offices. At present, only this last is mandatory—and then only after graduation. The first two kinds of "internship" would be of great help in giving the young architect a multidimensional concept of how buildings are actually put together and how they affect their inhabitants. Finally, education of the average citizen as a building consumer is also urgently required: our educational system should equip him with a clear understanding of his needs as a human being and his birthright as an American. A big program, perhaps, but the minimum indicated.

REFERENCES

1. Turpin C. Bannister, ed., *The Architect at MidCentury: Evaluation and Achievement* (New York: Reinhold, 1954), p. 4.

2. Letter, Joseph Watterson, Editor, *Journal* of the American Institute of Architects, Washington, D.C., April 24, 1964.

3. Author's own estimate; at the time of writing, the AIA had not yet completed its first exhaustive survey of the national profession.

4. *1963–64 Report on Enrollment* (Washington, D.C.: Association of Collegiate Schools of Architecture).

5. *List of Accredited Schools of Architecture: 1963–64* (Washington, D.C.: National Architectural Accrediting Board, June 1, 1963).

6. Watterson, *op. cit.*

7. Bannister, *op. cit.*, Table 57, Appendix.

8. *Ibid.*, Table 53.

9. *Architectural Forum* (New York) Vol. 120, no. 4 (April, 1964), p. 38.

10. Henry Saylor, *The AIA's First Hundred Years* (Washington, D.C.: The Octagon, 1957), p. 38.

PENN KIMBALL

Journalism: Art, Craft or Profession?

AMONG THOSE who gather, write and edit the news for a living, the highest compliment is to be called a "pro." It is the mark of a respected journeyman in a demanding craft. The pro handles a fast-breaking world crisis with the same deft touch he brings to a ponderous city budget. Such skills are highly mental. A pro has the gumption to stand up for what is right and, under pressure, sensitivity in judging what is fair. Good newspapermen, good broadcasters, good magazine writers—the "pros" in the business of journalism—are acutely aware of their responsibility to the public interest. Successful journalists, moveover, circulate these days in the loftiest salons of The Establishment. Presidents curry their favor. Business leaders seek their company. Universities honor them with citations and degrees. The prestige of such practitioners as James Reston, Walter Lippmann, Edward R. Murrow, Howard K. Smith and Theodore H. White is as high as that enjoyed in any of the learned and traditional professions.

Yet it is hard for journalists to take seriously the idea that there really exists a "profession" of journalism. Some of this is self-deprecation, such as that practiced by self-styled country boys about to take over the city. There is an inverse snobbery about their work among newspapermen, especially the more successful. "So, the fact has got to be faced," the Alsop brothers of Groton, Harvard and Yale write disarmingly, "newspaper reporting is a craft or trade, like undertaking, which it sometimes resembles."[1] The status of journalism as a profession thus stands in double jeopardy. The journalist is himself conscious of the unprofessional quality of some ventures in his chosen field. The ground rules set forth by those who would classify him as a marginal member in professional ranks, on the other hand, strike some journalists as irrelevant and even susceptible to sham.

The iconoclastic view is partly explained by the newsman's occupational aversion to pretension. His job exposes him to both the best and the worst of life; he is not inclined to concede anyone a halo without first probing around for a concealed strand of wire. The nobility of professional codes and examples of selfless service by the general run of professional people of his experience are duly registered. But so are the mundane frailties of human character, not excepting his own. An impressionable cub reporter's very first job is likely to be covering police and the courts. There he sees too many third-raters at the bar, too many corrupt politicians on the bench, too many defendants pushed around to stand in much awe of even the more venerable professions. When his career takes him on to the State House, he is likely to get an intimate glimpse of the lobbyists for some of the newer, would-be professions. Behind the platitudes he often detects crass self-interest advanced in the guise of professionalism.

Public acknowledgement of their prestige is a sustaining element for those professions that have come to be "recognized." A journalist's ego, however, is often buffeted by popular scorn. "Journalese" is a synonym for vulgarization of the language. "Journalistic," to many academic savants, means the same as superficial. "Just newspaper talk" is an effective phrase for politicians trying to discredit a rumor. If journalism is thoroughly American in its breezy impertinence toward those who take themselves too seriously, it suffers the reciprocity of being too easily dismissed.

Stanley Walker, the late city editor of the New York *Herald Tribune,* complained in his "Notes on a Noble Calling" of popular conceptions of the Fourth Estate: "The ordinary American newspaper reporter, in the O. Henry era and later, was identified in the popular mind as a low and irresponsible rake with misshapen and unnatural images in his head, a flask of gin on his hip, scant carfare in his pocket, dandruff on his coat-collar, a leer in his eyes, and headed straight for Hell or Seattle."[2] Professional pride, in such circumstances, can be eroded by self-doubt. There is a hang-dog air about some members of the working press who are too quick to apologize that they are only trying to earn a living. The defensive posture is not unknown among some publishers. Their ears burn when journalism is criticized, although their pocketbooks freeze when improvements are suggested.

The upgrading of news in recent times in Washington and on the international front has helped to upgrade both the pay and

prestige of journalists. The white-collar dignity of the modern newsman makes him more eligible to be thought of in the same terms
as teachers, civil servants and dentists. Yet he tends to resist the
thought. Even the word "journalist" itself is somewhat suspect. It
has a foreign flavor, for it is often used by politicians who write for
subsidized journals on the side. It smacks of drawing rooms rather
than of shoe leather. It has a dilettante ring for a vocation still
not far removed from the smell of printer's ink in the back shop.
Americans prefer to call themselves reporters, writers, rewritemen,
deskmen, editors—or just plain newspapermen. When they do not
work for newspapers, they will call themselves reporters or correspondents whenever they can.

The priority of merit among writers of news has been set forth
by the late A. J. Liebling, who used to conduct a column on "The
Wayward Press" for the *New Yorker* magazine, in the following—
descending—order:

1. The reporter, who writes what he sees.
2. The interpretive reporter, who writes what he sees and what he
construes to be its meaning.
3. The expert, who writes what he construes to be the meaning of
what he hasn't seen.[3]

The complication of labels in the field noted by Mr. Liebling and
the development of the newer mass media have generated the need
for new descriptions for everybody involved in chronicling current
events. A more generic term than the lexicon of the newspaper
office is required to cover the activities of news broadcasters,
syndicated columns, newsmagazines and such. Journalist and journalism are still the best anyone has come up with.

On the business and advertising side of the various media one
hears mention of the "communications industry," an idea disturbingly suggestive of an assembly line punching out aspirin com-
mercials. There are Schools and Institutes of Communication these
days, too. The bodies of knowledge being pursued therein are
subject to a good deal of dispute. Most working journalists would
rather drop dead than call themselves "communicators" of anything.
Mr. Liebling has explained this, too.

Communication means simply getting any idea across and has no
intrinsic relation to truth. It is neutral, or the weapon of a political
knave or the medium of a new religion. . . . Its general and increasing
substitution, in the schoolman's jargon, for harmless old Journalism dis-
turbs me. . . .

Q. What do you do for a living?
A. I am a communicator.
Q. What do you communicate? Scarlet fever?[4]

The search for truth, then, should be the drive of the journalist, although his deadlines deny him the luxury, enjoyed by scholars, always to await ultimate truth. Sharing what he digs up with an audience is as important to him as discovering it. The journalist who cannot get his story out is like a bird with a broken wing.

We are dealing here with a point of view about one's work, a frame of mind, an attitude. A private conscience is more central to professional conduct perhaps than public credentials. Journalism has its own quota of knaves and sycophants, some of whose office walls are adorned with testimonials or photographs of the powerful. There are also, happily, a decent proportion of working stiffs with a nose as true as a bird dog's for any scent of wrongdoing. As a searcher after truth, racing the daily deadline, the conscientious journalist is in need of extraordinary help. A systematic approach as rigorous as a scientist's is indispensable to pierce the fogs enveloping the important news. A delicate ethic is required to weigh, for example, an individual's right to privacy against the public's right to know. Can there be a science to something so perversely unpredictable? Can there be a professional ethic in the absence of a profession?

The questions are germane because when enough journalists become either unreliable or irresponsible the social consequences can be grave. Doctors may bury their individual mistakes; lawyers' errors, the jest runs, merely create clients for other lawyers. But even the peccadillos of journalists, as well as their more serious transgressions, are visited upon the public at large. James Reston, chief Washington correspondent of *The New York Times,* has measured the relative risks thusly: "The doctor affects the physical well-being of his patients; the reporter affects the mental well-being of his reader. . . . Like the doctor, he has the opportunity to poison them, and the main difference, it seems to me, is merely that the reporter can poison more of them quicker than the doctor."[5]

This special relationship between journalism and the mental well-being of our society is recognized in the Constitution, which specifically prohibits government encroachment upon freedom of the press. A free press is such an integral part of the American system of government that the benefits are often taken too much for granted. As watchdog for the public interest, the press is guardian of the principle of popular control. The reporter who keeps nipping at the heels of the government bureaucracy is performing a service the voter cannot perform for himself. The mass media, whether you like them or not, are the principal channels for most of the facts, figures, policy statements and policy criticisms upon which the dialogue of democracy depends. Television has become the main instrument for bringing citizens into contact with the personal dimensions of their public officials. Magazines of opinion, columnists, broadcast discussion programs provide the yeast, the leavening process, by which a nation as large and heterogeneous as ours can assimilate new ideas.

In the established professions the right of the state to participate in the examination and licensing of new members is part of a collaboration for upholding standards. The idea of giving any agency of government similar power to license journalists, however, is unthinkable. The pressures already brought to bear to interrupt or deflect the free flow of information are formidable enough. But as long as entry into a career in journalism carries no compulsory period of specialized training, as long as there is no recognized test for the right to practice, journalists will forever be set apart from the ranks of the formal professions.

To be different is not, in itself, to be inferior. One importance of the license is the leverage it gives to the professional schools. Since a compulsory degree usually precedes the right to apply to be licensed, the educators for the licensed professions have first crack at the future practitioner. The view of the Alsop brothers that they engage in a trade, not a profession, is based partly on this question of initiation:

> Newspaper reporting is not a profession, despite the complacent belief of a good many reporters who have achieved the upper brackets. You may go to journalism school before you become a reporter. You may save valuable time there, learning things in school that you would otherwise learn on the job. But you can still achieve a fair measure of success as a reporter without any of the long, specialized prior training that is the mark of a professional man. . . .
> It is a trade, of course, that has its own well-defined requirements. All reporters need sturdy constitutions, good feet and some feeling for the English language.[6]

The education of journalists is a controversial topic both on the campus and in the trade. Journalism schools and departments find themselves, too, in a defensive position. They suffer the disdain of academic colleagues who cannot identify what has fashionably come to be called "the discipline." This makes journalism courses subject to the withering criticism of being merely "trade school." Some members of the working press, on the other hand, look askance at what they describe as the "academic approach" to practical needs—the latter defined as a guaranteed supply of well-mannered young men who can write fast, clean copy with a minimum of spelling errors.

At another level, it is stoutly maintained that a "liberal arts" education, not too specifically defined, is the optimum preparation in itself for a future journalist. Everything else, as the Alsops suggest, can eventually be learned on the job—provided one's feet hold out. Some of the sting has been taken out of the debate by journalism graduates who have won their spurs in all of the media. Employers now systematically recruit from the self-styled professional schools. But the role of the professional school in the non-profession of journalism remains ambiguous. It is time, perhaps, to clarify it, if only because the issues involve a better understanding of what journalism is all about.

Preparation for journalism, as a matter of fact, puts broader demands on education than does that for most professional careers. One reason is the journalist's role as a generalist in an ever more specialized culture. The curriculum appropriate for a superior journalist is terrifyingly broad. Another educational challenge is posed by the journalist's special role as an observer of human events. He needs a tight discipline over his mind and emotions, since he is expected to engage himself in life without losing his perspective. And if the foregoing were not enough, the journalist faces the final creative challenge of making this knowledge and experience interesting and significant to as wide an audience as possible. Society's need for the generalist is intensified by the dilution of liberal arts education in the era of the educational explosion. (One graduate teacher of journalism has been heard to describe his job as "teaching remedial English to Harvard graduates.") Specialization has proceeded so far in some subjects that only specialists within the specialty can communicate with one another.

Somewhere between the technical prose of a narrow expertise and the false clarity of oversimplification is an area of broad, meaningful communication. It falls to the journalist to be able to talk intelligently with both the specialist and the public. He has to win the confidence of the former without losing the ear of the latter. The

247

perfect journalist, then, needs a sense of history, even if he cannot command the details of an epoch. He must be familiar with the rigor of science without necessarily being able to perform the proof. He should see politics in the patterns of the political scientist, business trends in the context of economic theory, international affairs in the stream of social change. What good is a political reporter without an eye for constitutional protections? How far can the roving correspondent go who cannot speak the language?

The ideal of the Renaissance Man, unhappily, is rarely realized, as even the gifted Benjamin Franklin was forced to admit two centuries ago in the first number of the *Pennsylvania Gazette:*

> We are fully sensible, that to publish a good News-Paper is not so easy an Undertaking as Many People imagine it to be. The Author of a Gazette (in the Opinion of the Learned) ought to be qualified with an extensive Acquaintance with Languages, a great Easiness and Command of Writing and Relating Things clearly and intelligibly, and in a few words; he should be able to speak of War both by Land and Sea, be well acquainted with Geography, with the History of the Time, with the several Interests of Princes and States, the Secrets of Courts, and the Manners and Customs of all Nations. Men thus accomplished are very rare in this remote Part of the World; and it would be well if the writer of these Papers could make up among his Friends what is wanting in himself.[7]

The education of a journalist is of necessity an ongoing process. The good ones never stop learning, refreshing themselves. But the "discipline," its area of generalized and systematic knowledge, is as all-inclusive as human thought.

As a generalist, the journalist should be continually looking for relationships—relating what he sees with everything else he ever knew, and relating that to an audience he can never know. The mind of the journalist should aim outward. One of the great difficulties in the training of young journalists is to shake them out of the rut of egocentricity. Too many youngsters seem fascinated only by their own interests, one of the by-products of early specialization. The urge for self-expression runs more strongly than the willingness to tackle something new. Journalists, on the other hand, are often called upon to cover subjects far removed from their private, personal bents. A journalist cannot turn up his nose at such an assignment. He just digs in and learns. And he had best learn fast.

Good reporting, therefore, entails a great deal more than a B.A. degree in some useful phase of the liberal arts plus a stout constitution. The reporter is part of an interdependent communication process. That is one reason why the behavioral sciences have figured so prominently in the new curricula in journalism. Insights into human behavior, human prejudice, social and cultural patterns are essential equipment. The tragedy and comedy of life is in human relationships. Prior knowledge in the academic disciplines is helpful, but the content of truth cannot be divorced from its expression. Assuming him to be a well-educated man in the best sense of the word, a reporter also requires a set of mind to enable him to use what he knows. While it is true that some are able to accomplish this feat intuitively, most are less fortunate. In a sense the reporter must learn to master two opposite psychological states. One is the capacity to immerse himself in the stories he is sent to cover so completely that he actually relives them. The other is to be able to detach himself from these same intense involvements, to stand outside the experience and place it in perspective for the reader.

There is a fiction that good journalists hold themselves aloof from life. They cannot do this and also truly understand the people and events they cover. Without involvement they would be unable to share the full dimensions of those experiences with their audience. It is the recognition of common experience that makes a story "connect" with the lives of others. Sensitivity, empathy—however it is described—a faculty for identifying with other human beings is often the ingredient that separates the vivid story from the drab, the superficial from the penetrating truth. Sending an Ivy League graduate on a story in a Harlem tenement may be as important a part of his development as his reading the Fourteenth Amendment. But just going there is not enough. He must learn to respond.

Newsmen who boast that they have learned everything on the job are often the kind who shield themselves from reality behind an air of cynicism. The cynics write around the real story. Their copy is mechanical. The aggressive stereotype seen in so many movies about the press is another fraud. Aggressiveness and cynicism in a reporter are defense mechanisms which rob him of his skills. A journalist without a heart is an empty writer. A journalist who is *all* heart, on the other hand, is an undisciplined writer. And in journalism the key professional quality is: control. It takes control to extricate oneself from an overpowering experience and still be able to write it, as did more than one reporter in Dallas on the day of President Kennedy's assassination. The ability to analyze, to evaluate, to put something in context—even to suspend judgment until all the evidence is in—is the self-discipline to detach oneself from the emotional pulls of the situation. A journalist should be skeptical, though not cynical. His critical faculties are his best armor against one-sidedness in a world where truth tends to be many-sided.

This is something different from what used to be known in the trade as "objectivity." Heywood Broun, who was fired a generation ago for expressing too much outrage over the Sacco-Vanzetti case, confessed his own inability to meet that standard:

> It has been said that the perfect reporter ought to be patterned more or less along the physical and chemical lines of a plate glass window. It is not his function to take the light from the sun and shade into blue, green, yellow or even red. He is an associate member of the light brigade, and when cannon roar from the right or left his mission is to keep precisely in the middle of the road in the hope that he will find the truth, which is always said to lie between the two. . . . I fear I am not glass, either clear or opaque. When hit the result is something other than "Tinkle! Tinkle!"[8]

The cult of objectivity took a bad beating during the era of the late Senator Joseph R. McCarthy, when the press found itself spreading outrageous falsehoods merely by following the accepted techniques of "objective" reporting. These techniques assumed that the reporter could escape responsibility as long as he could attribute the information in his story. But the televised hearings in Washington that preceded the Senator's downfall conveyed something to the audience that had been lacking in print.

The interpretation of events and the personalities who shape events is much more difficult, nevertheless, than one would judge from the hostility of some intellectuals toward the mass media. Alistair Cooke, American correspondent for the Manchester *Guardian,* has pointed out the paradox in the position of some campus critics of the press:

> There is a very odd and enduring contradiction between the prejudice of the intelligentsia that today's journalism is a debased form of literature and history and the steady belief of historians that yesterday's journalism is one of the most authentic of documentary sources. . . .
> Journalism is good and bad; it is not bad because it is journalism but because it is abominably written; that is to say, its material is tritely observed, crudely felt and foggily communicated. The same may be said of a great many medical papers, historical monographs, and nearly all sociological treatises. In truth, the journalist is merely the scapegoat of all professionals who put pen to paper.[9]

The generalist is not, as some say, someone who knows less and less about more and more. The power to range over the whole complex of life requires a high degree of concentration. The discipline is as rigorous as the methodologies of any of the narrow specialties. Few are born with the gift. It has to be instilled. A point of view toward one's work, the development of habits to stand outside prejudice, including one's own, the drive to understand and to communicate that understanding—these are the goals of professional training. The schoolmen seek to develop men and women capable of understanding their own vocational activities in a larger social and moral context. A professional attitude can be cultivated most vigorously perhaps in an educational institution, whose own first loyalties are toward society.

Equipped with enough initial knowledge at least to ask intelligent questions, armed with a frame of mind that can relate to any situation while assessing it with detachment, the journalist must finally write the story so as to capture the attention, interest and understanding of the reader. That, of course, is an art. It is an uncertain art, on no less an authority than E. B. White, whose own felicitous prose graces the pages of the *New Yorker* magazine.

Who can confidently say what ignites a certain combination of words, causing them to explode in the mind? Who knows why certain notes in music are capable of stirring the listener deeply, though the same notes, slightly rearranged, are impotent. These are high mysteries. . . .

There is no satisfactory explanation of style, no infallible guide to good writing, no assurance that a person who thinks clearly will be able to write clearly, no key that unlocks the door, no inflexible rules by which the young writer may shape his course. He will often find himself steering by stars that are disturbingly in motion.[10]

One hears of child prodigies in music, even in mathematics. But good writers have to age. The chemistry of this process, as Mr. White points out, is pretty mysterious. One ingredient, certainly, is a fierce desire to write in the first place. As far as journalism is concerned, the enlightenment of others is the source of the highest gratification. A journalist with weak motivation is lost from the start. There is no such thing as going through the motions on a challenging assignment. On this point, Mr. White is firmly on the side of the committed: "Style takes its final shape more from attitudes of mind than from principles of composition. . . . If one is to write, one must believe—in the truth and worth of the scrawl."[11] Thus we are led once more to the journalist's strength of will. The requirements of writing are demanding and often painful to the young. They must learn to walk before they can begin ballet, and the tendency is toward impatience.

251

There is no way, of course, to separate good writing from its content. Journalism textbooks—and city editors—frequently harp on the so-called "rules" of newswriting. Those who try to teach the forms of journalism independent of the substance are like those who imagine they are painting pictures when they fill in the numbered spaces on a prefabricated chart. Substance should dictate the form, and the substance *is* journalism.

The artistry of the "pro" is his ability to use a slice of life to illustrate the whole, to relate the reader to the event as if he himself were there, to unravel the complicated idea by some illuminating illustration. The agonies of composition are multiplied for the journalist by the tyranny of the deadline. The opportunities for polishing his words are rare. The psychic rewards of a story well told are thus correspondingly increased. Mr. White's former colleague, A. J. Liebling, has conveyed some of the frustration and elation of the task in this account of the reporter's artistic struggle:

> To understand perfectly a new country, new situation, the new characters you confront on an assignment is impossible. To understand more than half, so that your report will have significant correlation with what is happening, is hard. To transmit more than half of what you understand is a hard task, too, far beyond the task of the so-called creative artist, who if he finds a character in his story awkward can simply change its characteristics (Even to sex, *vide* Proust and Albertine. Let him try it with General de Gaulle!) It is possible, occasionally, to get something completely right—a scene or a pattern of larceny, or a man's mind. These are reporters' victories, as rare as pitchers' home runs.[12]

The journalist, as artist, suffers a grievous handicap in comparison with fellow artists. He does not control his medium as the painter and poet can control theirs. A landscape is an affair between the painter and his canvas. He is limited only by inspiration and talent. A poet can scribble happily, or unhappily, in a garret, and for him the act of putting pen to paper is creatively satisfying. The journalist, on the contrary, spends his life usually as one employee among many, separated from the final product by a chain of command and subject to the control of a corporate authority. Thomas Griffith, a former West Coast newspaperman now high on the pyramid of Time, Inc., has characterized the limitation bluntly: "A journalist may have the duty, but often does not have the opportunity to tell the truth as he sees it. He is a hired man, and because he is, his is not a profession."[13]

The professional ideal of an individual in practice for himself

252

for a number of clients has been modified greatly by a steady flow of professionals of all kinds into large business organizations. But the journalist has little choice. The logistics of publishing and broadcasting are based on group effort. Working in the company of others, as opposed to free, individual enterprise, is not necessarily demeaning. The camaraderie among journalists is one of the attractions of the vocation. The esprit of a first-class journalistic institution is strong. When the New York *Times* or a network news operation turns its staff loose on a big story, the collective coverage adds up to something more than the mere sum of the parts. Group journalism, as developed on magazines, has made creative contributions in many areas of newsgathering. Looking at the same event from the perspective of several capitals, for example, has advantages over the single reporter anchored to one spot. The interplay of minds in a joint story conference sometimes sparks a better idea than any originally brought into the room by anyone. The specialization through which good writers can concentrate on writing, while others perform the more mundane tasks, has upgraded both the style and the content of journalism.

Yet, as everyone knows who has sat on a committee trying to draft a report, many minds do not make light work of writing. The journalist is rarely free of his colleagues, and the flow of copy through the mill of mass media organizations can be frustrating and—worse—distorting. Many hands, some heavy, may be laid upon a story before it sees the light of day. Since truth does not come packaged conveniently in blacks and whites, the tendency of the homogenizing process is toward gray. The shading of a sentence, one word in the headline, one deletion in a quote can make all the difference. When one considers the thousands of "facts" reported in each edition of a newspaper, magazine or broadcast, the wonder is not the number of errors but the scarcity. Try asking your neighbors to report something all in the neighborhood have seen. The collective eye of journalistic processing screens out an enormous quantity of error, false emphasis, bad taste and dullness. That it does not catch it all, sometimes even the most glaring, is indicative not so much of willful prejudice as of the toughness of the task.

John Gordon, editor of the London *Sunday Express,* is credited with having pinpointed a familiar complaint of readers in this memo to his staff: "I do not wish to be hypercritical, but the plain fact is—and we all know it to be true—that whenever we see a story in a newspaper concerning something we know about, it is more often wrong than right."[14] The tendency of laymen is to attribute such error to the evil motives or irresponsibility of those who represent the press. It would be naïve to gloss over the deliberate obfuscation that occasionally occurs in the press. But it is just as revealing oftentimes to analyze the awesome complexity of the news itself together with the large-scale organizations needed to report it.

Writing nearly twenty-five years ago, H. L. Mencken lamented the changes in the reporter's life since he first began covering Baltimore at the turn of the century:

> In my day a reporter who took on an assignment was wholly on his own until he got back to the office, and even then he was little molested until his copy was turned in at the desk; today he tends to become a homunculus at the end of a telephone wire, and the reduction of his observations to prose is commonly farmed out to literary castrati who never leave the office, and hence never feel the wind of the world in their faces or see anything with their own eyes.[15]

The newsmagazine writer who works exclusively at second hand or the newscaster who rips and reads the wire service reports are the dwarfs in today's technological forest. And even the man who is feeling the wind, say, in Saigon must thread his way through a maze of intrigue, rumor, censorship, officialdom and downright confusion.

The further the flow of information from its source, the greater the danger that group effort may distort it. And group editing can have a stultifying effect on boldness and originality. Second-guessing the man on the scene, the indoor sport among *Time* magazine's hired men, demoralizes the reporter as well as dilutes the truth. The sheer weight of technology in journalism's newest medium, television, furthermore, has created burdens never encountered by the newsman who gets by with strong feet and a sharp pencil. A television news documentary requires the logistics of an amphibious landing combined with the delicacies of directing a play. The number of people who get into the act is sometimes ludicrous. In the conception, production and editing of a network show the story needs to be nursed like a violet in the path of a steamroller. Whatever his medium, the journalist works in a power structure that has a good deal of control, immediate and potential, over both his output and his livelihood. The life of the twentieth-century organization man has been analyzed at length, but the organization man whose job it is to inform the public is under special stress.

Journalistic enterprises offer their product directly to one public while asking other sources to share a part of the cost. In broadcasting in America the public, of course, pays nothing. Most newspapers today devote more than half their space to advertising. An economic structure involving two different sets of customers, each indispensable in his own way to the life of the enterprise, creates a ticklish ethical and business problem. Sometimes a dishonest publication makes a great deal of money. Sometimes a laudable example of editorial integrity fails. The hired men of journalism function at widely differing levels of independence within their hierarchies. Other consciences than those of the reporter are brought to bear upon editorial decisions. The work of the journalist is particularly exposed to pressure because he operates in a public arena; when he treads on a toe, the act is acutely visible. An angry reader or an angry advertiser is swift to react.

The wickedness of overt advertising influence on the press tends to be exaggerated, although the real estate, food and travel pages of some of our most prestigious publications are suspiciously promotional. A corporation as secure as General Motors has been known to withdraw advertising to register its displeasure over editorial matter. Television sponsors back away from controversial reportage as from leprosy. But the forces grinding away at the integrity of the news are usually more subtle. The most insidious force of all is the self-censorship of the organization underling who imagines he knows how to please the boss. The boss, himself, is sometimes the victim of social, economic and political bias—spontaneously and sincerely felt. The publisher who picks up his viewpoints from his golfing companions and passes them on to a key subordinate on the make can poison the well more thoroughly than open sewage.

The cloudy nature of truth complicates office debates over editorial justice. The issue is seldom so clear cut as to banish every doubt. The reporter fighting for publication of what he knows in his bones to be right is on somewhat less sure ground than an evangelist preacher; he gets few signs from Heaven. The fascinating thing about journalists is not how many crumble under the strain but how many stand up to the challenge. War correspondents have forfeited their credentials rather than knuckle under to pressure from the military brass. Broadcasters like Elmer Davis and Edward R. Murrow have dared to battle powerful politicians. In the South in recent years more than one editor and publisher have stood together to resist an advertising boycott of their anti-segregationist efforts.

The little, less spectacular engagements that go on between rank-

and-file reporters and the front office, between the man on the beat and the man on the desk, between a conscientious newsman and a nervous news source—these perhaps result in the most important victories of all. What makes the hired man stick his neck out? T. S. Matthews, once editor of *Time*, fondly recalls those "sea-green incorruptibles who acknowledged no authority but some inner light of their own. . . . They gave their editors more trouble than anybody, but they made the whole undertaking worthwhile."[16] The "inner light," presumably, is what warms the figure standing vigil in a cold rain to check out one last vital fragment of the yarn. It illuminates the typewriter in the lap of the man riding a campaign bus through the sticks. It shines like a beacon when the angry mob closes in threateningly or when an icy executive puts through a tough phone call of complaint to the boss.

Journalism in such circumstance becomes not just a job, but a calling. Wickham Steed, a distinguished correspondent and editor of *The Times* of London, felt compelled to explain: "Journalism is something more than a craft, something other than an industry, something between an art and a ministry. Journalists proper are unofficial public servants whose purpose is to serve the community."[17] This sense of responsibility to the community, the loyalty to the public as client above all other loyalties, is the principal professional claim of the working journalist. Public service, in fact, turns out to be one of the overriding motivations of young people contemplating a future in journalism. Great reporters at the pinnacle of their careers retain an almost missionary zeal.

One of the high satisfactions of being a journalist is that it is a pursuit in which one can have impact on one's surroundings, whether the scale be large or small. The journalist helps shape his own times. This gives meaning to life. There is no lack of public service to be performed, though too frequently there is a lack of management drive to expand journalism's time-cherished franchise "to afflict the comfortable and comfort the afflicted." The apprentice journalist who abandons the field feels frustrated more often by what he is given—or not given—to do than he is tempted by money alone. The managers of our press institutions are going to have to devote more thought to providing their most promising prospects with maximum opportunities for personal satisfaction on the job.

Journalism cannot make it possible for everybody to find jobs in Washington or on foreign assignment any more than can every lawyer practice exclusively before the United States Supreme Court.

On a local level, the run of the news that needs to be covered is not universally of noble proportions. There is, alas, such a thing as a dull and routine assignment. In what occupation is there not? Something comes over the competent journalist, however, who is given his head by his superiors to write what he must write now and then. Even the routine acquires a glow at the hands of a "pro" with the opportunity as well as the duty to tell the truth. He fairly itches to dig through dusty files to document a hunch of official corruption. He will burn the midnight oil to unravel the rate structure of a public utility. Like applause to an actor, the chance to develop his own story makes everything else worthwhile.

Most of the large questions confronting journalism these days involve the use of its freedoms in the public service. There are, first, questions concerning whether its economic self-interests are interfering with its social responsibilities. What is the effect of the trend toward single ownership of newspapers in local communities, or joint ownership of newspapers and television stations, on the Jeffersonian ideal of a free marketplace of ideas? Do newspapers allot too much space to trivia and the sensational? Do the broadcast media cater to the least common denominator for advertising revenue at the expense of their obligation to the public interest?

Then there are doubts concerning journalism's ability and willingness to provide key areas of coverage. To what extent has the fantastic growth of our military-industrial complex outstripped the capacity of the press to cover it? Are we staffing the vital centers of world news, especially the emerging underdeveloped nations, sufficiently to provide a consistent flow of adequate information?

The vested interests of the press, itself, are sometimes seen as in conflict with its service to the public. Is the press intruding so much in the mass coverage of such dramatic stories as Premier Khrushchev's visit or President Kennedy's assassination or the national political conventions as to influence the news it is supposed to record? Are the rights of defendants to fair trial being compromised by competitive pre-trial publicity in the mass media?

The issue has also been raised whether the reflexes of editors are attuned to the flow of present-day events. Is there too much crisis reporting, too much emphasis on controversy at the expense of less spectacular understanding and interpretation? Is there a "Cold War psychosis" in press coverage of the relations between East and West or a reckless contribution by some segments of the press to dangerous international tensions?

Such questions—none simple to solve—loom as large in our
times as the mass media themselves. The press, wedded to the principle of self-regulation yet strategically linked to the public interest,
finds itself in an anomalous position. If it fails to work out its own
answers to its own weaknesses, society shares the consequences. If
the community seeks to impose its remedies, freedom is imperiled.
The top management of our press, broadcasting and publishing enterprises is quick to raise the spectre of outside interference. The
internal influence for reform exercised in other fields by their professional elite—judges, scholars, medical boards—has no exact counterpart in a business environment. And top management in the corporate structure of journalism is not necessarily trained in matters
of editorial discretion. This puts a special burden on the men and
women who deal directly with the news. If the working journalist,
as we have seen, has only indirect control over his medium and a
subordinate position in the power hierarchy of his livelihood, is he
really in a position to exert a constructive influence on journalism's
realization of its responsibilities?

He can and he does. A top journalist, for example, builds up a
broad personal following. When his freedom of action is threatened
within his own organization, the possibility of public disclosure is
a useful ally. A newsman working at more ordinary levels is, nonetheless, in the mainstream of public life in his community. He can
be extremely well informed on issues subject to office dispute. If his
superiors must resort to raw power to win their point, they risk the
morale of their entire staff. The effectiveness of the individual in
upholding high professional standards begins with his determination to fight for them. The goal is to be respected, if not loved. The
best journalists are not always the most popular ones.

The weakness of the individual journalist's position is in matters
reaching beyond his personal relationships—the pressures of competition, large scale economic forces, the impetus of powerful interest groups. Here is where action by the collective body of practitioners can at least reinforce the solitary struggle. The association of
the committed for the betterment of their endeavors is the basis of
every profession. The process of the professionalization of journalism in America has been the gradual evolution from the tramp reporter to the socities of newsmen that now exist in every state.

A professional ethic can take form without formal machinery or
an elaborate code. Professionalization is a human process, a feeling
that comes over a person when he behaves in concert with his own

conscience. Journalism has always attracted a maverick type who would rather be right than be rich. The object is to extend the breed. It is in this connection that schools of journalism have a useful mission to perform. For they are in a strategic position to orient individuals about to meet the practical tests of professional pride. Without some moral armor, the journalist is a sitting target for disillusion. Mid-career education for journalists has been another factor in rekindling the ideals of many practitioners who go back to the job with a renewed regard for what ought to be done. The alumni of the Nieman program at Harvard, for example, have become a kind of lobbying force within the trade.

There are other influences at work inside the ranks that indicate an emerging professionalization. Organizations such as the Associated Press Managing Editors and the Radio and Television News Directors do a shirt-sleeved review of their own day-to-day performances. The traditional gulf between editorial staff and business management is being bridged by an increasing crossover from editorial experience to managerial posts. One result is a new sensitivity toward professional standards in management ranks. Network news organizations have demonstrated the leverage of a professional model by taking a leaf from their print brethren to seek autonomy and editorial control over their own news reports. Since broadcast journalism has been expanding so spectacularly, its need for standards may be the most strenuous of all. Critical journals like *Nieman Reports* and *Columbia Journalism Review* supply a framework for evaluating the media independent of competitive bias. In an age when every businessman, even the most powerful, is self-conscious about his "image," the Lords of the Press are becoming eager for good notices.

The journalist laboring in the vineyards needs no longer to go it alone. There are a growing number of professional meetings where he can mingle and exchange ideas with his opposite numbers. If he cannot legitimately lay claim to a profession, he nevertheless goes right on growing more professionally minded. The attitude that the whole endeavor belongs within his sphere of concern is the mark of the modern-day "pro." He sees himself working not merely for a single organization but as part of a brotherhood to shore up the foundations of an honest press. It is a loose federation, singularly devoid of ritual or by-laws. But the newsmen who belong can recognize one another in whatever small town or far corner of the earth they chance to meet.

REFERENCES

1. Joseph and Stewart Alsop, *The Reporter's Trade* (New York: Reynal, 1958).

2. Stanley Walker, *City Editor* (New York: Frederick A. Stokes, 1934).

3. A. J. Liebling, *The Press* (New York: Ballantine Books, 1961).

4. *Ibid.*

5. James Reston in *The Newspaper*, by members of the staff of the New York Times (New York: Charles Scribner's Sons, 1945), p. 94.

6. Alsop, *op. cit.*

7. Frank Luther Mott, *American Journalism* (New York: Macmillan, 1941).

8. Heywood Hale Broun (ed.), *Collected Edition of Heywood Broun* (New York: Harcourt, Brace, 1941).

9. Alistair Cooke in *Bedside Guardian* (New York: Ives Washburn, 1959).

10. E. B. White, *The Elements of Style* (New York: Macmillan, 1959).

11. *Ibid.*

12. Liebling, *op. cit.*

13. Thomas Griffith, *The Waist-High Culture* (New York: Harper & Brothers, 1959).

14. T. S. Matthews, *The Sugar Pill* (New York: Simon and Schuster, 1959).

15. H. L. Mencken, *Newspaper Days, 1899–1906* (New York: Alfred A. Knopf, 1941).

16. T. S. Matthews, *op. cit.*

17. Wickham Steed, *The Press* (London: Penguin Books, 1938).

Notes on Contributors

WILLIAM ALONSO, born in 1933, is Assistant Professor of Regional Planning at Harvard University and the Acting Director of the Center for Urban Studies. His book on the economics of urban structure, *Location and Land Use,* will be published later this year.

BERNARD BARBER, born in 1918, is Professor and Chairman of the Department of Sociology at Barnard College, Columbia University. His publications include *Science and the Social Order* and *Social Stratification.* He is Chairman of the Columbia University Council on Research in the Social Sciences as well as Advisory Editor of *Technology and Culture.*

JOHN J. BEER, born in 1927, is Assistant Professor of the History of Science at the University of Delaware. In 1959 he published *The Emergence of the German Dye Industry.*

JOHN CONWAY, born in 1916, was until 1963 Master of Leverett House and Lecturer in History at Harvard University. He will spend the academic year 1963–1964 at All Souls College, Oxford, writing a comparative study of American and Canadian politics.

JAMES MARSTON FITCH is Professor of Architecture at Columbia University. He is the author of several books, including *American Building: The Forces That Shape It* and *Architecture and the Esthetics of Plenty,* as well as many papers in the professional and scientific press of the United States and Europe. He has recently been studying the preservation of historic monuments in various countries of Europe, the Middle East and Africa in preparation for teaching a graduate course in that subject at Columbia.

PAUL A. FREUND, born in 1908, is University Professor at Harvard University. He is Editor-in-Chief of a history of the Supreme Court which was commissioned by Congress. He published *The Supreme Court of the United States* in 1961.

JAMES M. GUSTAFSON, born in 1925, is Professor of Christian Ethics at Yale University Divinity School. His publications include *The Advancement of Theological Education,* together with H. R. Niebuhr and D. C. Williams; and *Treasure in Earthen Vessels: The Church as a Human Community.*

EVERETT C. HUGHES, born in 1897, is Professor of Sociology at Brandeis University. He is the president of the American Sociological Association. Among his many published works, particular attention ought to be given to *Boys in White: Student Culture in Medical School* and *Men and their Work.*

SAMUEL P. HUNTINGTON, born in 1927, is Professor of Government at Harvard University. He has published *The Soldier and the State: The Theory and Politics of Civil-Military Relations* and *The Common Defense: Strategic Programs in National Politics.* He has edited *Changing Patterns of Military Politics.*

PENN T. KIMBALL, born in 1915, is presently Professor in the Graduate School of Journalism at Columbia University. A graduate of Princeton and of Balliol College, Oxford, where he was a Rhodes Scholar, he also engaged in advanced study in government and sociology at Yale and Columbia Universities. His career in journalism included positions as Senior Editor of the *New Republic*, 1947; Assistant to the Sunday Editor, *New York Times*, 1951–1954; Senior Editor of *Collier's*, 1955–1956. He is a member of the National Press Club and of the American Association of Public Opinion Research.

W. DAVID LEWIS, born in 1931, is Lecturer in History at the University of Delaware. He is also Fellowship Coordinator of the Eleutherian Mills-Hagley Foundation. He has published articles in various historical journals.

KENNETH S. LYNN, born in 1923, is Professor of English at Harvard University. He will spend 1963–1964 as Visiting Professor at the University of Madrid. He has published *The Dream of Success* and *Mark Twain and Southwestern Humor*; he has edited *The Comic Tradition in America* and *The American Society*.

JAMES HOWARD MEANS, born in 1885, is a retired academic physician who is interested in Medicare, thyroidology and the history of medicine. His publications include *Thyroid and Its Diseases, Doctors, People and Government* and "too many papers to list."

C. RICHARD SODERBERG, born in Ulvöhmamn, Sweden, in 1895, became in 1960 Institute Professor Emeritus of the Massachusetts Institute of Technology, with which he had been associated since 1938. His entry into education was preceded by a career in industry, which, apart from a short period in shipbuilding, was concerned with electric and mechanical power machinery. During his academic career, his professional work has dealt chiefly with problems of aircraft and rocket propulsion. His many honors include awards from the United States Army and Navy and from the Air Force, medals and awards from professional societies, and honorary degrees. Member of many learned societies and institutes, he is the author of articles on dynamics, vibrations, design of turbines and generators, and engineering education, the two most recent being "The Trends in Engineering Education—Do They Concern the Power Industry?," *Proceedings of the American Power Conference*, Vol. XXIX, 1962, and "Mechanical Properties in Relation to Design Requirements," *Metallurgical Reviews*, Vol. I, Part I, 1956.

ALMA S. WITTLIN, is now a Scholar of the Radcliffe Institute for Independent Study and consultant of Educational Services, Inc. Her publications include *The Museum, its History and its Tasks in Education*, 1949, in Routledge and Kegan Paul's series Sociology and Social Reconstructions, edited by Karl Mannheim.

NORMAN E. ZINBERG, born in 1921, is Assistant Director, Psychiatric Service, Beth Israel Hospital, Boston; he is also Clinical Associate in Psychiatry at the Harvard Medical School. He has published extensively in medical and psychiatric journals and recently edited *Normal Psychology of the Aging Process*.

INDEX

Accreditation, 41, 61, 98, 99, 214–215; *see also* Certification, Licensing
Acculturation, 171
Acheson, Dean, 194, 195
Adams, Henry, 189, 190
Adolescence, 5
Adventures of Ideas, v
Advertising, 255
Advocate, 35, 40
Agricola, 207
Agriculture, 206, 211
Air Force, 132, 133, 134, 136, 137; *see also* Military
Air Force Academy, 137
Air Force Institution of Technology, 135
Alienist, 162
Allinsmith, Wesley, 94, 101
Alsop, Joseph, 196
Alsop brothers, 243, 246, 247
American Association of Theological Schools, 86
American Bar Association, 41, 237
American Education Research Association, 106
American Engineering Council, 214
American Foreign Policy—Freedom and Restraints, vi
American Institute of Aeronautics and Astronautics, Inc., 214
American Institute of Architects, 234, 239
AIA Journal, 234
American Institute of Chemical Engineers, 214
American Institute of Mining, Metallurgical, and Petroleum Engineers, 214
American Institute of Planners, 174
American Law Institute, 45

American Management Association, 23
American Medical Association, 29, 30, 50, 51, 65, 237
American Psychoanalytic Association, 155, 156
American Public Health Association, 69
American Society for Engineering Education, 213, 214
American Society of Civil Engineers, 214
American Society of Mechanical Engineers, 214, 215
Anaesthesiology, 10
Anderson, Admiral George W., Jr., 143
Anti-Americanism, 194
Anti-Semitism, 161
Apothecary, xii
Apprentice, 52, 104; *see also* Internship
Archaeology, 6
Architect, 171, 173, 182, 206, 231–241
    activities of, 231–233
    client relationship of, 235–236, 237
    definition of, 234
    income of, 235
    journals of, 234
    licensing of, 234, 239
    organization of, 234–235
    supply of, 234
    training of, 234, 239, 240
Ark of the covenant, 201
Army, 132, 136, 137, 138; *see also* Military
Armytage, Walter H. G., 208
Arthur, Chester, 194
Artist, 231, 252, 253, 254
Associated Press Managing Editors, 259

263

Index

Index

Index

Index

New York State Teachers Association, 99
New York Times, The, xiv, 245, 253
New Yorker, 244, 251
Newcomen steam engine, 208
Nieman Reports, 259
Nitze, Paul, 145, 194
Nixon, Richard M., 142, 156
Nobel Prize, 19, 38, 122
Noise of Solemn Assemblies, 83
North, Robert D., 101
NATO, 193

Oberndorf, C. P., 158
"Occupational Licensing in the States," 99
Officers Candidate Schools, 137, 138
Ohio State University, 102
"On Psychoanalysis," 158
Ong, Walter J., Fr., 74
Organization, professional, *see* Institutionalization
Organization Man, The, 84
Osler, William, Sir, 50, 55, 56, 57

Palmer, H. R., 209
Paramedicals, 9, 10, 59, 62, 63
Parliament (Britain), 105, 196, 200
Parsons, Talcott, 17
Pasteur, Louis, 55
Patent system, 208
Pathology, Virchowian, 162, 168
Peace Corps, 73
Peck, R. V., 105, 106
Pennsylvania Gazette, 248
Pennsylvania Hospital (Philadelphia), 50
Pennsylvania, University of, ix, 49
Pentagon, 144, 145, 147, 148
Perkin, William Henry, 111
Permanente, 67
Pestalozzi, Johann, 92
Peterson, Frederick, 158
Philadelphia, College of, 49
Pitt, William, 194
Pittsburgh, University of, 114
Polhem, Christopher, 207
Politician, 29, 186–202
   and corruption, 186, 189, 190
   idealism of, 191, 192, 194
   research of, 29
   status of, 194
   and world situation, 192–194
Politics, xii, 29–31, 142–143, 147, 149, 150, 171, 172

city planning and, 171, 172
   clergy and, xii
   military and, 142–143, 147, 149, 150
Population, density of, 64
Prestige, *see* Status
Prince, Morton, 158
Princeton University, ix
Probation officer, 4
Proctor, 35
Professions, The, xiv
Progressives, 193
Protestantism, 70, 71, 72–73, 74, 75, 76, 77, 79, 80, 81–83, 84, 85–87, 88–89
   minister, 71, 72–73, 74, 79, 81–83, 85–87, 88–89
      authority of, 81–83
      recruitment of, 87, 88–89
      role of, 72–73, 74
      training of, 85–87
      women, 88
Psychiatrist, xii, 154–169
   academic, 158
   child, 155
   consultation of, 166
   neurological, 162
   patient relationship of, 164, 167
   referral to, 154, 163
   relationship to medicine, 63, 154–155, 162, 164, 167–168
   relationship to social sciences, 155
   relationship to teacher, 106–107, 165, 166–167
   research of, 168
   training of, 154, 163
Psychoanalysis, 155–156, 157, 158, 159, 160, 161, 167
   acceptance in U.S., 157–163
   value of, 164
Psychoanalyst, 163
Psychologist, 5, 6, 161
Psychotherapy, 160, 168
Public relations, 4, 25
Public health, 4, 5, 48, 69, 199, 209
Public School Administration, 97
Pupin, Michael, 113
Putnam, James J., 158

Qualifications, professional, 7, 8, 95, 101, 204
Quasi professions, 22; *see also* Paramedicals
Quattlebaum, Charles A., xiv
Queen Mary, 176

Index

DATE DUE